SPOTLIGHT ON LITERACY

The Road To Independent Reading

W9-BLS-641

Integrate reading with all other language arts.

11 Daily Language Activities Transparencies
Grades 1–6 Daily language activities to provide brief regular practice and reinforcement of grammar, mechanics, and usage skills.

12 Grammar Minilessons
Grades 1–6 Teacher's book of lessons, practice, and writing applications for grammar, mechanics, and usage.

13 Grammar Practice Book
Grades 1–6 Additional practice opportunities for objectives presented in the *Teacher's Planning Guide 5-Day Grammar Plan.* (Answer Key also available)

14 Spelling Activity Book
Grades 1–6 Writing activities and extension ideas for extra practice or for homework/parent involvement. (Teacher's Guide also available)

15 Writing and Language Handbook
Grades 1–6 Student reference book with focus on writing process and writing models, study skills, and language skills. Includes a writing, language, and literary manual.

16 Writing Process Transparencies
Grades 1–6 Full-color transparencies to model each stage of the writing process.

Give explicit skill instruction as needed.

ABC Cards
Grades K–1 Textured letter forms in upper-case and lowercase provide tactile learning.

Alphabet Posters
Grades K–1 Colorful posters to display letters of the alphabet with well-illustrated pictures representing the beginning sound made by each letter.

Literacy Launch Practice Book
Grade 1 Activities for teaching sound/symbol relationships of letters and basic comprehension strategies.

Literature Activity Book
Grade K Colorful activities for exploring print, practicing phonics, and responding to literature.

17 Phonics Activity Book
Grades 1–2 Focus on vowel sounds, phonograms, blends, digraphs, and key phonetic elements. (Teacher's Guide also available)

Phonics Support Blackline Masters
Grades 1–2 Explicit phonics lessons including teaching lessons and blackline masters.

18 Practice Book
Grades K–6 Practice opportunities with phonics, instructional vocabulary, comprehension and vocabulary strategies, study skills, and story comprehension. (Teacher's Guide also available)

19 Reteaching Blackline Masters
Grades 1–6 Reteaching opportunities for each assessed skill.

20 Vocabulary Strategy Blackline Masters/Transparencies
Grades 1–6 Activities for developing concepts and vocabulary found in the literature. (Available in blackline master or transparency format)

Word Building Kit
Grades 1–2 Letters, blends, digraphs, and phonograms that students use to manipulate language and build words.

Word Masks
Grades K–2 A teaching tool used to frame or isolate words, letters, and phrases.

Spotlight on Literacy Enables You to:

◆ *Reach all students through award-winning and unabridged literature.*

◆ *Teach all skills your students need to achieve success in reading.*

◆ *Assess student progress through ongoing, easy-to-use evaluations.*

◆ *Minimize planning time with a comprehensive, easy-to-use Teacher's Planning Guide.*

LITERATURE:

Provide access to literature for all students.

1 Anthology/Unitized Pupil Editions
Grades 1–6 Thematically organized collections of trade book literature. (Grades 1–5 are available in a soft-cover unitized format or a single-volume hardcover anthology for each level. Grade 6 is available as a hard-cover anthology only.)

Big Book of Alphabet Rhymes and Chimes
Grade K Familiar rhymes, chimes, and poems to assist in letter and sound instruction.

Big Book of Poems
Grade K Theme-related poems which offer opportunities for teachers to tie print to oral language.

Big Book of Rhymes and Chimes
Grades 1–2 Rhymes for the phono-grams presented in instructional lessons.

Big Book of Songs
Grade K Well-known songs that are used to introduce the major concept for each thematic unit.

Big Book of Songs and Poems
Grade 1 Songs and poems that are used to extend and enrich children's experiences with literature.

Big Books/Little Books
2 *Grades K–1* Big book/little book versions of the pupil's trade book literature.

Learning Centers
Grades 1–3 Learning centers that rein-force language, reading, and writing skills. Each kit includes eight hands-on activities that explore the theme of the unit.

3 Multilanguage Support Blackline Masters
Grades 1–6 Selected literature translated into five languages (Spanish, Hmong, Vietnamese, Cantonese, and Cambodian). Includes introduction with suggestions for use by teachers and classroom aides.

4 Read Alouds, Plays, and Choral Readings
Grades 1–6 Collection of read alouds, plays, poems, and choral readings, from cultures throughout the world, thematically related to the literature in the *Anthology/Unitized Pupil Editions*.

Rhyme and Chime Strips
Grade K Illustrated strips for each nursery rhyme in the *Big Book of Alphabet Rhymes and Chimes,* to allow students to explore language patterns, concepts of print, and high-utility vocabulary.

Sing and Read Books
Grade K Emergent reading books that contain familiar songs or refrains taken from the theme song of each unit.

5 Spotlight Books: Comprehension
Grades 3–6 Stories and articles that encourage students to apply the skills and strategies they are learning.

6 Spotlight Books: Literacy Support
Grades 1–2 Emergent readers and independent reading books linked to the content of the main selections.

7 Spotlight Books: Phonics and Decoding
Grades 1–2 Patterned language books for applying phonics and decoding strategies and reinforcing phonograms and spelling patterns.

8 Spotlight Books: Theme
Grades 3–6 High-interest books related to the unit and selection themes.

9 Spotlight Books: Vocabulary
Grades 3–6 Books to reinforce the instructional vocabulary in a new context.

10 Spotlight Books: Vocabulary/ Comprehension
Grades 1–2 Stories that encourage students to practice instructional vocabulary and apply the skills and strategies they are learning.

Story Strips
Grade 1 Story strips for the literature selections to allow students to explore language patterns, concepts of print, and high-utility vocabulary.

Teacher's Read Aloud Anthology
Grade K A collection of stories, folk tales, and poems from various cultures that supports the theme of each unit.

Theme Big Books
Grades 1–3 Big books to set the unit theme and make content-area connections.

Trade Book Library
Grades 1–6 Thematically related fiction and nonfiction trade books at different reading levels.

Zoo-Be-Doo: A Literacy Launch Big Book/Little Book
Grade 1 Trade books to help introduce and reinforce concepts of print, sound/symbol relationships, and comprehension strategies. (Available in both big book and little book format)

MANAGEABILITY:

Manage resources easily—TEACH more, plan less.

21 ESL/Second-Language Teacher's Guide
Grades 1–6 Parallel teaching lessons for core literature; designed for students acquiring English.

22 Graphic Organizers for Reading and Writing
Grades 1–6 Graphic models to organize information from reading and listening and to generate information for writing and speaking. (Available in blackline master or transparency format)

23 Home Involvement Activities
Grades 1–6 Literature-specific activities for core selections in English and Spanish.

Homewords
Grade K A newsletter with family-centered articles and activities that establish cross-curricular and home/school connections.

Literacy Launch Teacher's Planning Guide
Grade 1 Teaching ideas to help build background for phonics and comprehension activities included in the *Literacy Launch Practice Book.*

24 Macmillan/McGraw-Hill Staff Development Guide
Grades K–6 Teacher-oriented guide with background articles and classroom practice ideas.

25 Teacher's Planning Guide
Grades K–6 Thematic planning guide for integrated language arts instruction, with phonics, vocabulary, spelling, grammar, writing, and trade book lessons.

Theme Big Book Lessons
Grades 1–3 Lessons for theme-support and content-area big books. Lessons focus on shared, paired, and group reading and include teaching ideas for students acquiring English.

INTEGRATED ASSESSMENT:

Assess student progress at any stage of instruction.

26 Diagnostic/Placement Evaluations Blackline Masters/Teacher's Manual
Grades 1–6 Easy-to-use assessment instruments that supply teachers with information for making placement and instructional decisions. These evaluations include Individual Reading Inventory/ Running Record and Decoding and Phonics Inventory.

Early Literacy Assessment Blackline Masters/Teacher's Manual
Grades K–1 Group and individual assessments of students' print awareness, phonemic awareness, letter and word recognition, vocabulary, comprehension, writing, story retelling, and story response.

27 Increase Your Testing Power for Standardized Tests
Grades 1–6 Practice tests for reading, language arts, and mathematics to prepare students for standardized tests.

28 Performance Assessment Handbook
Grades K–6 A guide for implementing performance-based assessment.

29 Progress Assessment
Grades 1–6 Formal assessments in both written-response and multiple-choice formats for reading, writing, listening, and study skills. Includes assessment by unit as well as pre-book, mid-year, and end-year assessments. (Teacher's Manual also available)

30 Selection and Unit Assessments
Grades 1–6 Quick multiple-choice assessments of skills/strategies and vocabulary for each selection, with cumulative unit assessments based on short reading passages. (Teacher's Manual also available)

COMPONENT CHART GRADES K–6

	K	1	2	3	4	5	6
LITERATURE RESOURCES							
Anthology (hardcover)		■	■	■	■	■	■
Big Book of Alphabet Rhymes and Chimes	■						
Big Book of Poems	■						
Big Book of Rhymes and Chimes		■	■				
Big Book of Songs	■						
Big Book of Songs and Poems		■					
Big Books	■	■					
Little Books	■	■					
Sing and Read Books	■						
Theme Big Books		■	■	■			
Trade Book Library		■	■	■	■	■	■
Unitized Pupil Editions (softcover)		■	■	■	■	■	
Zoo-Be-Doo: A Literacy Launch Big Book/Little Book		■					
TEACHER'S MATERIALS							
Daily Language Activities Transparencies		■	■	■		■	■
ESL/Second-Language Teacher's Guide		■	■	■		■	■
Graphic Organizers for Reading and Writing (Blackline Masters)*		■	■	■		■	■
Graphic Organizers for Reading and Writing (Transparencies)*		■	■	■		■	■
Homewords	■						
Literacy Launch Teacher's Planning Guide		■					
Macmillan/McGraw-Hill Staff Development Guide*	■	■					■
Multilanguage Support Blackline Masters		■	■	■		■	■
Read Alouds, Plays, and Choral Readings		■	■	■		■	■
Teacher's Planning Guide	■	■	■	■		■	
Teacher's Read Aloud Anthology	■						
Theme Big Book Lessons		■	■	■			
Vocabulary Strategy Blackline Masters		■	■	■		■	■
Vocabulary Strategy Transparencies		■	■	■		■	
Writing Process Transparencies		■	■	■		■	
ASSESSMENT							
Diagnostic/Placement Evaluations Blackline Masters/Teacher's Manual*		■	■	■		■	■
Early Literacy Assessment Blackline Masters/Teacher's Manual	■	■					
Increase Your Testing Power for Standardized Tests		■	■	■	■	■	■
Performance Assessment Handbook	■	■	■	■	■	■	■
Progress Assessments (Teacher's Manual also available)		■	■	■		■	■
Selection and Unit Assessments (Teacher's Manual also available)		■	■	■		■	■
MANIPULATIVES, PHONICS, PRACTICE AND SUPPORT RESOURCES							
ABC Cards	■	■					
Alphabet Posters	■	■					
Grammar Minilessons			■	■		■	■
Grammar Practice Book (Answer Key also available)			■	■	■	■	■
Home Involvement Activities		■	■	■			
Learning Centers		■	■	■			
Literacy Launch Practice Book		■					
Literature Activity Book	■						
Mini Pocket Charts		■	■				
Phonics Activity Book (Teacher's Guide also available)		■	■				
Phonics Support Blackline Masters		■					
Pocket Chart	■						
Pocket Chart Stand	■						
Practice Book (Teacher's Guide also available)	■	■	■	■		■	■
Reteaching Blackline Masters		■	■	■		■	■
Rhyme and Chime Strips	■						
Spelling Activity Book (Teacher's Guide also available)		■	■	■		■	■
Spotlight Books: Comprehension				■	■	■	■
Spotlight Books: Literacy Support		■	■				
Spotlight Books: Phonics and Decoding		■	■				
Spotlight Books: Theme				■	■	■	■
Spotlight Books: Vocabulary				■	■	■	■
Spotlight Books: Vocabulary/Comprehension		■					
Story Strips		■					
Word Building Kit			■				
Word Masks	■	■	■				
Writing and Language Handbook		■	■	■		■	■
MULTIMEDIA							
CLOZE Reading Audiocassettes		■					
Listening Library Audiocassettes	■	■	■	■	■	■	■
MediaWeaver (CD-ROM/Floppy Disc)							■
Multimedia Literature (CD-ROM)					■	■	■
Sights & Sounds (CD-ROM)	■	■	■				
Sing a Sound Audiocassettes	■						
Sing and Read Audiocassettes	■						
Songs and Stories Audiocassettes	■						
Story Lane Theater Videos	■	■	■	■	■	■	■
Story Web™: Multimedia Literature for the Primary Grades (CD-ROM)		■	■				
'Tronic Phonics™ (CD-ROM)		■	■				

*Denotes a single component that spans the grade levels

MULTIMEDIA:

Experience literature in new, exciting ways.

31 CLOZE Reading Audiocassettes
Grade 1, Levels 1–3 CLOZE reading of the selections in Levels 1-3 to offer repeated reading opportunities that take advantage of the predictable language of the literature.

32 Listening Library Audiocassettes
Grades K–6 Dramatic readings of selected literature and poems that enhance students' literary awareness and access to the literature. Include authentic voices for multicultural selections.

33 MediaWeaver
Grade 6 A writing tool to enable students to turn their written documents into dynamic projects by adding art, sound, photographs, and movies. (Available in both CD-ROM format and on floppy disc)

34 Multimedia Literature
Grades 3–6 CD-ROM selections from *Spotlight on Literacy.* Each module contains background building activities, interactive reading strategies, and a writing tool.

35 Sights & Sounds
Grades K–2 An interactive phonics program for emergent readers.

Students can explore the sounds of our language — letters and phonograms — and learn to connect these sounds with print. (Available in both CD-ROM format and on floppy disc)

36 Sing a Sound Audiocassettes
Grade K Familiar songs and recordings to support phonemic awareness and phonics instruction in beginning sounds, both for initial consonants and for vowels.

37 Sing and Read Audiocassettes
Grade K A collection of traditional and contemporary songs taken from the *Big Book of Songs,* plus a reading of each of the *Sing and Read Books.*

38 Songs and Stories Audiocassettes
Grades K–6 A collection of theme songs, story songs, sound effects, and multicultural storytellings that are thematically related to the literature

in the *Anthology/Unitized Pupil Editions.*

39 Story Lane Theater Videos
Grades K–6 Video presentations of folk tales, artists interviews, and suggestions for reading strategy instruction.

40 Story Web™: Multimedia Literature for the Primary Grades
Grades 1–2 Featuring selections from *Spotlight on Literacy.* Each module contains background building activities, interactive reading strategies, a 5-step phonics lesson, and a writing tool.

41 'Tronic Phonics™
Grades 1–2 A fun, motivating way to teach, practice, and review phonograms. Each module features a selection from the *Spotlight Books: Phonics and Decoding* with a 5-step phonics lesson and an opportunity to "make a book."

42 Web Site
Visit Macmillan/McGraw-Hill's Home Page at **http://www.mmhschool.com**

Spotlight on Literacy Enables Your Students to:

◆ *Experience success in reading through high-interest, multilevel literature.*

◆ *Become independent readers through phonics, skills, and strategy instruction.*

◆ *Develop Language Arts competency through lessons and activities for spelling, writing, grammar, listening, speaking, and viewing.*

◆ *Increase knowledge through engaging and integrated technology.*

GRADE 1 ◆ LEVEL 4 ◆ UNIT 2

SURPRISES

ALONG
THE WAY

**Macmillan
McGraw-Hill**

NEW YORK   FARMINGTON

Macmillan/McGraw-Hill
A Division of The McGraw-Hill Companies

Macmillan/McGraw-Hill
1221 Avenue of the Americas
New York, New York 10020

Printed in the United States of America
ISBN 0-02-181154-7 / 1, L.4, U.2
3 4 5 6 7 8 9 WEB 02 01 00 99 98 97

The Authors

Spotlight on Literacy

Dr. Virginia Arnold

Dr. Arnold Webb

Dr. James Hoffman

Dr. James Flood

Dr. Karen D. Wood

Dr. Diane Lapp

Mr. Michael Priestley

Dr. Elaine Aoki

Dr. Josefina Villamil Tinajero

Dr. Miriam Martinez

Dr. Carl B. Smith

Dr. Annemarie Sullivan-Palincsar

Dr. William Teale

Anthology

THEME FOCUS: Life is full of surprises.

CONTENTS

Fantasy

Realistic/Fiction

Folk Tale

Realistic/Fiction

Flexible Grouping Options

See **Suggested *5-Day* Lesson Planners** for:
One Monday Morning, 140C–D
You'll Soon Grow into Them, Titch, 180C–D

Seven Blind Mice, 212C–D
The Surprise Family, 256C–D

GROUPING OPTIONS	PART 1 — DAY 1 FOCUS ON READING	PART 2 — DAYS 2-3 READ THE LITERATURE	PART 3 — DAYS 4-5 EXTEND SKILLS IN CONTEXT
Whole Group	**Prepare to Read** Evaluate Prior Knowledge **Vocabulary** Vocabulary, activity 1 **Grammar** **Spelling** **Phonics and Decoding** Develop Phonemic Awareness	**Strategic Reading** Set Purposes; Read and Teach **Respond to the Literature** Choose from among suggested response activities. **Grammar** **Spelling** **Phonics and Decoding** Discover the Spelling Pattern Choose from among suggested blending activities.	**Writing** Writing Process **Grammar** **Spelling** **Study Skills** **Phonics and Decoding** Writing Reading
Extra Support	**Prepare to Read** Build Background **Vocabulary** Oral Language Activities **PRACTICE BOOK** **Grammar** **GRAMMAR MINILESSONS** **Phonics and Decoding** 'TRONIC PHONICS™	**Strategic Reading** Read Aloud **LISTENING LIBRARY** **Respond to the Literature** Choose from among suggested response activities, **READER RESPONSE CARD**, and **PRACTICE BOOK**. **RETEACHING BLM** **Phonics and Decoding** Choose from among suggested blending activities. 'TRONIC PHONICS™	**Meeting Individual Needs** Spotlight: **LITERACY SUPPORT BOOK** **PHONICS AND DECODING BOOK** **VOCABULARY/COMPREHENSION BOOK** **Skills in Context** Choose from skills and strategies lessons. Vocabulary Review **Writing** Writing Projects **Phonics and Decoding** **PHONICS ACTIVITY BOOK** 'TRONIC PHONICS™
Challenge	**Prepare to Read** **Vocabulary** Vocabulary, activity 2 **Spelling** Challenge Words **Phonics and Decoding** **PHONICS SUPPORT BLM**	**Strategic Reading** Read Independently **Respond to the Literature** Choose from among suggested response activities and **READER RESPONSE CARD**. **Writing About the Theme** **Phonics and Decoding** **PHONICS SUPPORT BLM**	**Vocabulary** Vocabulary Strategy **Writing** Writing Projects **Across the Curriculum** Curriculum activities using different learning styles **Phonics and Decoding** 'TRONIC PHONICS™
Second-Language Support	**Vocabulary** Oral Language Activities **PRACTICE BOOK** **ESL/SECOND-LANGUAGE TEACHER'S GUIDE** with Phonics Lessons **"One Monday Morning"** is available in Spanish in **Cuentamundos**.	**Strategic Reading** Read Aloud **LISTENING LIBRARY** **MULTILANGUAGE SUPPORT BLM** **Grammar** Meeting Individual Needs **ESL/SECOND-LANGUAGE TEACHER'S GUIDE** with Phonics Lessons	**Meeting Individual Needs** **MULTILANGUAGE SUPPORT BLM** **Across the Curriculum** Curriculum activities using different learning styles **ESL/SECOND-LANGUAGE TEACHER'S GUIDE** with Phonics Lessons

Meeting Individual Needs

Multilevel Resources

SPOTLIGHT: PHONICS AND DECODING

EASY   AVERAGE

TRONICS & PHONICS   All titles are available on CD-ROM with a variety of phonics activities.

SPOTLIGHT: LITERACY SUPPORT

EARLY INTERVENTION

EASY

SPOTLIGHT: VOCABULARY/COMPREHENSION

EASY

INDEPENDENT READING

TRADE BOOK LIBRARY

EASY   AVERAGE

The Cow That Went OINK
written and illustrated by
Bernard Most

AVERAGE   CHALLENGE

Theme Resources

THEME
BigBook

Take children on an underwater expedition with the story *Fish Faces,* and explore the surprises of the deep blue sea.

READ ALOUDS, PLAYS, AND CHORAL READINGS

Share these short read-aloud pieces and plays before or after children read the corresponding unit selection.

ESL SECOND-LANGUAGE TEACHER'S GUIDE

This guidebook provides theme-related teaching ideas and literature activities for children acquiring English and other children who need extra language support.

SONGS AND STORIES AUDIOCASSETTES

Use the unit theme song "Surprise! Surprise!" to introduce the theme; play it often during the unit.

 ### TRADE BOOK LIBRARY

Encourage independent reading with *The Cow that Went Oink* and *Pet Show!* Multilevel reading experiences are suggested. **Complete lessons are also provided.**

LEARNING CENTERS

The **Literacy Explorers Learning Center** for this unit reinforces language, reading, and writing skills. It includes a poem poster and eight hands-on activities (on four laminated Activity Cards) that explore the theme of **surprises**. In addition, each Center has a Teacher's Guide that includes:

• Tips for using Center materials
• Grouping suggestions
• Support for second-language learners
• Assessment guidelines
• Extension ideas
• Blackline masters

CREATE CENTERS

Reading Center Display children's favorite books. Add the books from the Trade Book Library as well. Include books and other writing that children have created.

Writing Center Provide various writing tools. Surround children with multiple print modes such as magazines, advertisements, and food labels to serve as models for writing.

Language Center Include Big Books, and the Word Building Kit to encourage children to explore print.

Curriculum Centers Use the Theme Connections activities listed on page **138/139E** for ideas on Science, Art, Math, Music, and Social Studies Centers.

Theme Connections

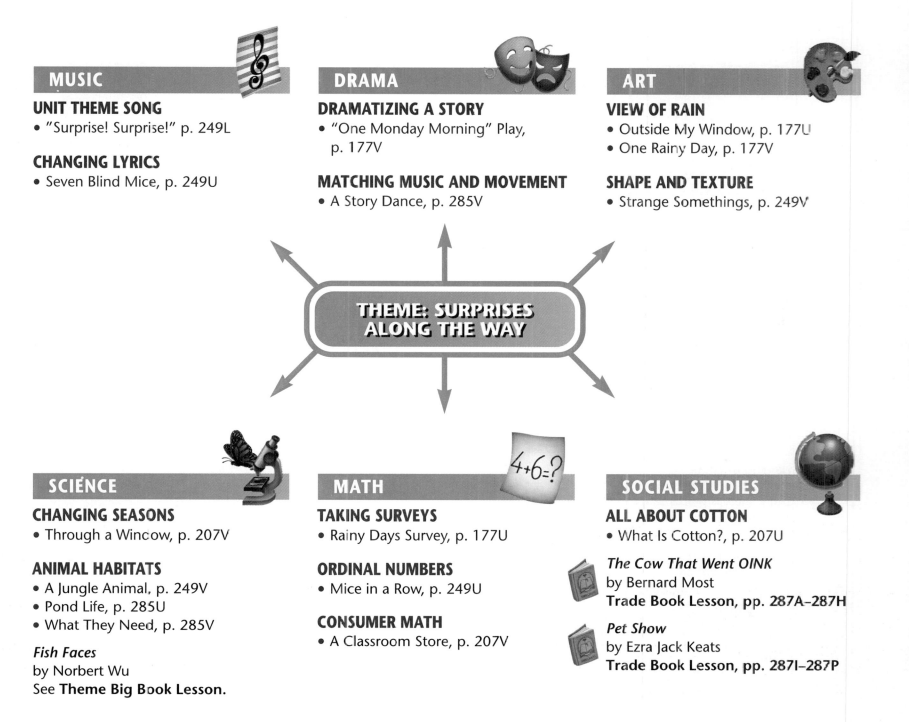

MUSIC

UNIT THEME SONG
- "Surprise! Surprise!" p. 249L

CHANGING LYRICS
- Seven Blind Mice, p. 249U

DRAMA

DRAMATIZING A STORY
- "One Monday Morning" Play, p. 177V

MATCHING MUSIC AND MOVEMENT
- A Story Dance, p. 285V

ART

VIEW OF RAIN
- Outside My Window, p. 177U
- One Rainy Day, p. 177V

SHAPE AND TEXTURE
- Strange Somethings, p. 249V

THEME: SURPRISES ALONG THE WAY

SCIENCE

CHANGING SEASONS
- Through a Window, p. 207V

ANIMAL HABITATS
- A Jungle Animal, p. 249V
- Pond Life, p. 285U
- What They Need, p. 285V

Fish Faces
by Norbert Wu
See **Theme Big Book Lesson.**

MATH

TAKING SURVEYS
- Rainy Days Survey, p. 177U

ORDINAL NUMBERS
- Mice in a Row, p. 249U

CONSUMER MATH
- A Classroom Store, p. 207V

SOCIAL STUDIES

ALL ABOUT COTTON
- What Is Cotton?, p. 207U

The Cow That Went OINK
by Bernard Most
Trade Book Lesson, pp. 287A–287H

Pet Show
by Ezra Jack Keats
Trade Book Lesson, pp. 287I–287P

MULti-AGe Classroom

The theme Surprises Along the Way is compatible
with themes in other grade levels.
Kindergarten: FIND IT OUT!
Grade 2: EUREKA!

MULTICULTURAL PERSPECTIVES

Encourage students to describe some of
their own cultural traditions. Have them
share anything they find surprising in other cultures.

Theme Bibliography

ONE MONDAY MORNING

The House That Jack Built
Illustrated by Emily Bolam 1992, E.P. Dutton
Bold, childlike, and amusing pictures illuminate this familiar cumulative verse. **VERY EASY**

The Napping House
Audrey Wood, illustrated by Donald Wood 1984, Harcourt Brace & Co.
In the napping house there is a cozy bed and in it is a snoring granny, a dozing dog, and others. All sleep peacefully until a small flea comes along. **EASY**

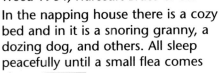

The Bag I'm Taking to Grandma's
Shirley Neitzel, pictures by Nancy Winslow Parker 1995, Greenwillow Books
In simple verse, we see a little boy's idea of what to pack for his short visit to Grandma's. **AVERAGE**

This Is the Bread I Baked for Ned
Crescent Dragonwagon, illustrated by Isadore Seltzer 1989, Macmillan
In swinging rhythmic verse, Glenda tells us of all the different kinds of food that she has prepared for Ned.

CHALLENGE

Abuela (Grandmother)
A. Dorros 1991, Dutton
Rosalba and her grandmother have a surprising adventure.

SPANISH **CHALLENGE**

YOU'LL SOON GROW INTO THEM, TITCH

♪ Mary Wore Her Red Dress
Adapted and illustrated by Merle Peek 1985, Clarion
Based on a Texas folk song, the narrative tells of Katy Bear's animal friends who, wearing variously colored clothing, gather and have a party.

VERY EASY

Jesse Bear, What Will You Wear?
Nancy White Carlstrom, illustrated by Bruce Degen 1986, Macmillan
In rhymed verse, we see Jesse Bear awaken, follow him through his day, and watch him go to sleep at night.

EASY

The Jacket I Wear in the Snow
Shirley Neitzel, pictures by Nancy Winslow Parker 1989, Greenwillow Books
A cumulative poem humorously demonstrates the frustration of layers of winter clothes. **AVERAGE**

Just My Size
May Garelick, pictures by William Pene du Bois 1990, HarperCollins
A girl remembers the beautiful coat she owned that was made into many things—a jacket, a vest, a knapsack—when it became too small for her to wear. **CHALLENGE**

Agú, agú, agú (Murmel, Murmel, Murmel)
Robert N. Munsch 1989, AP (Lectorum)
Robin makes a surprising find—a baby in a sandbox.

SPANISH **CHALLENGE**

TECHNOLOGY RESOURCES

A Boy Creates (Encyclopaedia Britannica Educational Corporation) Video, 10 Min. A boy creates a sculpture that comes alive.

Spelunx and the Cave of Mr. Seudo (Broderbund) Computer software Macintosh, IBM. Students visit a wonderful world that holds a surprise behind each door.

Harold's Fairy Tale (Weston Woods) Video or film, 8 Min. Harold draws himself into a castle and has a king, fairy, and giant for company.

The Human Body (National Geographic Educational Services) CD-ROM Macintosh, Windows. A tour of the body, showing how it works and how it grows.

Whistle for Willie (Weston Woods) Video, 6 Min. Willie wants to learn to whistle in order to call his dog and to prove he's growing up.

You Are Growing Day by Day (Encyclopaedia Britannica Educational Corporation) Video, 8 Min. A program that explains how children grow, emotionally and physically.

Books for All Levels and Curriculum Areas

ART   MULTICULTURAL HEALTH MATH MUSIC SCIENCE SOCIAL STUDIES

SEVEN BLIND MICE

Mouse Paint
Ellen Stoll Walsh 1989, Harcourt Brace Jovanovich

Three white mice find three jars of paint and experiment with mixing colors. The little mice are expressive and completely charming.

VERY EASY

Come Out and Play Little Mouse
Robert Kraus 1987, Greenwillow Books

Imaginative and amusing drawings support the story of how a persistent cat finally lures a mouse and the surprising way in which the mouse is saved.

EASY

Mouse Count
Ellen Stoll Walsh 1991, Harcourt Brace Jovanovich

This charming story tells how ten courageous and clever mice outwit a greedy snake. Delightful and witty collage illustrations support the text.

AVERAGE

The Picnic
Ruth Brown 1993, Dutton Children's Books

A family picnic seen from the animals' point of view. Rich, imaginative drawings make this book a treasure; it is also a fine impetus for story writing.

CHALLENGE

Adelaide
Tomi Ungerer 1983, Lectorum

A winged kangaroo sees the world and lands in Paris.

SPANISH **AVERAGE**

THE SURPRISE FAMILY

I Had a Cat
Mona Rabun Reeves, illustrated by Julie Downing 1989, Bradbury Press

A joyful little girl has a huge family of pets. When their numbers become overwhelming, however, she finds suitable homes for them all.

VERY EASY

Is Your Mama a Llama?
Deborah Guarino, pictures by Steven Kellogg 1989, Scholastic

The baby llama asks the other animals, "Is your mama a llama?" Their replies give hints as to what kinds of animals their mamas are.

EASY

Aunt Nina and Her Nephews and Nieces
Franz Brandenburg, illustrated by Aliki 1983, Greenwillow

Aunt Nina's nieces and nephews come to visit. A surprise in the form of a family of new kittens means delightful presents for all.

AVERAGE

The Kitten Who Thought He Was a Mouse
Miriam Norton, illustrated by Garth Williams 1982, Artist's & Writer's Guild Book

A family of field mice adopt a newborn kitten found in their nest, and raise him as one of their own children.

CHALLENGE

Petunia
Roger Duvoisin 1977, Shen's Books and Supplies

A barnyard adventure. **CHINESE**

Whazzat? (Adapted from the folk tale "The Six Blind Men and the Elephant") (Encyclopaedia Britannica Educational Corporation) Video, 10 Min. Six clay figures think that the elephant they are touching is something else.

Kick Me (Encyclopaedia Britannica Educational Corporation) Video, 8 Min. Two legs that are always kicking things run into giant trouble and then must run for their lives.

Designer Puzzles (MECC) Computer software Apple II. A collection of enjoyable learning puzzles.

The Dog Who Had Kittens (Pied Piper/AIMS Multimedia) Video, 14 Min. A dog gets a surprise family.

Stellaluna (Reading Rainbow/GPN) Video, 30 Min. A baby bat is raised by a family of birds.

Copycat Dog (Troll Associates) Video, 9 Min. A dog acts like each of the farm animals he encounters.

Overview

☑ These core skills are tested in the Unit Progress Assessment.

	PHONICS/DECODING CONCEPTS OF PRINT	COMPREHENSION STRATEGIES	VOCABULARY AND STUDY SKILLS	SPELLING/GRAMMAR, MECHANICS, AND USAGE
One Monday Morning	Directionality, 147 Capital Letters, 151 ☑ Short Vowels: /u/-*ut*, 153 ☑ Consonant Blends: /dr/*dr*, 175 ☑ Long Vowels: /ā/-*ame*, 177G–177I Rhyming, Blending, 177J	☑ Make Predictions, 140–177B, 157 ☑ Cause and Effect, 149 ☑ Make Inferences, 159 ☑ Distinguish Between Fantasy and Reality, 165 Self-Monitoring Strategies, 167 Second-Language Support, 151, 152, 156	Language Support, 140F Instructional Vocabulary, 140G Compound Words, 169 Content Words, 173 Vocabulary Review, 177K Study Skills: ☑ Use Reference Sources, 177S	5-Day Spelling Plan, 177Q–177R Long Vowel Patterns *came, same, game, name, frame* Challenge Words: *just, home* 5-Day Grammar Plan, *Come* and *Came*, 177O–177P Second-Language Support, 177O
You'll Soon Grow into Them, Titch	☑ Short Vowels: /i/-*ig*, 185 ☑ Consonant Blends: /kl/*cl*, 199 Quotations, 205 ☑ Long Vowels: /ō/-*old*, 207G–207I Rhyming, Blending, 207J	☑ Character, Plot, Setting, 180–207B, 203 ☑ Problem and Solution, 183 ☑ Sequence of Events, 193 ☑ Summarize, 195 ☑ Use Illustrations, 197 Second-Language Support, 191, 198	Language Support, 180H Instructional Vocabulary, 180I Contractions, 191 Vocabulary Review, 207K Study Skills: ☑ Use Graphic Aids, 207S	5-Day Spelling Plan, 207Q–207R Long Vowel Patterns *old, gold, told, sold, cold* Challenge Words: *him, new* 5-Day Grammar Plan, *Say* and *Said*, 207O–207P Verbs (Present and Past Tense), 187 Second-Language Support, 207O
Seven Blind Mice	☑ Long Vowels: /ī/-*ice*, 215 Capital Letters, 217 Quotation Marks, 223 ☑ Consonant Blends: /hw/*wh*, 241 ☑ Long Vowels: /ī/-*ide*, 249G–249I Rhyming, Blending, 249J	☑ Make Predictions, 212–249B, 221 ☑ Use Illustrations, 219 ☑ Sequence of Events, 227 Self-Monitoring Strategies, 231, 237 Draw Conclusions, 235 ☑ Spatial Relationships, 243 Second-Language Support, 217, 220	Language Support, 212F Instructional Vocabulary, 212G Vocabulary Review, 249K Study Skills: ☑ Use Parts of a Book, 249S	5-Day Spelling Plan, 249Q–249R Long Vowel Patterns *side, wide, slide, ride, hide* Challenge Words: *first, find* 5-Day Grammar Plan, *Go* and *Went*, 249O–249P Verbs (*Is* and *Are*), 245 Second-Language Support, 249O
The Surprise Family	☑ Long Vowels: /ī/-*ide*, 261 Directionality, 265 ☑ Consonant Blends: /sw/*sw*, 275 ☑ Long Vowels: /ā/-*ay*, 285G–285I Rhyming, Blending, 285J	☑ Character, Plot, Setting, 256–285B, 271 ☑ Problem and Solution, 259 Self-Monitoring Strategies, 277 ☑ Summarize, 279 ☑ Compare and Contrast, 281 Second-Language Support, 260, 270	Language Support, 256F Instructional Vocabulary, 256G Unfamiliar Words, 267 Vocabulary Review, 285K Study Skills: ☑ Follow Directions, 285S	5-Day Spelling Plan, 285Q–285R Long Vowel Patterns *away, anyway, bay, day, say* Challenge words: *every, only* 5-Day Grammar Plan, *Was* and *Were*, 285O–285P Second-Language Support, 285O

Unit Vocabulary Review, 287R

WRITING	LISTENING, SPEAKING, VIEWING	INTEGRATED CURRICULUM	TECHNOLOGY RESOURCES	MULTILEVEL RESOURCES
Journal Writing, 140H, 177A From Reading to Writing, 167, 177 Writing: Exaggeration, 177 Writing About the Theme, 177A Writing Process: Place Description, 177M Writing Projects, 177N	Listening, Speaking, Viewing, 177L Read Aloud, "La Hormiguita," a folk tale Second-Language Support, 177L Reading Fluency, Choral Reading, 155	Respond to the Literature, 177A Multicultural Perspectives, 163, 177T Visual Arts, 145 Across the Curriculum, 177U–177V	*The Game* ☑ Long Vowels: /ā/-ame Film/Video, *Harold's Fairy Tale* (Weston Woods) *Spelunx and the Cave of Mr. Seudo* (Broderbund) Song and Stories Audiocassette, "*Little Prince*," 177L	*One Sunny Morning* Early Intervention, 177E *The Game* ☑ Long Vowels: /ā/-ame, 177F *The Apple Mystery* Vocabulary ☑ Make Predictions, 177F *The Cow that Went OINK* ☑ Make Predictions, 177F
Journal Writing, 180J, 207A From Reading to Writing, 205, 207 Writing: Characterization, 207 Writing About the Theme, 207A Writing Process: Character Description, 207M Writing Projects, 207N Unit Writing Process: Description, 211A–211H	Listening, Speaking, Viewing, 207L Read Aloud, "The Emperor's New Clothes," a fairy tale Second-Language Support, 207L	Respond to the Literature, 207A Multicultural Perspectives, 201, 207T Across the Curriculum, 207U–207V	*Old Jack Fold* ☑ Long Vowels: /ō/-old *Sights and Sounds* ☑ Long Vowels: /ō/-old Film/Video, *Whistle for Willie* (Weston Woods) *The Human Body* (Nat'l Geo. Ed. Serv.) Songs and Stories, "*Seeds*," 207L	*Sarah's Surprise* Early Intervention, 207E *Old Jack Fold* ☑ Long Vowels: /ō/-old, 207F *Good Idea, Mikey!* Vocabulary ☑ Character, Plot, Setting, 207F
From Reading to Writing, 223, 233, 235, 249 Writing: Fable, 249 Writing About the Theme, 249A Writing Process: Explanation, 249M Writing Projects, 249N Journal Writing, 212H, 249A	Listening, Speaking, Viewing, 249L Read Aloud, "Test of a Friendship," a folk tale Second-Language Support, 249L Reading Fluency, Choral Reading, 225, 239	Respond to the Literature, 249A Multicultural Perspectives, 247, 249T Visual Arts, 229 Across the Curriculum, 249U–249V	*What a Ride!* ☑ Long Vowels: /ī/-ide Film/Video, *Whazzat?* (Encyclopaedia Britannica Educational Corporation), *Kick Me* (Encyclopaedia Britannica Educational Corporation) *Designer Puzzles* (MECC)	*Elephant Boy*, 249E Early Intervention *What a Ride!* ☑ Long Vowels: /ī/-ide, 249F *Rover* Vocabulary ☑ Make Predictions, 249F *Fish Faces* ☑ Use Illustrations, 249F
Journal Writing, 256H, 285A From Reading to Writing, 285 Writing: Story, 285 Writing About the Theme, 285A Writing Process: Description, 285M Writing Projects, 285N	Listening, Speaking, Viewing, 285L Read Aloud, "Lion and the Ostrich Chicks," a folk tale Second-Language Support, 285L You may want to have children perform "Just Like This" from Read Alouds, Plays, and Choral Readings.	Respond to the Literature, 285A Multicultural Perspectives, 285T Visual Arts, 273 Across the Curriculum, 285U–285V Unit Theme Review, 287Q	*Molly May* ☑ Long Vowels: /ā/-ay Film/Video, *The Dog Who Had Kittens* (Pied Piper/AIMS Multimedia), *Stellaluna* (Reading Rainbow/GPN), *Copycat Dog* (Troll Associates) Songs and Stories, "*Shaiu Ya* (Little Duck)," 285L	*Beak-a-Boo*, 285E Early Intervention *Molly May* ☑ Long Vowels: /ā/-ay, 285F *Just the Same* Vocabulary ☑ Character, Plot, Setting, 285F *Pet Show* ☑ Character, Plot, Setting, 285F

Cooperative Project

PROJECT: SKITS ABOUT SURPRISES

Children explore the theme of unexpected happenings by creating and performing their own skits about surprising events.

PROJECT MATERIALS
- note paper
- self-stick paper
- supplies for making simple props, such as boxes, paper bags and plates, yarn, construction paper, markers, crayons, scissors, glue

SUGGESTED ROLES
- Note Taker
- Stage Manager
- Director
- Clean-up Manager

STEP 1 INTRODUCE THE PROJECT
Before reading the first selection

Ask children to tell about plays they have seen. Explain that they will create and perform skits about surprising events that happen to people. Teams can brainstorm ideas and the **note taker** can record them.

STEP 2 CREATE THE SKIT
After reading the first selection

Teams choose an event from their list to turn into a skit. Then children draw pictures of the scenes and place them in order. Team members can write dialog on self-stick paper and attach it to the pictures. The **clean-up manager** supervises the clean-up.

STEP 3 COMPLETE THE SKIT
After reading the second selection

Team members can choose parts to act out and a **director** to oversee rehearsals. The **stage manager** can supervise prop making. Children should improvise additional dialog as they rehearse.

STEP 4 FINAL REHEARSALS
After reading the third selection

Teams continue to rehearse. Have **directors** check that the story is clear and complete. The **stage manager** can supervise prop set-up.

STEP 5 PERFORM THE SKIT
After reading the fourth selection

Invite teams to perform their skits. After the performance, encourage children to talk about the surprising things that happened. Teams may evaluate their own work.

See **page 287Q** for informal assessment suggestions.

Unit Assessment Plan

INFORMAL

INFORMAL ASSESSMENT

- Comprehension, 154, 158, 160, 164, 176, 177B, 192, 196, 200, 206, 207B, 224, 232, 238, 248, 249B, 266, 272, 276, 284, 285B

SCORING RUBRICS

- Cooperative Project, 287Q
- Selection Writing Process, 177M, 207M, 249M, 285M
- Unit Writing Process, 211H

PORTFOLIO ASSESSMENT

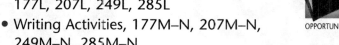

PORTFOLIO

OPPORTUNITIES

- Listening, Speaking, Viewing Activities, 177L, 207L, 249L, 285L
- Writing Activities, 177M–N, 207M–N, 249M–N, 285M–N
- Cross-Curricular Activities, 177U–V, 207U–V, 249U–V, 285U–V

PRACTICE BOOK

- Comprehension
    Cause and Effect, 199
    Make, Confirm or Revise Predictions, 201, 223
    Make Inferences, 202
    Distinguish Between Fantasy and Reality, 203
    Problem and Solution, 209
    Sequence of Events, 212, 224
    Summarize, 213, 237
    Use Illustrations, 214, 222
    Character, Plot, Setting, 216, 235
    Spatial Relationships, 226
    Compare and Contrast, 238

- Phonics and Decoding
    Short Vowels and Phonograms, 200, 210, 234
    Long Vowels and Phonograms, 206, 218, 221, 228, 233, 240
    Consonant Blends, 204, 207, 211, 215, 219, 225, 229, 236, 241

FORMAL

SELECTION TESTS

- Comprehension and Vocabulary
    One Monday Morning, 13–14
    You'll Soon Grow into Them, Titch, 15–16
    Seven Blind Mice, 17–18
    The Surprise Family, 19–20

UNIT PROGRESS ASSESSMENT*

- Comprehension
    Cause and Effect, 6
    Make, Confirm or Revise Predictions, 8
    Make Inferences, 6
    Distinguish Between Fantasy and Reality; Use Illustrations, 7
    Problem and Solution, 6, 7
    Sequence of Events, 7
    Summarize, 8
    Character, Plot, Setting, 6
    Spatial Relationships, 7
    Compare and Contrast, 7
- Phonics and Decoding
    Short Vowels and Phonograms, 12
    Long Vowels and Phonograms, 12
    Consonant Blends, 12

DIAGNOSTIC/PLACEMENT EVALUATIONS BLM

- Individual Reading Inventory, 7–14
- Running Record, 15–22
- Phonics and Decoding Inventory, 85–87

PERFORMANCE ASSESSMENT HANDBOOK

- Portfolios, 9–23
- Evaluation Forms and Checklists, 69–70, 82–93
- Self-Assessment Forms, 71–81

* Page numbers are for Multiple-Choice Tests. Written Response Tests are also available.

One Monday Morning

Selection Summary

It is a rainy day, and a bored little boy imagines that "the king, the queen, and the little prince" have come to visit him. They return every day for a week adding a new member to their entourage with each visit. But the boy is never home until the sun shines high in the sky and the fantasy ends.

Linking Skills to Literature

Key Comprehension Strategies/Skills

☑ **MAKE, CONFIRM, REVISE PREDICTIONS**

MAKING, CONFIRMING, REVISING PREDICTIONS
A party of royalty and its subjects return time and again to pay a visit, only to be turned away every time. Children will use their natural interest in repetition to learn the pattern of this story and predict its repeating outcome.

INTERACTING WITH THE TEXT

ENGAGE THE READER Children will have an opportunity to interact with the text by making and confirming their predictions of the story's outcome. Each child will record his or her predictions in a daily chart.

See **pages 140H** and **140**, where the story pages begin.

WRITER — ILLUSTRATOR

URI SHULEVITZ

Uri Shulevitz came to New York from Israel in 1956 and studied painting at the Brooklyn Museum Art School. He began writing his own books following a suggestion from the editors at a publishing company.

Uri sees the process of putting a book together as similar to the game of "telephone." The story goes through many stages, continually incorporating small changes until the end result looks entirely different from the original idea.

Other Books by Uri Shulevitz
- *Secret Room* (Farrar, Straus, Giroux, 1993)
- *The Strange and Exciting Adventures of Jeramiah Hush* (Farrar, Straus, Giroux, 1986)
- *The Treasure* (Farrar, Straus, Giroux, 1979)

Suggested Lesson Planner
With Flexible Grouping Options

WEEK AT A GLANCE	PART 1 — DAY 1 FOCUS ON READING	PART 2 — DAY 2 READ THE LITERATURE
◆ Reading **◆ Writing** **◆ Listening, Speaking, Viewing**	Preview the Selection, 140E ● Build Background, 140E Graphic Organizer Transparency/BLM 31 ● Oral Language Activities, 140F *See also* ESL/Second-Language Teacher's Guide, 187–196 Vocabulary, 140G Instructional Vocabulary *cook* *queen* *prince* *visit* *return* *knight* Vocabulary Transparency/BLM 5 Practice Book, 198 If you wish to have children begin reading the selection at this point, see page 140H.	Set Purposes, 140H Journal Writing Suggestions for Reading, 140H ● Read Independently ●● Read Aloud ● Read Together Read and Teach Teach Strategic Reading, 140H–177 ☑ Make, Confirm, Revise Predictions
◆ Phonics and Decoding	☑ Develop Phonemic Awareness for *-ame*, 177G Long *a*: Lessons and Practice ● Phonics Support BLM 24, 80	☑ Discover the Spelling Pattern *-ame*, 177Q
◆ Spelling	For a detailed 5-day lesson plan for spelling, see pages 177Q–177R. Pretest (long *a*), 177Q Word in dark type appears in the story. **came** *same game name frame* Spelling Activity Book, 91	● Challenge Words *just home* Explore the Pattern, 177Q–177R Spelling Activity Book, 92
◆ Grammar, Mechanics, and Usage	Daily Language Activity: *Come* and *Came* 1. The king comes to visit on Monday. (came) 2. Many people come with him. (came) 3. He comes to visit on Tuesday, too. (came) Grammar Practice Book: *Come* and *Came*, 91 ● Grammar Minilessons: 21–22 See pages 177O–177P	Daily Language Activity: *Come* and *Came* 1. The king came every day. (comes) 2. The queen came, too. (comes) 3. They came with the little prince. (come) 5-Day Grammar Plan: *Come* and *Came*, 177O–177P Grammar Practice Book: *Come* and *Came*, 92

Flexible Grouping Options
- ● Extra Support
- ● Challenge
- ● Second-Language Support
- ☑ These core skills are tested in Unit Progress Assessment.

PART 3

DAY 3 — READ THE LITERATURE	DAY 4 — EXTEND SKILLS IN CONTEXT	DAY 5 — EXTEND SKILLS IN CONTEXT
Respond to the Literature Journal Writing, 177A ● Writing About the Theme, 177A Practice Book, 205 Comprehension Checkpoint, 177B ☑ Make, Confirm, Revise Predictions Graphic Organizer Transparency/BLM 30 ● Reteaching ☑ Make, Confirm, Revise Predictions, 157 Practice Book, 201 Vocabulary Selection Assessment Selection Assessment/Unit Progress Assessment, Levels 4/5	Skills in Context New York City Facts, 143 Technique, 145 Directionality, 147 ☑ Cause and Effect, 149 Practice Book, 199 Capital Letters, 151 ● ☑ Short Vowels and Phonograms: /u/-*ut*, 153 Practice Book, 200 Choral Reading, 155 ● ☑ Make, Confirm, Revise Predictions, 157 Practice Book, 201 ●●● Multilevel Resources, 177D–177F Vocabulary, 177K Listening, Speaking, Viewing, 177L Across the Curriculum, 177U	Skills in Context ☑ Make Inferences, 159 Practice Book, 202 Modeling and Partner Reading, 161 World Leaders, 163 ☑ Fantasy and Reality, 165 Practice Book, 203 Ask Questions, 167 Compound Words, 169 Narrative Point of View, 171 Content Words, 173 ● ☑ Consonant Blend /dr/-*dr*, 175 Practice Book, 204 Exaggeration, 177 Writing Process: Place Description, 177M ●● Writing Projects, 177N Study Skills/ Reading Resources: Use Reference Sources, 177S Multicultural Perspectives Fun without the Sun, 177T Across the Curriculum, 177V
☑ Decoding Strategies: Blending Activities, 177H Practice Book, 206 s|ame g|ame fr|ame	☑ Writing with the Phonogram, 177I ● Phonics Activity Book, 105–106	☑ Reading with the Phonogram, 177I ☑ Maintain Consonant Blend: *pr*, 177J Practice Book, 207 ● Phonics Activity Book, 107–108 'TRONIC PHONICS™
Constructing Words, 177R Work with Meaning, 177R Spelling Activity Book, 93	Spelling and Writing, 177R Spelling Activity Book, 94	Posttest, 177R Spelling Activity Book, 95
Daily Language Activity: *Come* and *Came* 1. A knight comes to see me on Wednesday. (came) 2. A royal guard comes, too. (came) 3. They come with the king and queen. (came) Writing Application: Story, 177P Grammar Practice Book: *Come* and *Came*, 93	Daily Language Activity: *Come* and *Came* 1. The royal cook came next. (comes) 2. Then came the royal barber. (comes) 3. All the visitors came at the same time. (come) Quick Write: Thank You Note, 177P Grammar Practice Book: *Come* and *Came*, 94	Daily Language Activity: *Come* and *Came* 1. The royal jester comes on Saturday. (came) 2. A little dog comes on Sunday. (came) 3. They all come to say hello. (came) Grammar Practice Book: *Come* and *Came*, 95; Answer Key and Grammar Assessment, 22

Prepare to Read

PREVIEW THE SELECTION

AUTHOR, ILLUSTRATOR
Read **page 177.** Discuss with children how the author, who is also the illustrator, got the idea for this story.

GENRE: FANTASY
Encourage children to preview the illustrations and text to predict what kind of story this is. Do the characters seem real or make-believe? What about the events? How can children tell?

EVALUATE PRIOR KNOWLEDGE

SUNNY AND RAINY DAYS
Brainstorm with children a list of fun things to do on a sunny day, and a list of fun things to do on a rainy day. Create a chart or display **GRAPHIC ORGANIZER TRANSPARENCY/BLM 31.**

Sunny Day Fun	Rainy Day Fun
go on a picnic	play cards
take a walk	paint pictures
go swimming	read
play baseball	cook
go to the park	watch videos

ACTIVITIES FOR BUILDING BACKGROUND

MAKE IT REAL: DAYDREAMING
Invite children to sit by a window and look outside for a few minutes. Let them daydream about other things they could be doing that day. Encourage children to pantomime what they are thinking and have classmates guess the various activities.

INTEGRATING

SPELLING AND GRAMMAR

SPELLING
You may want to present the spelling pretest of words with /ā/-*ame*. See **pages 177Q–177R** for the 5-Day Spelling Plan.

PHONICS AND DECODING CONNECTION
See lesson on Long Vowels and Phonograms: /ā/-*ame* on **pages 177G–177I.**

GRAMMAR
See **pages 177O–177P** for Daily Language Activities. A 5-Day Grammar Plan is also presented.

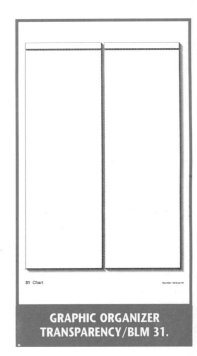

GRAPHIC ORGANIZER TRANSPARENCY/BLM 31.

ORAL LANGUAGE ACTIVITIES

DESCRIBING FAMILY MEMBERS
Invite children to bring in photographs or draw pictures of family members or friends who visit them or whom they visit on special occasions. Children can describe who each person is and how they are related.

Children who don't speak English can be paired with bilingual children who speak their language. Have bilingual children help translate for their partners.

QUESTION AND ANSWER
To encourage further discussion, ask children questions about people who visited them or whom they visited. Let children ask questions about their classmate's pictures.

After all presentations, have children share what they think makes visits from their friends and family special. Do they see some relatives more than others? Have any of them been to a reunion with their extended family?

NONVERBAL RESPONSE
Encourage children to use facial expression and gestures to communicate their feelings about a special visit.

TEACHING
TIPS

If some children can not think of someone who has visited them, have them tell about someone to whom they would like to pay a surprise visit.

LANGUAGE DEVELOPMENT

You may want to present the following words, idioms, and phrases to children who need language support:

in that case, p. 149
we shall return, p. 149
knight, p. 151
royal guard, p. 155
royal cook, p. 159
royal barber, p. 163
royal jester, p. 167
just dropped in, p. 174

ESL/SECOND-LANGUAGE TEACHER'S GUIDE
A full teaching lesson for students acquiring English is available in the ESL/SECOND-LANGUAGE TEACHER'S GUIDE.

Vocabulary

INSTRUCTIONAL VOCABULARY

cook	a person who makes food ready to eat
queen	a woman who rules a country
prince	the son of a king or queen
visit	to go to see someone
return	to come back or to go back
knight	a soldier for a king or queen

VOCABULARY ACTIVITIES

WORD CHART

PARTNER

As you present the vocabulary, have children determine whether each word names a person or shows an action. Then have them brainstorm other naming and action words. Create a chart or use **VOCABULARY STRATEGY TRANSPARENCY/BLM 5.**

Word Chart

Words That Name People	Words That Show Action
cook	visit
queen	return
prince	
knight	

PERSONAL EXPERIENCE

GROUP

After you present the vocabulary, invite groups to discuss when they have used these words. For example, what stories or fairy tales have they read with a queen or a knight in them? Children can use the glossary to check definitions.

WORDS IN CONTEXT

ONE

For more vocabulary practice, assign **PRACTICE BOOK, page 198.**

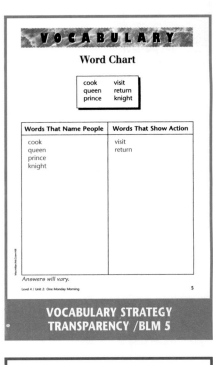

VOCABULARY

Word Chart

cook	visit
queen	return
prince	knight

Words That Name People	Words That Show Action
cook	visit
queen	return
prince	
knight	

Answers will vary.

Level 4 / Unit 2: One Monday Morning

5

VOCABULARY STRATEGY TRANSPARENCY /BLM 5

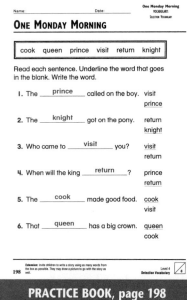

Name: _____ Date: _____

One Monday Morning
VOCABULARY:
Selection Vocabulary

ONE MONDAY MORNING

cook queen prince visit return knight

Read each sentence. Underline the word that goes in the blank. Write the word.

1. The ___prince___ called on the boy. visit
   prince

2. The ___knight___ got on the pony. return
   knight

3. Who came to ___visit___ you? visit
   return

4. When will the king ___return___? prince
   return

5. The ___cook___ made good food. cook
   visit

6. That ___queen___ has a big crown. queen
   cook

Extension: Invite children to write a story using as many words from the box as possible. They may draw a picture to go with the story as well.

198

Level 4
Selection Vocabulary 6

PRACTICE BOOK, page 198

Strategic Reading

SET PURPOSES

JOURNAL WRITING

Encourage children to discuss and record their reasons for reading this selection. Children may read to

• find out what happens one Monday morning.

• see what this rainy day is like.

• discover who the funny-looking characters are.

ENGAGE THE READER

Opportunities to role-play story characters are provided in the Strategic Reading suggestions. As children read, they can also record and confirm their predictions about the story on a chart that lists every day of the week, starting with Monday.

Day	What I Predict	Was My Prediction Right?
Monday		

As they read, children can note in their journals their reactions and any comments they may want to explore. Invite children to refer to their journals and their prediction charts in their after-reading discussions **(pages 177A–177B)**.

OPTIONS

⏱ **MANAGEMENT**
TIPS

Books for Meeting Individual Needs, **pages 177D–177F,** offer teaching suggestions for working with groups of children who have specific needs.

SUGGESTIONS FOR READING

READ INDEPENDENTLY

Invite independent readers to read the selection silently, noticing the predictability of events in the story.

READ ALOUD

Read the story aloud or play the **LISTENING LIBRARY AUDIOCASSETTE.** Encourage children to listen for repetitive phrases.

READ TOGETHER

Invite children to read the selection with a partner. Pair children of different reading levels and have them take turns reading each page.

READ AND TEACH

☑ **Make, Confirm, or Revise Predictions**

Use the comprehension strategy beginning on **page 140** as you and your children read the literature, or use the strategy after any other Suggestion for Reading option.

Comprehension

STRATEGIC READING

☑ **MAKE, CONFIRM, OR REVISE PREDICTIONS**

Share the comprehension strategy that will be focused on.

When you read a story, sometimes you can guess, or predict, what will happen next. Clues in the story, such as pictures and words, help you to guess. You can also use what you already know to help you make predictions. As you read, you find out if you were right, if you were close, or if you really weren't on track. If your predictions are not right, you can change them as you read. Predicting is one way of getting really involved in a story.

TEACHING
TIPS

Explain to children that as they read, you will model how readers use this strategy. Tell children they will have a chance to use the strategy, too.

ONE MONDAY MORNING

Text and pictures by Uri Shulevitz

140

141

Skills in Context

Comprehension

STRATEGIC READING

1 **MAKE PREDICTIONS** What is the weather like? Look back at the picture of the boy on the cover. What do you think he's thinking? Do you think the boy will stay home or go out? Let's write our prediction on the chart in the column next to Monday.

Day	What I Predict	Was My Prediction Right?
Monday	The boy will stay home.	

2 Where have you seen these words before? **(on the cover)** Let's read them together.

142

One Monday morning

143

Skills in Context

New York City Facts

Remind children that the setting of this story is New York City. Then share these facts:

- New York City is the most populous city in the United States.

- There are only eight states (not including New York State) that have more people than New York City.

- The city stands mostly on three islands.

- Some of the world's tallest skyscrapers can be found in New York City.

- The Statue of Liberty, one of the largest statues on Earth, is on a small island in New York Harbor.

- More books and clothes are made in New York City than in any other city in the country.

MEETING INDIVIDUAL NEEDS

Challenge
Invite children to discover facts about their own city or town and share them with the class.

Comprehension

STRATEGIC READING

3 **MAKE PREDICTIONS** Do you know who this is? I wonder where he is walking with his umbrella. Where do you think he is going? How does he look?

the king,

144

Skills in Context

Technique

Draw attention to the contrast between the dreary rain on **pages 144–145** and the vibrant colors the illustrator used for the royal visitors on **pages 146–147**. Point out how the wonderful colors used for the royal visitors make them seem lively.

Encourage children to glance at the rest of the illustrations to discover how the number of characters seems to be growing as the story progresses. This technique helps to build the pace of the story and adds more excitement to each royal visit.

Invite children to look through other books to see how color and size are used to add excitement.

145

Comprehension

STRATEGIC READING

4 Who are these characters? **(the queen and the little prince)** Follow the words and let's read them together.

5 Who is the character we only see part of? **(the king)** How can we tell? **(by his clothing, his crown, and his umbrella)**

PHONICS AND DECODING

/ā/-ame as in *came*, **page 147** See Phonics and Decoding lesson on Long Vowels and Phonograms: /ā/-*ame* on **pages 177G–177I.**

146

the queen, and the little prince came to visit me.

147

Skills in Context

Directionality

Ask children to look at **page 146.** Explain that this is the page that we would normally read next, but there aren't any words on this page.

Then read aloud **page 147** with the class, pointing to each word. Place a green self-stick paper circle to the left of the text on the page. Tell children that this is where we begin to read.

Ask children to point to the words as you read together, tracking the print across the page with your fingers.

Comprehension

STRATEGIC READING

6 **CONFIRM PREDICTIONS** Was your prediction right? Let's write a check in the last column if our prediction was right. Let's write an X in the last column if our prediction was not right.

Day	What I Predict	Was My Prediction Right?
Monday	The boy will stay home.	X

Do you think the boy knew that the king, the queen, and the little prince were coming to visit him? **(no)** Why do you think that? **(because the boy wasn't home)** Where was he? **(standing on line at a bus stop)**

7 **MAKE PREDICTIONS** Do you think another character will join the group of visitors? Who might that be?

But I wasn't home.

148

7

So the little prince said,

"In that case we shall return on Tuesday."

149

Skills in Context

COMPREHENSION

✔ Cause and Effect

INTRODUCE Discuss with children that when something happens, it often causes something else to happen.

DEVELOP/APPLY You might wish to model how readers think about cause and effect.

THINK ALOUD When I read, I can see how one thing makes another thing happen. In this story, the royal visitors arrive at the boy's home on Monday. But the boy isn't there. This causes another event: The royal visitors decide to come back on Tuesday.

Ask children to find more cause-and-effect relationships in the story.

CLOSE Ask children to share examples of causes and effects in their own lives with the class.

Name: _____ Date: _____ One Monday Morning

WHAT IS THE CAUSE?

Read the question. Look at the picture. Underline the answer.

Effect	Cause
1. Why did the milk spill?	The cup was too full. The knight bumped the cup. The cup was too tall.
2. Why did the queen go away?	No one was home. The king said to go away. The prince was late.
3. Why did the queen call the knight?	He tells good stories. She wants the dragon to go away. The king is missing.
4. Why did the cook run in?	He saw a mouse. The food was not cooked. The pot was running over.

Level 4/Unit 2
ORGANIZE INFORMATION: Cause and Effect   199

PRACTICE BOOK, page 199

See also RETEACHING BLM, page 121

SKILLS TRACE

CAUSE AND EFFECT

Tested: Progress Assessment: Level 4 Unit 2

Review: Level 3: 177, Level 4: 27, 111, 149,
                  Level 5: 95
Practice Book: 109, 159, 186, 199, 273
Reteaching BLM: 83, 90, 111, 121, 182

Comprehension

STRATEGIC READING

8 **CONFIRM PREDICTIONS** What have you noticed about the weather? **(The sun is out now.)** Do you think the boy will be home today? Let's write our prediction in the column next to Tuesday.

Day	What I Predict	Was My Prediction Right?
Monday	The boy will stay home.	X
Tuesday	The boy will not be home.	

On Tuesday morning the king, the queen, the little prince,

150

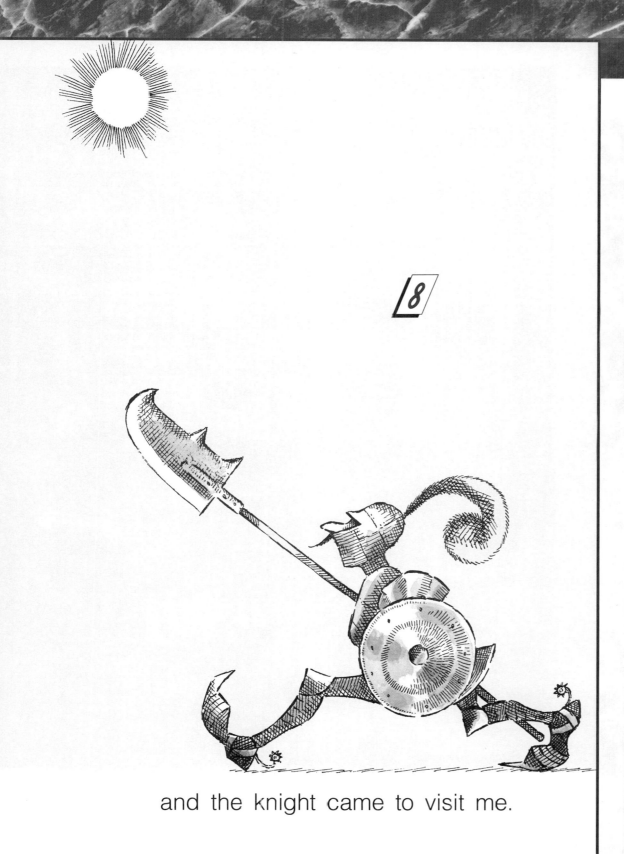

and the knight came to visit me.

151

Skills in Context

CONCEPTS OF PRINT

Capital Letters

Reread **page 150** with children. Remind them that the days of the week appear throughout the story. Ask children to notice what is special about how they are written. Elicit that each day of the week always begins with a capital letter.

Encourage children to find words that name the other days of the week in the story. Invite them to create a list of the days they find. Explain to children that the days of the week always begin with capital letters.

Ask children what other kinds of words always begin with capital letters.

SECOND-LANGUAGE SUPPORT

Invite children to practice writing their names, making sure that they start with capital letters. They may also write the names of their pets or the streets where they live.

Comprehension

STRATEGIC READING

9 **CONFIRM PREDICTIONS** It looks like the boy is on a train! Our prediction was right! Let's put a check on our chart.

Day	What I Predict	Was My Prediction Right?
Monday	The boy will stay home.	X
Tuesday	The boy will not be home.	✔

This leads me to think that he probably won't be home on Wednesday morning, either. What do you think?

10 **MAKE PREDICTIONS** When the royal visitors return on Wednesday, do you think someone else will be with them? Who do you think it's going to be?

Day	What I Predict	Was My Prediction Right?
Monday	The boy will stay home.	X
Tuesday	The boy will not be home.	✔
Wednesday	The princess will be with them.	

Let's write this prediction on our chart, and then we'll see if we're right.

But I wasn't home.

152

So the little prince said,

"In that case we shall return on Wednesday."

153

Skills in Context

☑ Short Vowels and Phonograms: /u/-ut

INTRODUCE Write the word *nut* on the chalkboard and read it with children. Underline the letters *ut*.

DEVELOP/APPLY Invite children to read **page 152** and find the word that ends in *ut*. Draw the outline of a walnut on the chalkboard and write *but* inside. Have children suggest other short *u* words with the *ut* spelling pattern. Write the words inside the walnut. Then read all the words together.

CLOSE Invite children to work with a partner to write a sentence using one of the *-ut* words.

CUT WORDS

Look at the picture. Choose the word that completes the sentence and tells about the picture.

1. The prince has a ___cut___ on his hand.   cut / nut

2. Who lives in this ___hut___?   rut / hut

3. The door is ___shut___.   shut / cut

4. The animal will eat the ___nut___.   but / nut

5. I want to skate, ___but___ I can't.   but / rut

PRACTICE BOOK, page 200

See also RETEACHING BLM, page 122

SKILLS ✕ TRACE

SHORT VOWELS AND PHONOGRAMS: /u/-*ut*

Tested: Progress Assessment: Level 4 Unit 2

Introduce:	Level 3: 39
Review:	Level 4: 153
Practice Book:	112, 200
Reteaching BLM:	64, 200

Comprehension

STRATEGIC READING

11 **CONFIRM PREDICTIONS** If you predicted that a new character would show up with the king, the queen, the little prince, and the knight, you were right! Who did you predict that character would be? Let's put a check on our chart to show if our prediction was right. Point to the new visitor. **NONVERBAL RESPONSE**

Day	What I Predict	Was My Prediction Right?
Monday	The boy will stay home.	X
Tuesday	The boy will not be home.	✔
Wednesday	The princess will be with them.	X

12 Now look at all of these characters! Do you think they're having fun going to visit the boy? Let's role-play the characters and act out their Wednesday morning visit. **ROLE-PLAY**

INFORMAL ASSESSMENT

Observe if children recognize the predictability of the text.

To help children Make, Confirm, or Revise Predictions, see Reteaching lesson on page 157.

154

On Wednesday morning
the king,
the queen,
the little prince,
the knight,
and a royal guard
came to visit me.

155

Skills in Context

Choral Reading

You may wish to model fluent reading of **page 155**. Then have children:

- read the page aloud as a group.

- form two groups and take turns reading the page.

Encourage children to practice reading the page together until their reading is fluent.

Comprehension

13 Do you wonder why the boy is never at home when his company comes? Where was he this time? **(at the laundromat)**

14 MAKE PREDICTIONS Who always talks for the royal visitors? **(the little prince)** What does he always say? **("In that case we shall return on . . .")** On what day of the week will they come to visit next? **(Thursday)**

But I wasn't home.

156

14

So the little prince said,
"In that case we shall return on Thursday."

157

Skills in Context

RETEACHING
COMPREHENSION

☑ Make, Confirm, or
Revise Predictions

INTRODUCE Discuss with children how one event can help readers guess, or predict, what happens later.

DEVELOP/APPLY Model how to make predictions when reading:

THINK ALOUD When I read page 156, I tried to figure out what the visitors would do when they discovered the boy wasn't home. I guessed that the prince would say they would return the next day, since this is what he always says. Then, I read the next page and saw that I was right. If I was wrong, I would have checked to see if I missed any clues.

CLOSE Invite children to draw a picture of who they predict will return on Thursday.

		One Monday Morning
Name:	Date:	COMPREHENSION Page... Make, Confirm, or Revise Predictions

WHAT'S NEXT?

Look at the picture. Draw what could happen next.

1.		a baby bird
2.		people raking or a bare tree
3.		the boy with a haircut
4.		an ear of corn

Level 4
Make, Confirm, or Revise Predictions

PRACTICE BOOK, page 201

See RETEACHING BLM, page 123

SKILLS ╳ TRACE

MAKE, CONFIRM, REVISE PREDICTIONS
Tested: Progress Assessment: Level 4 Unit 2

Review: Level 4: 85, 140, 157, 177B, 221
Practice Book: 177, 201, 233
Reteaching BLM: 104, 123, 141

Comprehension

STRATEGIC READING

15 **MAKE PREDICTIONS** As I read this story, I notice a pattern. Every day of the week the royal visitors go to visit the boy and he is not at home. From the pattern of the story, I predict that he will be out doing something. I also can predict that every day a new visitor will join the others. What do you think happens next? Where will the boy be on Thursday? Let's write what we think next to Thursday.

Day	What I Predict	Was My Prediction Right?
Monday	The boy will stay home.	X
Tuesday	The boy will not be home.	✔
Wednesday	The princess will be with them.	X
Thursday	The boy will not be home.	

16 Who was the new visitor on Thursday? **(the royal cook)** Were you surprised? Why or why not?

SELF ASSESSMENT

Encourage children to reflect on their reading by asking themselves these questions.

• Can I figure out what may happen next by the way the words are repeated?

• How have the pictures helped me understand the story?

To help children Make, Confirm, or Revise Predictions, see Reteaching lesson on page 157.

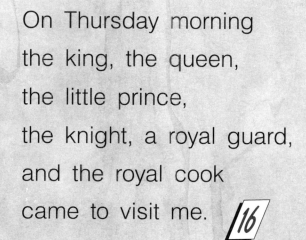

On Thursday morning
the king, the queen,
the little prince,
the knight, a royal guard,
and the royal cook
came to visit me. 16

159

Skills in Context

COMPREHENSION

☑ Make Inferences

INTRODUCE Help children realize that when they make inferences, they think about what they have read and what they already know in order to understand story events better.

DEVELOP/APPLY Ask children to use the text and illustrations to make an inference about how the royal visitors are feeling as they return for the fourth time to visit the boy. Have them explain their reasoning. Did they use clues in the text or in the illustrations? Did they draw on their own experience? Record children's responses on chart paper.

CLOSE Have children discuss how making inferences can help them understand what the characters are like. Encourage children to make inferences based on another story event.

PRACTICE BOOK, page 202

See RETEACHING ELM, page 124

Comprehension

STRATEGIC READING

17 **CONFIRM PREDICTIONS** Did you predict that the boy wouldn't be home again? What helped you make your prediction?

Let's show if our prediction was correct. Remember, it's okay if your predictions are not always right.

Day	What I Predict	Was My Prediction Right?
Monday	The boy will stay home.	X
Tuesday	The boy will not be home.	✔
Wednesday	The princess will be with them.	X
Thursday	The boy will not be home.	✔

18 Why do you think the king is wiping his brow? How do you think he feels? How do you think the other royal visitors feel? Who wants to be the king and tell and show us how he is feeling now? **ROLE-PLAY**

INFORMAL ASSESSMENT

Use **pages 153–160** to informally assess children's ability to sequence events.

But I wasn't home.

160

So the little prince said,
"In that case we shall return on Friday."

161

Skills in Context

Modeling and Partner Reading

Pages 159–161 provide an excellent opportunity for children to practice fluent reading. Read each page aloud, using different voices for the narrator and for the little prince. Be sure to pause at commas, varying tone as you read off the various character names on **page 159.** Then have children model your reading.

Children can practice reading the modeled passages with a partner, monitoring each other's

- accuracy.
- expressiveness.
- use of punctuation.

Comprehension

STRATEGIC READING

19 How many visitors do you see now? (Seven)

20 **MAKE PREDICTIONS** It's almost the end of the week. I wonder if the boy is going to be home. What do you predict? What makes you think that? Let's write our prediction on the chart next to Friday.

Day	What I Predict	Was My Prediction Right?
Monday	The boy will stay home.	X
Tuesday	The boy will not be home.	✔
Wednesday	The princess will be with them.	X
Thursday	The boy will not be home.	✔
Friday	The boy will not be home.	

162

On Friday morning
the king, the queen,
the little prince,
the knight, the royal guard,
the royal cook,
and the royal barber
came to visit me.

163

Skills in Context

World Leaders

Explain to children that most countries have a leader who is chosen by the people of that country. Then explain that kings and queens are leaders of countries who are not chosen by the people but who inherit their positions from their families. When a king or queen dies or becomes too old to do the job, the throne is passed down to a son or daughter who becomes the next king or queen.

Share with children that today a few countries still have kings or queens as leaders. Add that some countries have both a royal leader and someone who is chosen by the people. Remind them that the United States has a leader, chosen by the people, called a president.

Here are some examples of countries that have kings and queens as leaders:

- King: Belgium, Cambodia, Jordan
- Queen: Denmark, England, the Netherlands

Comprehension

21 **CONFIRM PREDICTIONS** Did you predict correctly? Where was the boy? (at the store) Let's put a check to show we were right.

Day	What I Predict	Was My Prediction Right?
Monday	The boy will stay home.	X
Tuesday	The boy will not be home.	✔
Wednesday	The princess will be with them.	X
Thursday	The boy will not be home.	✔
Friday	The boy will not be home.	✔

22 **MAKE PREDICTIONS** As soon as I saw that the boy wasn't home, I knew exactly what the little prince was going to say! How do you think I knew what his words would be?

Use **pages 164–165** to observe if children are using text and picture clues to predict what might happen next.

To help children Make, Confirm, or Revise Predictions, see Reteaching lesson on page 157.

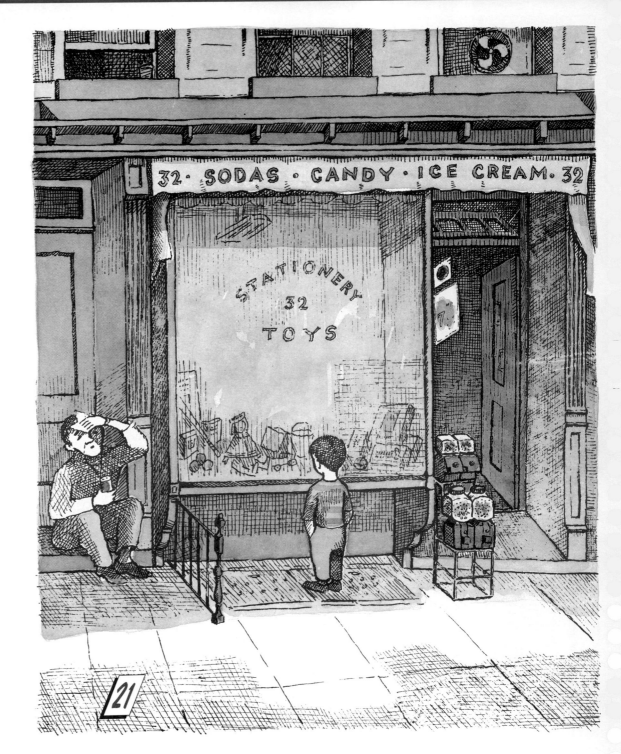

But I wasn't home.

164

So the little prince said,

"In that case we shall return on Saturday."

165

Skills in Context

COMPREHENSION

✍Distinguish Between Fantasy and Reality

INTRODUCE Explain to children that sometimes stories tell about things that happen in real life. Stories can also tell about things that are make-believe. Ask children to talk about their favorite stories and whether they tell about real-life things or make-believe things.

DEVELOP/APPLY Have children look at the illustrations on **pages 164–165**. Then have them talk about which things in the picture are real and which are make-believe.

CLOSE Invite children to turn to **page 176** to find out where the boy got the idea for the make-believe characters. Then have them draw a picture of someone who might really visit the boy.

Name: _____ Date: _____

One Monday Morning
COMPREHENSION: Distinguish
Between Reality and Fantasy

WHAT IS REAL?

Read each sentence. Put an **X** under **Real** if the sentence tells something that could really happen. Put an **X** under **Make-believe** if the sentence tells something that could not really happen.

	Real	Make-believe
1. The cook made a big cake.	X	
2. A prince got a yellow cat.	X	
3. The alligator talked to the boy.		X
4. The goose sang a song.		X
5. The king wore a crown.	X	
6. A cat rode a horse with wings.		X
7. A knight called to the dragon.		X
8. The barber cut the bug's hair.		X
9. The guard watched for danger.	X	
10. A tailor sewed some pants.	X	

Level 4
Distinguish Between Reality and Fantasy

Extension: Invite children to write three more sentences, some of which could really happen and some of which could not really happen. 203

PRACTICE BOOK, page 203

See RETEACHING BLM, page 125

SKILLS ⟩ TRACE

DISTINGUISH BETWEEN FANTASY AND REALITY

Tested: Progress Assessment: Level 4 Unit 2

Introduce:	Level 2: 127
Review:	Level 4: 165, Level 5: 31, 51, 81
Practice Book:	85, 203, 249, 258, 269
Reteaching BLM:	49, 125, 162, 169, 178

Comprehension

STRATEGIC READING

23 Look how high they are! Do you see the number of the floor at the edge of the picture? What number is it? **(five)** How do you think the visitors feel after climbing up five flights of stairs? **(They're probably very tired.)**

24 **MAKE PREDICTIONS** Who is the newest visitor? **(the royal jester)** Who can predict from the picture what his job is? Let's have someone do something silly like the royal jester. **ROLE-PLAY**

SOCIAL STUDIES CONNECTION

Hundreds of years ago, the antics of court jesters made kings and queens laugh and forget their royal troubles. Jesters were like members of the royal family. Sometimes they were called Fools, but most jesters were very clever. In the 1600s, you needed a license to be a jester!

On Saturday morning
the king, the queen,
the little prince,
the knight, a royal guard,
the royal cook,
the royal barber,
and the royal jester
came to visit me.

24

167

Skills in Context

Ask Questions

Let children know that when they read a sentence or part of a story that doesn't make sense, it sometimes helps to stop and ask themselves questions and to think about how to answer the questions. You may want to use the following Think Aloud to demonstrate the strategy.

THINK ALOUD *There were so many characters on **page 167** that I got confused. I stopped and asked myself, "Who is the new visitor on Saturday morning?" I reread the page slowly. Then I checked back to Friday morning. This helped me understand that the royal jester was the new visitor.*

Encourage children to skim through the story and ask themselves questions about parts that they don't understand.

Invite children to write their own versions of **page 167.** Invite them to include characters who might show up at their houses.

Comprehension

STRATEGIC READING

25 Did the visitors find the boy home on Saturday morning? (no) Where was he? (He was out flying a kite.) How do the visitors look now?

26 **MAKE AND CONFIRM PREDICTIONS** Tomorrow is Sunday. Let's write what happened on Saturday and what you think will happen on Sunday on our chart.

Day	What I Predict	Was My Prediction Right?
Monday	The boy will stay home.	X
Tuesday	The boy will not be home.	✔
Wednesday	The princess will be with them.	X
Thursday	The boy will not be home.	✔
Friday	The boy will not be home.	✔
Saturday	The boy will not be home.	✔
Sunday	The boy is finally at home.	

But I wasn't home.

168

So the little prince said,

"In that case we shall return on Sunday."

169

Skills in Context

Compound Words

Write the word *Sunday* on a card. Have children find the word in the selection. Cut the word into two parts, explaining that Sunday is a compound word made up of two smaller words: *sun* and *day*.

On the chalkboard, make a chart. Have children match a word in the first column to a word in the second column to make a compound word.

Column 1	Column 2
rain	ball
back	coat
sun	flower
base	box
mail	pack

Discuss the meanings of the compound words children form.

Comprehension

STRATEGIC READING

27 There's the king ringing the boy's doorbell at last! What do you think the royal visitors are thinking as they wait outside his door? (They're probably hoping that he's home so they don't have to climb up all of those stairs one more time!)

28 MAKE PREDICTIONS We can't see all of the royal visitors on these pages. Who do you think is in line behind the royal guard? Who will the new visitor be?

On Sunday morning the king, the queen,
the little prince, the knight,
a royal guard,

Skills in Context

Narrative Point of View

Discuss with children the importance of recognizing who is telling a story and how that affects what the reader knows about the characters and story events.

THINK ALOUD *When I read a story, I try to figure out who is telling the story. I remember that I'm seeing things the way that character sees them. While reading **page 171**, I realize that I can't seem to tell who is telling the story. There don't seem to be any clues. So I read on. The author writes, "And I was home." That reminds me of other pages when the boy says, "But I wasn't home." As I look back in the story, I see that it's the boy who is telling the story.*

Have children look at **page 176**. Encourage them to discuss what is probably on the storyteller's mind.

Comprehension

STRATEGIC READING

29 **CONFIRM PREDICTIONS** Did you guess that the new visitor would be a little dog?

🌐 SOCIAL STUDIES CONNECTION

A "royal" dog is not such a far-fetched idea. American Presidents have had birds, rabbits, goats, snakes, guinea pigs, ponies, and lots of cats and dogs as pets. Have children find out if the President today has a pet. What would make a good Presidential pet?

172

the royal cook,
the royal barber,
the royal jester,
and a little dog
came to visit me.

173

Skills in Context

VOCABULARY

Content Words

Write the following words on the chalkboard: *jester, cook, barber, prince, king,* and *queen.* Discuss with children who each of these characters is and what each one does.

Then give each child a paper plate. Invite children to choose one of the people and draw his or her face on the front of the plate. On the back, have children write one thing about this person.

Children can use their paper-plate masks to role-play conversations with partners.

MEETING INDIVIDUAL NEEDS

Challenge

Encourage children to pretend they are members of the royal procession in the story. Have them write about who they are and what they would do if they were in a similar situation.

Comprehension

STRATEGIC READING

30 REVISE AND CONFIRM PREDICTIONS How did you think the story was going to end? How would you compare your prediction about the story ending to what really happened? Let's show if we predicted correctly on our chart.

Day	What I Predict	Was My Prediction Right?
Monday	The boy will stay home.	X
Tuesday	The boy will not be home.	✔
Wednesday	The princess will be with them.	X
Thursday	The boy will not be home.	✔
Friday	The boy will not be home.	✔
Saturday	The boy will not be home.	✔
Sunday	The boy is finally at home.	✔

31 How would you feel if all those royal people came to visit you? Looking at the picture, how do you think the boy feels?

TEACHING
TIPS

When text differs from the established pattern, children are likely to need more support. You might return to echo reading.

And I was home.

So the little prince said,

"We just dropped in to say hello."

174

Skills in Context

✔ Consonant Blends: /dr/ *dr*

INTRODUCE Ask children to read **page 174** with you. Emphasize the beginning blend in *dropped* as you read the word. Write the word *dropped* on the chalkboard.

DEVELOP/APPLY Draw several large drops of rain on chart paper. Encourage children to brainstorm other words that begin with the letters *dr*. Write one word inside each drop.

CLOSE Have children copy one of the words onto a sheet of paper, underline the beginning blend, and illustrate the word.

PRACTICE BOOK, page 204

See RETEACHING BLM, page 126

SKILLS ⬦ TRACE

CONSONANT BLENDS: /dr/ *dr*

Tested: Progress Assessment: Level 4 Unit 2

Introduce: Level 2: 149
Review: Level 4: 175
Practice Book: 94, 204
Reteaching BLM: 54, 126

Comprehension

STRATEGIC READING

32 Look at the cards, the doll on the windowsill, and the picture of the dog on the wall. Do they look like any of the characters in the story? Who? (all of the royal visitors)

ONGOING ASSESSMENT

☑ **MAKE, REVISE, OR CONFIRM PREDICTIONS**

Encourage children to personalize this strategy and its possible transfer to other situations by discussing these questions:

• Do you think making predictions and reading to find out if you were right is a strategy you would recommend to a friend?

• When might you use this strategy again?

176

FOR RESPONSE AND ASSESSMENT OPPORTUNITIES, *see pages 177A–177B.*

MEET
Uri Shulevitz

Uri Shulevitz was born in Poland. As a boy he lived in France. While there, he learned a French song about a little boy who is visited by the king. It begins with the words "One Monday morning the Emperor, his wife and his son the little prince came to visit me . . ." Mr. Shulevitz liked the song so much he decided to write a story about it. That story became *One Monday Morning*.

177

Skills in Context

WRITING

Exaggeration

Discuss with children what an exaggeration is. Elicit that when someone exaggerates they make something seem greater than it really is. Did the boy see all of the royal characters mentioned in the story? Explain that he did see these characters, but only on playing cards. He was exaggerating when he brought them to life and told the story of them visiting him. Explain that exaggerations often make stories more interesting and fun to read.

STRATEGY: CLUSTER Invite children to tell about a story they know that contained exaggeration. Encourage children to use word clusters when planning how to tell about their events. Each child can write the main idea in the center of a circle and then draw spokes off of the circle. On each spoke, they can write something about the event that they will exaggerate. This strategy will help prepare them for the writing process lessons on **pages 177M** and **211A–H.**

WRITING TRACE

Descriptive Writing
177, 177M, 207, 207M, 211A–211H
Strategies:
Cluster: 177, 177M, 211A–211H
List: 207, 207M

Respond to the Literature

PERSONAL RESPONSE

JOURNAL WRITING

Encourage children to use their journals to express any thoughts and questions they have about the selection. The journal can be used to capture how the story made them feel. The following questions may help them get started.

- What did you think of the royal visitors? Would you want them to visit you? Why or why not?
- What did you think of the illustrations? Which picture is your favorite?
- How did you like the ending of the story?

SMALL GROUP RESPONSE

JOURNAL ENTRIES

Children may work in small groups to discuss the selection. Encourage them to use their journals throughout the discussion.

READER RESPONSE CARD 1 is available to guide the discussion.

To check story comprehension you may want to assign **PRACTICE BOOK, page 205.**

WRITING ABOUT THE THEME

CRITICAL THINKING

Ask children to think about how **"One Monday Morning"** relates to the unit theme of Surprises Along the Way. Encourage children to discover that surprises happen every day of the week. A visit from a royal family can turn an ordinary day into a day full of surprises for everyone.

QUICK WRITE

Invite children to write a few sentences about a time when someone or something really surprised them. You may want to suggest that they pattern their writing after a favorite story's language pattern.

READER RESPONSE CARD **1**

Hattie and the Fox
pages 10–43

With a group, share your ideas about the story. You can talk about what you liked most. You can also talk about these questions.

- Did you write anything in your journal that you would like to share?
- Suppose a friend wanted to read this story. What would you tell that friend?
- Hattie knew something important, but no one would listen to her. Does that remind you of anything that has happened to you?
- In **"Hattie and the Fox,"** who really needed to Take a Closer Look? Why?

© 1997 Macmillan/McGraw-Hill

READER RESPONSE CARD 1, page T-3

Name: _____ Date: _____   One Monday Morning
COMPREHENSION
Story Comprehension

WHO CAME TO VISIT?

Many came to see the boy. Choose the letters beside the names of the visitors and write them next to the day or days they came.

a. king b. guard c. little prince d. barber
e. jester f. queen g. cook h. knight

1. Monday   a f c
2. Tuesday   a f c h
3. Wednesday a f c h b
4. Thursday   a f c h b g
5. Friday   a f c h b g d
6. Saturday   a f c h b
              g d e

Level 4/Unit 2
Story Comprehension   205

PRACTICE BOOK, page 205

Comprehension Checkpoint

ACTIVITIES

INFORMAL ASSESSMENT

☑ MAKE, CONFIRM, OR REVISE PREDICTIONS

PREDICTION CHART Display GRAPHIC ORGANIZER TRANSPARENCY/ BLM 30 or put the following chart on the chalkboard. Encourage children to expand their prediction charts to include information about what really happened in the story. This will give them an opportunity to reflect on their predictions. Invite children to finish their charts in groups. Then invite the groups to share what they added.

Day	What I Predict	Was My Prediction Right?	What Really Happened?
Monday	The boy will stay home.	✗	The boy was at a bus stop.
Tuesday	The boy will not be home.	✔	The boy was on the subway.
Wednesday	The princess will be with them.	✗	The new visitor was the royal guard.
Thursday	The boy will not be home.	✔	The boy was at the grocery.
Friday	The boy will not be home.	✔	The boy was at the store.
Saturday	The boy will not be home.	✔	The boy was out flying a kite.
Sunday	The boy is finally at home.	✔	The boy is finally at home.

ONGOING ASSESSMENT

COMPREHENSION

Assessment Checklist

• When you assess children's charts, check for **Foreshadowing**. Do children see how story clues and the repetitive story pattern are consistent with what does happen?

• Look for **Sequence**. Do children retell the story events in order?

• Look for **Understanding**. Did children understand the cumulative pattern of the story?

FORMAL ASSESSMENT

ONGOING ASSESSMENT

To test story comprehension and vocabulary, administer the multiple choice **Selection Assessment** for **"One Monday Morning"** in **SELECTION AND UNIT ASSESSMENTS** for Levels 4–5.

RETEACHING

ONGOING ASSESSMENT

For additional work with making, confirming, or revising predictions, use the Reteaching lesson on **page 157** or the **RETEACHING BLM, page 123.**

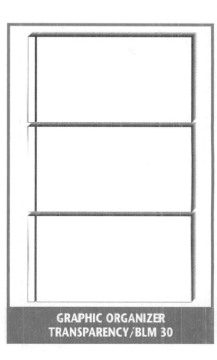

GRAPHIC ORGANIZER TRANSPARENCY/BLM 30

Extend Skills In Context

Literature-Based Instruction

To provide skills and strategies instruction to meet the needs of your children, select from these lessons.

☑ These skills are tested in the Unit Progress Assessment.

Meeting Individual Needs

*To provide additional literacy experiences tailored to specific students' needs and interests, use this literature and these resources. Activities are provided on **pages 177E-177F**.*

MULTILEVEL RESOURCES FOR FLEXIBLE GROUPING

EASY

SPOTLIGHT: LITERACY SUPPORT

EARLY INTERVENTION
COMPREHENSION:
Distinguish between Fantasy and Reality

PHONICS AND DECODING:
Long Vowels and
Phonograms: /ī/-ice

EASY **AVERAGE**

SPOTLIGHT: PHONICS/
DECODING

PHONICS/DECODING
☑ LONG VOWELS AND
PHONOGRAMS:
/ā/-ame

'TRONIC PHONICS

💿 Also available on CD-ROM

EASY

SPOTLIGHT: VOCABULARY/
COMPREHENSION

VOCABULARY
• cook
• queen
• prince
• visit
• return
• knight

COMPREHENSION
☑ MAKE, CONFIRM, OR REVISE
PREDICTIONS

EASY **AVERAGE**

TRADE BOOK LIBRARY

COMPREHENSION
☑ MAKE, CONFIRM, OR REVISE
PREDICTIONS

Meeting Individual Needs
Multilevel Resources

EASY

ONE SUNNY MORNING
by Beth Alley Wise
illustrated by Lizi Boyd

ONE SUNNY MORNING

EARLY INTERVENTION

REREAD A FAMILIAR BOOK

To reinforce a successful reading experience, have children read a familiar book, such as the **LITERACY SUPPORT BOOK** *At the Petting Zoo.*

READ A NEW BOOK

Preview the **LITERACY SUPPORT BOOK** *One Sunny Morning.* Point out illustrations, using story vocabulary such as *castle* and *king.*

Read aloud the story. Model how to determine whether the story is real or fantasy. After you read **page 5,** you might say, *"To decide if this story is real or fantasy, I need to think about whether the events in the story could really happen. Some things, like the boy building a sand castle, could really happen. But I know that crabs, starfish, and turtles can't talk. So, this story must be a fantasy.*

BUILD WORDS

Read from **page 3,** *This castle would be a nice home.* Ask children to think of words that rhyme with *nice.* Let them use the **Word Building Kit** to build rhyming words with the *-ice* phonogram.

For a full lesson on long vowels and phonograms: /ī/-*ice,* see Take a Closer Look, **pages 69G–69I.**

WRITE SENTENCES

Ask children to write 2–3 sentences about the story *One Sunny Morning.* Provide sentence starters such as, *"A boy _____.", "The crab _____."* or *"A big wave _____."* Invite children to share their sentences, comparing the ways they filled in the blanks.

Reinforce vocabulary by asking children to point out specific words in their sentences. Children can then illustrate their sentences.

READ INDEPENDENTLY

Have children reread *One Sunny Morning* independently. Invite them to look for picture clues that tell them whether this story is real or make-believe.

A boy builds a castle.

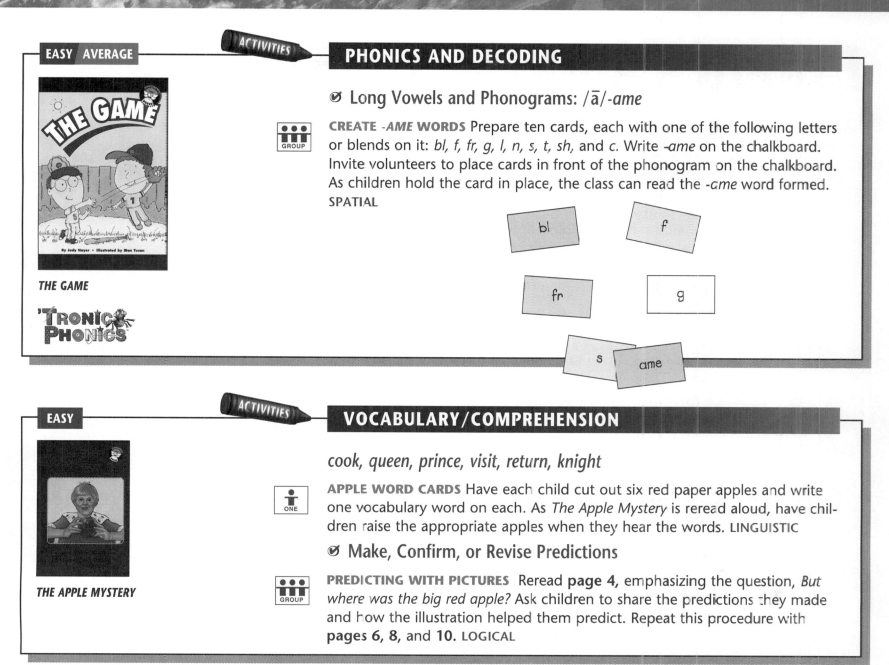

ACTIVITIES

EASY **AVERAGE**

PHONICS AND DECODING

THE GAME

'Tronic Phonics

⊘ **Long Vowels and Phonograms: /ā/-ame**

CREATE -AME WORDS Prepare ten cards, each with one of the following letters or blends on it: *bl, f, fr, g, l, n, s, t, sh,* and *c*. Write *-ame* on the chalkboard. Invite volunteers to place cards in front of the phonogram on the chalkboard. As children hold the card in place, the class can read the *-ame* word formed. **SPATIAL**

bl

f

fr

g

s

ame

EASY

ACTIVITIES

VOCABULARY/COMPREHENSION

THE APPLE MYSTERY

cook, queen, prince, visit, return, knight

APPLE WORD CARDS Have each child cut out six red paper apples and write one vocabulary word on each. As *The Apple Mystery* is reread aloud, have children raise the appropriate apples when they hear the words. **LINGUISTIC**

⊘ **Make, Confirm, or Revise Predictions**

PREDICTING WITH PICTURES Reread **page 4,** emphasizing the question, *But where was the big red apple?* Ask children to share the predictions they made and how the illustration helped them predict. Repeat this procedure with **pages 6, 8,** and **10. LOGICAL**

EASY **AVERAGE**

ACTIVITIES

COMPREHENSION

THE COW THAT WENT OINK

⊘ **Make, Confirm, or Revise Predictions**

SHARING PREDICTIONS Have children make two word cards: *MOO* and *OINK.* As you reread, invite them at appropriate points to hold up the card with the sound they expect to hear. After reading, ask children to tell about other points in the story when they made predictions. **KINESTHETIC**
Turn to **pages 287A–287H** for more teaching ideas for *The Cow That Went OINK.*

Phonics and Decoding /ā/ /el/ /ôr/

⊘ **Long Vowels and Phonograms: /ā/-*ame***

① DEVELOP PHONEMIC AWARENESS

READ THE LITERATURE
- Reread **pages 150** and **151** of **"One Monday Morning"** emphasizing the word *came* as you read. Introduce the **BIG BOOK OF RHYMES AND CHIMES**, and read the rhyme on **page 20**.

SAY THE RHYME
- Repeat the rhyme several times. Invite children to chime in.

- Say the words *game, came,* and *name,* explaining that these words rhyme.

- Ask children to listen to the following words and clap if they rhyme.

game/see	game/came	game/name	game/that
game/know	game/who	game/Jim	game/his

5-STEP PLAN

DECODING STRATEGIES:
RHYMING, BLENDING

1	DEVELOP PHONEMIC AWARENESS
2	DISCOVER THE SPELLING PATTERN
3	USE DECODING STRATEGIES
4	WRITING
5	READING

CONSONANT BLENDS

② DISCOVER THE SPELLING PATTERN

SHOW THE RHYME
- Display **page 20** in the **BIG BOOK OF RHYMES AND CHIMES**. Point out the word *name* at the bottom of the page and the underlined letters *ame*. Call on a volunteer to read the word.

- Read the rhyme, pointing to each word. Frame the words *game, came, James,* and *name,* and run your finger under the phonogram *-ame* in each.

- Then have children read the rhyme aloud with you and clap each time they see and hear a word with *-ame.*

For additional lessons and practice with long a, see **PHONICS SUPPORT BLM, pages 24** and **80.**

The Game

Let's play a game!
Let's see who else came!
Is that Jim or is it James?
Do you know his name?

name

BIG BOOK OF RHYMES AND CHIMES, page 20

SKILLS ⟩ TRACE

LONG VOWELS AND PHONOGRAMS: /ā/-*ame*

Tested: Progress Assessment, Level 4, Unit 2

Introduce:	Level 4: 177G
Review:	Level 5: 79
Practice Book:	206, 268
Reteaching BLM:	127, 177

ACTIVITIES

3 DECODING STRATEGIES: BLENDING ACTIVITIES

MODEL THE STRATEGY

- Write the phonogram *-ame* on chart paper or on the chalkboard. Model the blending strategy by blending *g* and the phonogram *-ame.*

   THINK ALOUD *Now I'm going to build words with* -ame. *Let's add* g *to make the word* game. *Listen as I blend the letters together:* g-ame. Ask children to use the blending strategy to blend *c-ame* and *n-ame.*

MAKE A WORD WALL

- Write the phonogram *-ame* on a large cut-out of a baseball diamond. Post the cutout on a classroom wall. Invite children to add words that rhyme with *game* to the Word Wall.

- Keep the Word Wall displayed so children can continue to add *-ame* words to it.

USE THE WORD BUILDING KIT

- Continue to model the blending strategy using the Word Building Kit. Insert cards containing the phonogram into the pockets of the mini-pocket chart.

- Put the letters *g, t,* and *s* in front of the phonogram and read the words with children, modeling the blending strategy.

- Let children build new words. Encourage them to use the blending strategy.

CONSONANT AND VOWEL PATTERNS: CVCe

- Write the word *game* on chart paper. Point out the consonant/vowel/consonant/*e* pattern of the word. Write the word *same* underneath. Point out the pattern again. Together, say the two words aloud, emphasizing the long *a* sound. Point out that in a one-syllable word with a consonant/vowel/consonant/*e* pattern, the vowel is usually long.

PRACTICE BOOK, page 206

See RETEACHING BLM, page 127

WORD BUILDING KIT

OPTIONS

INTEGRATING
SPELLING

SPELLING
To work with spelling words that contain the *-ame* phonogram, see the 5-Day Spelling Plan on **pages 177Q–177R.**

Phonics and Decoding /ā/ /el/ /ôr/

☑**Long Vowels and Phonograms: /ā/-*ame***

ACTIVITIES

④ WRITING

USE THE PHONOGRAM
- Encourage children to brainstorm sentences that contain words they have built from the phonogram *-ame*. Write their ideas on chart paper or the chalkboard. Children can pick a word or a sentence and draw a picture to go with it.

We can play the same game.

James came to tame the dog.

Name _____ Date _____

Look at each picture.
Read the sentence.
Circle and write the word that completes the sentence.

1. My friend **came** to my house.
came
name
same

2. His **name** is Ted.
same
flame
name

3. My name is **James**
Games
Tames
James

4. We like to play this **game**
game
tame
came

5. We do the **same** things.
name
same
came

105 Long Vowels and Phonograms: /ā/-ame

PHONICS ACTIVITY BOOK,
pages 105–106

ACTIVITIES

⑤ READING

READ "ONE MONDAY MORNING"
Tell children that they will keep encountering words with the phonogram *-ame* in books they read. Reread **"One Monday Morning"** together. Invite children to read or point to the word *came* whenever they see it.

READ "THE GAME"
Introduce small groups to "The Game." Children may predict what kind of game the book is going to be about. Then read the book together, emphasizing the *-ame* words.

'TRONIC PHONICS
"The Game" is also available in '**TRONIC PHONICS™** on CD-ROM. Children can work independently or in pairs to read the illuminated story, participate in blending activities, and write their own story.

SPOTLIGHT: PHONICS AND DECODING
The Game

☑ Consonant Blends: /pr/pr

DEVELOP PHONEMIC AWARENESS FOR /pr/pr

READ ALOUD
- Ask children to listen as you read **page 149** of **"One Monday Morning."** Emphasize the /pr/ sound in the word *prince*.
- Have children say the word *prince* and identify *pr* as the first sound in the word.

DEVELOP PRINT AWARENESS FOR /pr/pr

DISPLAY A SENTENCE
- Display the sentence from **page 149** of **"One Monday Morning."** Read it together, emphasizing the consonant blend /pr/ in the word *prince*.
- With a word mask, frame the letters *pr* in the word. Ask children to identify the letters and the beginning blend.
- Write the following list of words on the chalkboard: *princess, king, prize, royal, press,* and *queen.* Invite children to identify words that begin with the same sound as the word *prince*.

ACTIVITIES

READ AND WRITE

FIND OTHER WORDS
- Ask children to select a favorite story. Then, as you read it, invite them to listen for words that begin with the same blend as *prince*.

CREATE POSTERS
- Pairs of children can work together to create a poster. Have them cut out pictures from magazines of objects whose names begin with /pr/. If they prefer, they may draw pictures.
- Children can then paste the pictures on a large piece of oak tag.
- Help children label each picture on the poster.

prince   pretzel   prize

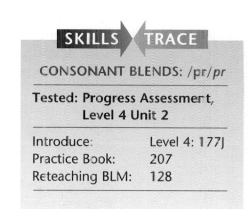

PRIZE WORDS

Look at the picture. Write the word that completes each sentence.

1. You have to _____practice_____ to play this well.
   practice   prize

2. Is the _____present_____ for me?
   pretty   present

3. Use this to _____press_____ your pants.
   press   print

4. The flower is very _____pretty_____
   pretty   prune

5. What is the _____price_____ of the car?
   present   price

PRACTICE BOOK, page 207

See RETEACHING BLM, page 128
See PHONICS ACTIVITY BOOK, pages 107–108

SKILLS TRACE

CONSONANT BLENDS: /pr/pr

Tested: Progress Assessment, Level 4 Unit 2

Introduce:	Level 4: 177J
Practice Book:	207
Reteaching BLM:	128

Vocabulary

ACTIVITIES

VOCABULARY REVIEW

cook	queen	prince
visit	return	knight

WORD RIDDLES

Have children write each vocabulary word on a separate index card. Read aloud the riddles below. Ask children to hold up the vocabulary word that answers each riddle. Have the class name the word together.

1. I dress in armor and am a soldier. Who am I? **(knight)**

2. I am a woman who wears a crown. Who am I? **(queen)**

3. I make breakfast, lunch, and dinner. Who am I? **(cook)**

4. I am what you do when you go to see someone. What word am I? **(visit)**

5. I am a word that means to go back and see someone again. What word am I? **(return)**

6. I am the son of a king or queen. Who am I? **(prince)**

cook

queen

prince

visit

return

knight

VOCABULARY STRATEGY   Inflectional Ending *-ed*

LINK TO LITERATURE

Ask children how adding *-ed* to drop on **page 174** changes the meaning of the word.

Write *dropped* on the chalkboard. Have children identify the base word. Elicit that in some words the last letter is doubled before the *-ed.* Review that *-ed* shows a past action.

EXPLORE

In small groups, have children complete these two sentences with the same verb, using *-ed* to show past tense: *Today we _____. Yesterday we _____.*

DISCUSS

Invite groups to share and act out their sentences. Ask children how they know when to use the *-ed* ending.

USE DIFFERENT MODALITIES

Have groups of children use drawings and demonstrations to show words with the inflectional ending *-ed* (for example: *clapped, hopped, skipped*).

Listening, Speaking, Viewing

LOOKING AT KINGS AND QUEENS

PARTNER Have children gather pictures of kings and queens found in fiction and nonfiction books, as well as those on different decks of playing cards. Encourage partners to compare the illustrations to the ones in **"One Monday Morning."** Have partners cast a vote for their favorite king and queen.

VIEWING TIP Encourage children to line up the pictures or cards side-by-side. This will help them focus on similarities and differences in the art.

ORAL LANGUAGE DEVELOPMENT

GROUP Have children gather in circles of four or five. Ask the first child in each circle to make up the name of a visitor and say: "_____ came to visit me, but I wasn't home." Have the next child repeat the first name and add a new name, saying "_____ and _____ came to visit me, but I wasn't home." Each child in the circle has to repeat the names of the visitors in order, and add his or her own new visitor to the end of the list.

TELLING A STORY

GROUP In small groups, have each child tell a story about something fun he or she has done on a rainy day. They may use props found in the classroom for their storytelling.

LISTENING AND SPEAKING TIPS Speakers should speak clearly and slowly so that others can understand them. Listeners should be attentive and raise their hands if they need the speaker to talk louder.

ADDITIONAL RESOURCES

GROUP **STORYTELLING** You may want to read aloud "La Hormiguita" from the book of **READ ALOUDS, PLAYS, AND CHORAL READINGS.** A recording is available on **SONGS AND STORIES AUDIOCASSETTES.**

ONE **LISTEN TO THE STORY** If children haven't already done so, they can listen to the **LISTENING LIBRARY AUDIOCASSETTE** for a dramatic reading of **"One Monday Morning."**

PARTNER **LISTEN TO THE SONG** Invite children to listen to the song "Little Prince" on the **SONGS AND STORIES AUDIOCASSETTES.**

PORTFOLIO

Use a tape recorder to keep a record of children's stories. You can also videotape children as they compare and contrast the pictures of the kings and queens.

OPPORTUNITIES

Writing

Writing Process: Place Description

Invite children to think of a favorite place. It may be a place they like to play when it rains. Encourage them to describe the place so others can see it in their minds. Ask them to recall how the setting in **"One Monday Morning"** was shown.

PREWRITING

STRATEGY: CLUSTER Suggest to children that they close their eyes and visualize the place they are going to describe. Prompt them to remember not only the things they see, but also smells and noises associated with this place. To help children organize their ideas, have them create a word cluster. Children can write "My Favorite Place" in a circle with other lines and circles branching off of it. Then they can jot down the words and phrases that relate to this place.

DRAFTING

Remind children that during the drafting stage, the most important thing is to get their ideas down on paper. Later, they can go back to check for punctuation and correct spelling.

REVISING

Ask children to read over their first drafts. Are their descriptions complete enough to create clear pictures of the places they are describing? What words or details might they want to add? Do their sentences seem choppy or do they seem to flow? Allow partners to read each other's work and give suggestions for improvement.

PROOFREADING

After children have finished writing, they should check their descriptions for spelling, grammar, and punctuation. If you have used the grammar lesson on **pages 177O–177P**, suggest that children make sure they have used the verbs *come* and *came* correctly.

PUBLISHING

Invite children to read their descriptions to the class. Encourage listeners to try to picture the place in their minds. Bind all the stories together in a class book entitled, "Our Favorite Places."

RUBRIC FOR PLACE DESCRIPTION	
4	**EXCELLENT** In this description the writer chose vivid words and images that give the reader a clear picture of a particular place.
3	**GOOD** This narrative describes a place, presenting and developing some important details.
2	**FAIR** This paper refers to a particular place but the description details may be too few or too fragmented to enable the reader to form a picture.
1	**POOR** This paper is not a description or it meets the criteria only minimally.

WRITING TRACE

Descriptive Writing
177, 177M, 207, 207M, 211A-211H
Strategies:
Cluster: 177, 177M, 211A-211H
List: 207, 207M

Writing Projects

TRONICS PHONICS *The **Make a Book** section allows children to write and illustrate their own stories.*

PROJECT 1

LABEL A PICTURE Draw pictures of the visitors you would like to have on a rainy day. They might be special friends, relatives, or someone you have not seen in a long time. Label your pictures with each person's name and the day of the week they visit.

EASY

PROJECT 2

RAINY DAY DESCRIPTION Imagine that it is raining. How does your neighborhood look on a rainy day? Are there lots of people outside? What color is the sky? Write a sentence or two describing the scene. You can draw pictures to illustrate your writing.

AVERAGE

PROJECT 3

CONTINUING THE STORY Describe some fun things the little boy might do with his imaginary guests. Will they play cards? Will they take the dog to the park? Write and illustrate one or two new pages to add to the story. **CHALLENGE**

GRAMMAR, MECHANICS, AND USAGE If you have already presented the grammar lesson on **pages 177O–177P** or in the **GRAMMAR MINILESSONS, page 21,** remind children to review their writing for correct usage of the verbs *came* and *come*.

SPELLING Encourage children to choose words from their writing that they want to learn to spell and add these to their personal spelling lists. See also the **SPELLING** lesson on **pages 177Q–177R.**

PORTFOLIO

OPPORTUNITIES

Invite children to choose samples from their writing to include in their portfolios.

5-Day Plan
Grammar

COME AND CAME

MEETING INDIVIDUAL NEEDS

Second-Language Support
English learners might have trouble with irregular verbs. Provide many oral practice opportunities with these verbs.

DAY 1

Daily Language Activity

Write the sentences on the chalkboard each day or use Transparency 5. Have children orally make each sentence tell about the past.

1. The king comes to visit on Monday. came
2. Many people come with him. came
3. He comes to visit on Tuesday, too. came

DAY 2

Daily Language Activity

Present these sentences and have children orally make each sentence tell about now.

1. The king came every day. comes
2. The queen came, too. comes
3. They came with the little prince. come

TEACH *COME* AND *CAME*

FROM THE LITERATURE

INTRODUCE Read the sentence on **pages 143–147** of "**One Monday Morning.**" Ask children whether the action word *came* tells about something happening now or in the past. (the past)

"One Monday morning the king, the queen, and the little prince came to visit me."

USE THE CORRECT VERB

DEVELOP/APPLY Write *come, comes,* and *came* on the chalkboard. Then read the following sentences, helping children identify whether they are talking about the present or past. Help children recall why some verbs that tell about now end with *s* and others don't.

The king *comes* to my house. The other visitors *come* with him. They *came* yesterday, too.

Invite the children to make up other sentences about the royal visitors using *come, comes,* or *came.*

SUMMARIZE

CLOSE Help children list rules for *come* and *came.*

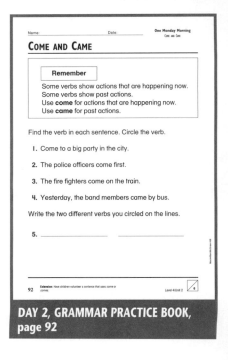

SPECIAL FORMS FOR PAST TENSE

Remember

Most past-tense verbs end in **ed.**
Some verbs have special forms to tell about the past.

The verb in each sentence tells about the past. Write the verb on the line.

1. My friend lived on my street. _____

2. He moved to a new city. _____

3. A letter came from me. _____

4. My friend was happy. _____

DAY 1, GRAMMAR PRACTICE BOOK, page 91

COME AND CAME

Remember

Some verbs show actions that are happening now.
Some verbs show past actions.
Use **come** for actions that are happening now.
Use **came** for past actions.

Find the verb in each sentence. Circle the verb.

1. Come to a big party in the city.

2. The police officers come first.

3. The fire fighters come on the train.

4. Yesterday, the band members came by bus.

Write the two different verbs you circled on the lines.

5. _____

DAY 2, GRAMMAR PRACTICE BOOK, page 92

COME AND CAME
- Some verbs have special forms to tell about the past.
- The words *come* and *comes* tell about things that happen now.
- The word *came* tells about things that happened in the past.

DAY 3

Daily Language Activity

Present these sentences and have children orally make each sentence tell about the past.

1. A knight comes to see me on Wednesday. **came**
2. A royal guard comes, too. **came**
3. They come with the king and queen. **came**

WRITING APPLICATION

STORY

Have children write a story about a party or special event. Suggest that they tell who comes to the party.

GRAMMAR/MECHANICS CHECKLIST

In evaluating their writing children may want to be sure that:
- they have used *comes* to tell what one person or thing does now.
- they have used *come* to tell what more than one person or thing does now.
- they have used *came* to tell about things that happened in the past.

DAY 4

Daily Language Activity

Present these sentences and have children orally make each sentence tell about now.

1. The royal cook came next. **comes**
2. Then came the royal barber. **comes**
3. All the visitors came at the same time. **come**

QUICK WRITE

THANK-YOU NOTE

Have children pretend they are the little boy in the story and write a quick thank-you note to the royal visitors. After they finish, encourage them to check verb tenses.

DAY 5

Daily Language Activity

Present these sentences and have children orally make each sentence tell about the past.

1. The royal jester comes on Saturday. **came**
2. A little dog comes on Sunday. **came**
3. They all come to say hello. **came**

*See **page 21** of the* GRAMMAR MINILESSONS *for more information on* come *and* came.

FORM FOR THE PAST: CAME

> **Remember**
> Some verbs do not form the past by adding **ed.**
> Use **come** to tell about actions that happen now.
> Use **came** to tell about past actions.

Write the verb.

1. The knight came to visit. _____
2. He came to the home of the king. _____
3. Royal visitors came with him. _____
4. They came late at night. _____

DAY 3, GRAMMAR PRACTICE BOOK, page 93

USE COME OR CAME

> **Remember**
> Use **come** to tell about actions that happen now.
> Use **came** to tell about past actions.

Use **come**, **comes**, or **came** in each sentence. Underline the correct verb.

1. We often (come, comes) to the mountains.
2. We (comes, came) early last spring.
3. Summer (came, come) in June.
4. Many people (comes, come) to the mountains in the summer.
5. My friend (comes, come) every year.

DAY 4, GRAMMAR PRACTICE BOOK, page 94

PAST TENSE VERBS

> **Remember**
> Some verbs change their form when they tell about the past.
> The past tense of **come** is **came**.

Find each sentence with a past tense verb. Circle the first letter of that sentence.

1. We came early to the pool on Friday.
2. Sam comes late every Saturday.
3. Everyone came early on Sunday.
4. Tuesday he came early.

Write the first letters you circled.

5. _____ _____ _____

Use the letters to spell a word that answers the question.

6. How was the water in the pool? _____

DAY 5, GRAMMAR PRACTICE BOOK, page 95

5-Day Plan
Spelling

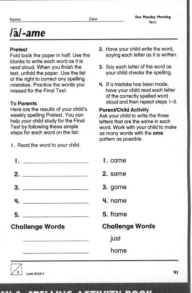

DAY 1, SPELLING ACTIVITY BOOK, page 91

DAY 1

BEGIN WITH A PRETEST

ASSESS PRIOR KNOWLEDGE: WORDS WITH /ā/-*ame*

Use the dictation sentences below and **page 91** of the SPELLING ACTIVITY BOOK for the pretest. A Student Record form is provided.

Allow children to correct their own papers. Ask them to pay special attention to the words they misspelled.

SPELLING WORDS /ā/-*ame*			CHALLENGE WORDS	
came	game	frame	**just**	**home**
same	name			

*Note: Words in **dark type** are from the story.*

DICTATION SENTENCES

SPELLING WORDS

1. The royal family <u>came</u> for a visit.
2. They all arrived on the <u>same</u> day.
3. When they got here, we played a <u>game</u>.
4. What is the prince's <u>name</u>?
5. I put the king's picture in a <u>frame</u>.

CHALLENGE WORDS

6. They <u>just</u> came by to play with me.
7. Will you be <u>home</u> tomorrow?

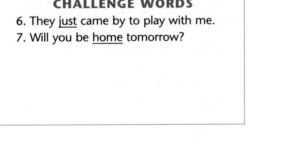

DAY 2, SPELLING ACTIVITY BOOK, page 92

DAY 2

EXPLORE THE SPELLING PATTERN

IDENTIFY THE PHONOGRAM PATTERN -*ame*

Write each Spelling Word on the chalkboard or chart paper. Encourage children to read the words with you. Ask them to identify the sound they hear and the spelling pattern that is the same in each word. Invite volunteers to circle the letters that make the sound in each word. (ame)

DAY 3

CONSTRUCTING WORDS

MAKE A PHONOGRAM SLIDE

Give each child a 6" tagboard sentence strip. Help each child to cut two 1" slits on the left side of the sentence strip. To the right of the slits, have them write the phonogram *-ame.* Next have them cut a 1" by 9" strip of tagboard and write on it the following letters vertically: *c, s, g, n,* and *fr.* Children then thread the 1"x 9" strip through the slits and identify the different words they can make by sliding it up and down.

ALPHABETICAL ORDER

WRITE DEFINITIONS

Remind children that words in the dictionary are always placed in alphabetical order. Invite partners to write each Spelling Word on a card. Have the pairs arrange the cards so that the words form an alphabetical list. Then invite them to write definitions on the cards in their own words.

The optional extension activity for the Challenge Word on **page 93** of the SPELLING ACTIVITY BOOK may be assigned on Day 3.

DAY 4

SPELLING AND WRITING

-ame GALLERY

Encourage children to create five colorful picture frames. Suggest that they use their imagination to write a sentence containing a Spelling Word inside each frame. The framed sentences can be hung on a bulletin board to create an "art gallery" featuring the phonogram *-ame.*

We played a fun game on the playground.

DAY 5

END WITH A POSTTEST

REASSESS CHILDREN'S KNOWLEDGE

Use **page 95** of the SPELLING ACTIVITY BOOK or the dictation sentences on **page 177Q** for the posttest. Have children record their scores on the Student Record form provided.

DAY 3, SPELLING ACTIVITY BOOK, page 93

DAY 4, SPELLING ACTIVITY BOOK, page 94

DAY 5, SPELLING ACTIVITY BOOK, page 95

Reading Resources
Study Skills

CALENDAR

For PUPIL EDITION, see page 289

Use Reference Sources

INTRODUCE Encourage children to remember which visitors arrived on each day of the week in the story. Explain that a **calendar** is very useful in helping keep track of time.

DEVELOP/APPLY Have children turn to the calendar on **page 291** in their anthologies. Ask for ideas about how a calendar could be used. Discuss how calendars can help us plan, remember appointments, and find out when holidays and special days occur.

Challenge volunteers to locate the name of the month, the days of the week, and the numbered days of the month. Do children recognize the holidays shown for the month of November? As a class, have children say the name of each day of the week aloud as they point to the words at the top of the calendar.

Have children look at the calendar to answer questions such as these:
• On what day of the week is the date November 10?

• On what day does the month begin? On what day does it end?
• How many Sundays occur in the month shown?

CLOSE Work together to make a one-month calendar on a large sheet of paper. Invite children to brainstorm a list of important days, such as birthdays, school events, or other special events. Let children mark these days on the calendar. They may also want to make a calendar to record events from the story "**One Monday Morning.**"

Multicultural Perspectives

FUN WITHOUT THE SUN

The boy in **"One Monday Morning"** plays an imaginative game to keep active during rainy weather. Although this is a fictional story, people throughout the world have devised ways to have fun indoors when the weather outdoors was bad.

European lords and ladies in the Middle Ages turned their vast halls into playgrounds where they played an early version of shuffleboard. Also highly popular were dice and card games of chance.

During hard winters on the Plains, the Arapaho played a guessing game in which players had to guess which stick in a pile was the shortest. They also entertained themselves telling stories around the fire and working on handicrafts such as bead work.

Like the Arapaho, the Inuit use the winter months to work on crafts.

Cold weather never stops the Arctic Inuit from having fun. They while away the endless winter months playing a variety of games. A favorite is a kind of cat's cradle, in which intricate designs are made by changing a loop of string from hand to hand. Like the Arapaho, the Inuit use the winter months to work on crafts. Whale bone sculpture is very popular.

The Japanese have a rich store of activities suitable for indoor entertainment. In the ancient art of paper folding, known as *origami*, children create everything from boats to cranes. Also popular is a board game called Go, in which players try to capture one another's territory.

Rainy Day Recreation

Have children work in small groups to create their own indoor activity. Have each group prepare rules and instructions. After children have shared their games with each other, you may wish to have a game fest in which children have an opportunity to play the games.

Across the Curriculum

ART

OUTSIDE MY WINDOW   ONE   30 minutes

Materials: drawing paper; pencils; watercolors; paintbrushes; smocks

DRAWING AND PAINTING

Children can make pictures of things that have been out in the rain.

- Children can show what happens to things when they are out in the rain, such as umbrellas, wet dogs, and puddles.

- Children can choose colors to use for their rain scenes. Help them to mix watercolors to get a rainy effect.

- Invite children to share their finished artwork.

SPATIAL

MATH

RAINY DAYS SURVEY   GROUP   2 days

Materials: paper; tape; crayons; posterboard

MAKING POSTERS

Children can survey others to find out about favorite rainy day activities.

- Discuss with children what they like to do on rainy days. Tape signs on the chalkboard that tell their ideas.

- Ask children to stand in front of the sign that shows what they would most like to do on a rainy day. Children can count and compare the number of class members in each line.

- Ask children to poll their friends and family to find out their five favorite things to do on rainy days. Have them bring in their lists and create a poster to show the number one choice.

LOGICAL/MATHEMATICAL/INTERPERSONAL

ART

GROUP

ONE RAINY DAY
1 day

Materials: pencils; crayons; mural paper

MAKING MURALS
Children can create a mural based on an original story.

- Invite children to sit in a circle and create a class story, beginning with the line "One rainy day when I was bored . . ." Encourage them to take turns adding one line at a time to the story. Prompts to begin the story may include: Who might be a possible character in your story? What might happen on a stormy, rainy day?

- Once the story is completed, have children work together to create a mural illustrating it.

- Suggest that children plan who will draw each part of the mural and how they want it to look when they are finished.

INTERPERSONAL/LINGUISTIC/SPATIAL

DRAMA

GROUP

"ONE MONDAY MORNING" PLAY
1–2 hours

Materials. "One Monday Morning"; construction paper; markers; tape

ACTING
Children can dramatize the story.

- Divide the class into groups of ten, covering all of the characters in the story. Invite one child to narrate the story as each group of performers acts out what is taking place.

- Children may wish to make construction paper crowns and hats to suggest those in the story.

- Encourage children to study the illustrations to get ideas for their characters' facial expressions and body language.

KINESTHETIC/INTERPERSONAL

Poetry

READING THE POEM

TEACHER READ ALOUD Before children look at the illustration, invite them to listen while you read the poem aloud. Encourage them to try to see what they hear in the poem. Then have children try sketching what they saw. You can play **"The Folk Who Live in Backward Town"** on the LISTENING LIBRARY AUDIOCASSETTE for a reading of the poem.

CHORAL READING The short length and simple rhyme scheme of this poem make it ideal for choral reading. Model fluent reading before the choral reading. Then read the poem with children.

LITERARY DEVICES AND TECHNIQUES

USE OF NONSENSE FOR HUMOROUS EFFECT Call children's attention to the way the writer took one silly idea—a place where everything is backward—and used it to create a whole world of other silly things. Ask children to recall the silly things the people did.

Read the poem again and, after the first two lines, ask children to change one word in each line to make the folks live in a normal town.

THE FOLK WHO LIVE IN BACKWARD TOWN

The folk who live in Backward Town
Are inside out and upside down.
They wear their hats inside their heads
And go to sleep beneath their beds.
They only eat the apple peeling
And take their walks across the ceiling.

Mary Ann Hoberman

POETRY TALK

Children can discuss their personal responses to the poem and talk about these and other questions in small groups.

• What do you think is the funniest thing the people in this poem do? Why?

• Would you like to live in Backward Town? Tell what you would do if you lived there.

PANTOMIME/DRAMA Children may enjoy acting out things they can do backward and then have classmates guess what the activities are.

MEET THE POET

ABOUT MARY ANN HOBERMAN
Children may be interested to know that Mary Ann Hoberman writes poems about growing up, seasons, and insects. She is working on a book of poetry that is all about animals. The pictures for this book will be drawn by her husband, who illustrates most of her poems. She has written other poetry, which can be found in the following collections: *All My Shoes Come in Twos, How Do I Go?*, and *Not Enough For the Babies.*

179

You'll Soon Grow into Them, Titch

Teacher's Read Aloud

Read the folk tale aloud to create interest for the story "You'll Soon Grow into Them, Titch."

Something from Nothing

a Jewish folk tale adapted by Phoebe Gilman

When Joseph was a baby, his grandfather made him a wonderful blanket . . .

. . . to keep him warm and cozy and to chase away bad dreams.

But as Joseph grew older, the wonderful blanket grew older, too.

One day his mother said to him, "Joseph, look at your blanket. It's frazzled, it's worn, it's unsightly, it's torn. It is time to throw it out."

"Grandpa can fix it," Joseph said.

Joseph's grandfather took the blanket and turned it round and round.

"Hmm," he said as his scissors went snip, snip, snip and his needle flew in and out and in and out, "There's just enough material here to make . . ."

. . . a wonderful jacket. Joseph put on the wonderful jacket and went outside to play.

But as Joseph grew older, the wonderful jacket grew older, too.

One day his mother said to him, "Joseph, look at your jacket. It's shrunken and small, doesn't fit you at all. It is time to throw it out!"

"Grandpa can fix it," Joseph said.

Joseph's grandfather took the jacket and turned it round and round.

"Hmm," he said as his scissors went snip, snip, snip and his needle flew in and out and in and out, "There's just enough material here to make . . ."

. . . a wonderful vest. Joseph wore the wonderful vest to school the very next day.

But as Joseph grew older, the wonderful vest grew older, too.

One day his mother said to him, "Joseph, look at your vest! It's spotted with glue and there's paint on it too. It is time to throw it out!"

"Grandpa can fix it," Joseph said.

Joseph's grandfather took the vest and turned it round and round.

"Hmm," he said as his scissors went snip, snip, snip and his needle flew in and out and in and out, "There's just enough material here to make . . ."

. . . a wonderful tie. Joseph wore the wonderful tie to his grandparents' house every Friday.

But as Joseph grew older, his wonderful tie grew older, too.

One day his mother said to him, "Joseph, look at your tie! This big stain of soup makes the end of it droop. It is time to throw it out!"

"Grandpa can fix it," Joseph said.

Flexible Grouping Options
- Extra Support
- Challenge
- Second-Language Support
- ✔ These core skills are tested in Unit Progress Assessment.

DAY 3 *READ THE LITERATURE*	DAY 4 *EXTEND SKILLS IN CONTEXT*	DAY 5 *EXTEND SKILLS IN CONTEXT*

Respond to the Literature
Journal Writing, 207A
● Writing About the Theme, 207A
Comprehension Checkpoint, 207B
✔ Analyze Character, Plot, Setting, 203
Character Chart: Character, Plot, Setting
Practice Book, 216
Graphic Organizer Transparency/BLM 30
● Reteaching
✔ Character, Plot, Setting, 203
Practice Book, 216
Vocabulary
Selection Assessment
Selection Assessment/Unit Progress Assessment, Levels 4/5

Skills in Context
✔ Problem and Solution, 183
Practice Book, 209
● ✔ Short Vowels and Phonograms: /i/-*ig*, 185
Practice Book, 210
● Verbs, 187
● Consonant Blends: /st/-*st*, 189
Contractions, 191
✔ Sequence of Events, 193
Practice Book, 212
✔ Summarize, 195
Practice Book, 213

● ● ● Multilevel Resources, 207D–207F

● ● Vocabulary, 207K
Listening, Speaking, Viewing, 207L
Across the Curriculum, 207U

Skills in Context
✔ Use Illustrations, 197
Practice Book, 214
● ✔ Consonant Blend: /kl/*cl*, 199
Practice Book, 215
Birthdays, 201
● ✔ Character, Plot, Setting, 203
Practice Book, 216
Quotations, 205
Characterization, 207
Writing Process: Character Description, 207M
● ● Writing Projects, 207N
Study Skills/Reading Resources, Use Graphic Aids, 207S
Multicultural Perspectives
Family Treasures, 207T
Across the Curriculum, 207V

✔ Decoding Strategies: Blending Activities, 207H
Practice Book, 218

g old   t old   c old

✔ Writing with the Phonogram, 207I
● Phonics Activity Book, 109–110

✔ Reading with the Phonogram, 207I
✔ Consonant Blends: *sw*, 207J
● Phonics Activity Book, 111–112
'TRONIC PHONICS™

Constructing Words, 207R
Work with Meaning, 207R
Spelling Activity Book, 98

Spelling and Writing, 207R
Spelling Activity Book, 99

Posttest, 207R
Spelling Activity Book, 100

Daily Language Activity: *Say* and *Said*
1. Yesterday Mary says, "What a cute baby!" (said)
2. Titch says, "What a small baby!" (said)
3. Pete says the baby was crying. (said)
Writing Application: Conversation, 207P
Grammar Practice Book: *Say* and *Said*, 98

Daily Language Activity: *Say* and *Said*
1. Titch said he will help with the baby. (says)
2. Mom said, "Good job!" (says)
3. Pete and Mary said they will help, too. (say)
Quick Write: Creating Dialog, 207P
Grammar Practice Book: *Say* and *Said*, 99

Daily Language Activity: *Say* and *Said*
1. Last week Dad says, "Look at the birds outside." (said)
2. Yesterday Pete says, "Have they hatched yet?" (said)
3. This morning Titch says, "Look at the baby birds." (said)
Grammar Practice Book: *Say* and *Said*, 100; Answer Key and Grammar Assessment, 23

Suggested Lesson Planner
With Flexible Grouping Options

WEEK AT A GLANCE	PART 1 — DAY 1 *FOCUS ON READING*	PART 2 — DAY 2 *READ THE LITERATURE*
You'll Soon Grow into Them, Titch by Pat Hutchins ◆ **Reading** ◆ **Writing** ◆ **Listening, Speaking, Viewing**	Preview the Selection, 180G ● Build Background, 180G Graphic Organizer Transparency/BLM 29 ● Oral Language Activities, 180H See also ESL/Second-Language Teacher's Guide, 196–204 Vocabulary, 180I Instructional Vocabulary *brother* *sister* *pants* *pair* *socks* *clothes* Vocabulary Transparency/BLM 6 Practice Book, 208 ┌─────────────────────┐ If you wish to have children begin reading the selection at this point, see page 180J. └─────────────────────┘	Set Purposes, 180J Journal Writing Suggestions for Reading, 180J ● Read Independently ● ● Read Aloud ● Read Together Read and Teach Teach Strategic Reading, 180J–207 ☑ Analyze Character, Plot, Setting 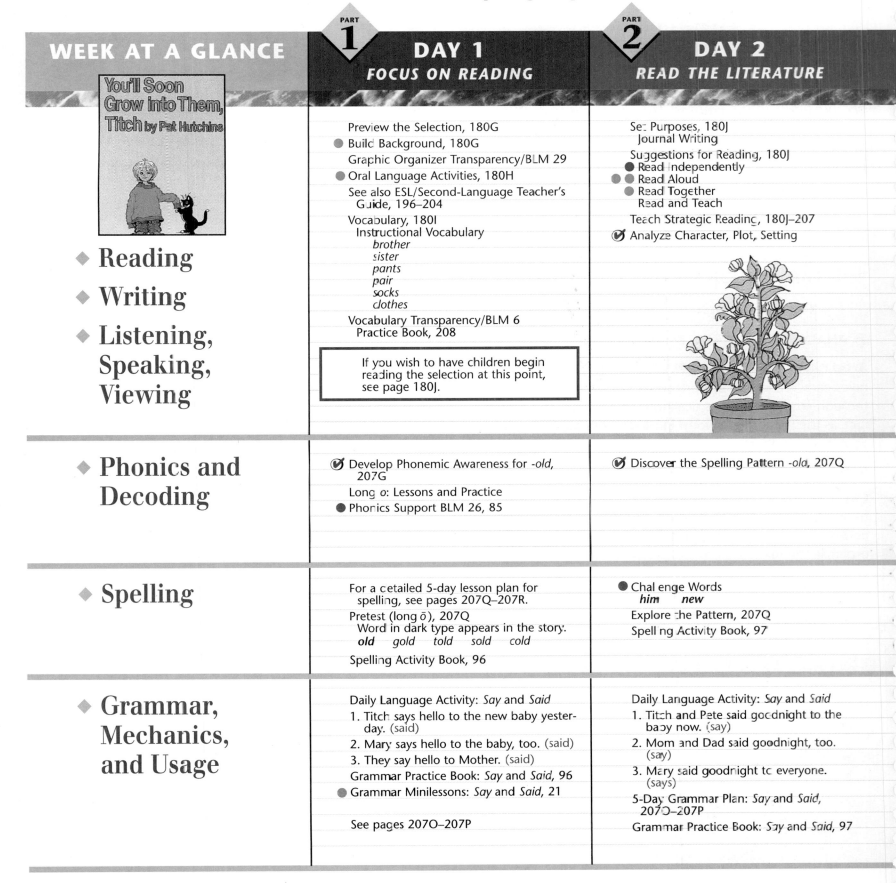
◆ **Phonics and Decoding**	☑ Develop Phonemic Awareness for *-old*, 207G Long o: Lessons and Practice ● Phonics Support BLM 26, 85	☑ Discover the Spelling Pattern *-old*, 207Q
◆ **Spelling**	For a detailed 5-day lesson plan for spelling, see pages 207Q–207R. Pretest (long ō), 207Q Word in dark type appears in the story. **old** gold told sold cold Spelling Activity Book, 96	● Challenge Words *him* *new* Explore the Pattern, 207Q Spelling Activity Book, 97
◆ **Grammar, Mechanics, and Usage**	Daily Language Activity: *Say* and *Said* 1. Titch says hello to the new baby yesterday. (said) 2. Mary says hello to the baby, too. (said) 3. They say hello to Mother. (said) Grammar Practice Book: *Say* and *Said*, 96 ● Grammar Minilessons: *Say* and *Said*, 21 See pages 207O–207P	Daily Language Activity: *Say* and *Said* 1. Titch and Pete said goodnight to the baby now. (say) 2. Mom and Dad said goodnight, too. (say) 3. Mary said goodnight to everyone. (says) 5-Day Grammar Plan: *Say* and *Said*, 207O–207P Grammar Practice Book: *Say* and *Said*, 97

WRITER   PAT HUTCHINS   ILLUSTRATOR

Selection Summary

Titch is the smallest in his family, but things are changing! Mother is expecting a baby, and Titch is growing out of his clothes. His older siblings pass on their hand-me-downs to him, and soon mom and dad notice that Titch needs his own clothing. When the baby comes, Titch realizes he now has a sibling who will soon grow into his clothes.

Pat Hutchins says, "I wrote *You'll Soon Grow into Them, Titch* for my son Sam. He has an older brother, Morgan. When Morgan grew out of his clothes, he gave them to Sam. Suddenly, we realized that Sam never had any new clothes of his own. So we went out and bought him his own new set of clothes."

About the pictures, Ms. Hutchins tells children, "The story is all about growing, so I put a bird's nest in the pictures. When Mother's baby is born, the baby birds have hatched."

Other Books by Pat Hutchins
- *Clocks and More Clocks* (Macmillan, 1994)
- *Little Pink Pig* (Greenwillow, 1994)
- *The Doorbell Rang* (Greenwillow, 1986)
- *Titch* (Macmillan, 1971)

Linking Skills to Literature

Key Comprehension Strategies/Skills

☑ **ANALYZE CHARACTER, PLOT, SETTING**

ANALYZING CHARACTER, PLOT, SETTING This selection gives early readers an opportunity to explore character through empathy. Titch is dealing with issues many children face as they examine a world in which they are often the youngest members.

INTERACTING WITH THE TEXT

ENGAGE THE READER Children will have an opportunity to interact with the text by analyzing the character, plot and setting. A story chart will be used as an aid to organize the text.

See **pages 180J** and **180**, where the story pages begin.

Joseph's grandfather took the tie and turned it round and round.

"Hmm," he said as his scissors went snip, snip, snip and his needle flew in and out and in and out, "There's just enough material here to make. . ."

. . . a wonderful handkerchief. Joseph used the wonderful handkerchief to keep his pebble collection safe.

But as Joseph grew older, his wonderful handkerchief grew older, too.

One day his mother said to him, "Joseph, look at your handkerchief! It's been used till it's tattered, it's splotched and it's splattered. It is time to THROW IT OUT!"

"Grandpa can fix it," Joseph said.

Joseph's grandfather took the handkerchief and turned it round and round.

"Hmm," he said as his scissors went snip, snip, snip and his needle flew in and out and in and out, "There's just enough material here to make . . ."

. . . a wonderful button. Joseph wore the wonderful button on his suspenders to hold his pants up.

One day his mother said to him, "Joseph, where's your button?"

Joseph looked. It was gone!

He searched everywhere but he could not find it. Joseph ran down to his grandfather's house.

"My button! My wonderful button is lost!"

His mother ran after him. "Joseph! Listen to me.

"The button is gone, finished, kaput. Even your grandfather can't make something from nothing."

Joseph's grandfather shook his head sadly. "I'm afraid that your mother is right," he said.

The next day Joseph went to school. "Hmm," he said, as his pen went scritch scratch, scritch scratch over the paper. "There's just enough material here to make . . ."

. . . a wonderful story.

Prepare to Read

PREVIEW THE SELECTION

AUTHOR, ILLUSTRATOR

Read **page 207.** How do you think the author's children felt after reading about the children in this story?

GENRE: REALISTIC FICTION

Invite children to look at the illustrations and tell what kind of story they think this is. Could the events shown in these pictures really happen? Do the children and parents look like real people?

EVALUATE PRIOR KNOWLEDGE

FAMILIES

Invite children to tell about sharing clothes and other objects with their older and younger siblings. Create a web or use **GRAPHIC ORGANIZER TRANSPARENCY/BLM 29.**

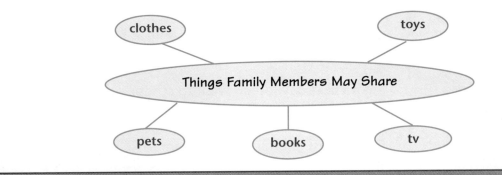

clothes

toys

Things Family Members May Share

pets

books

tv

ACTIVITIES FOR BUILDING BACKGROUND

MAKE IT REAL: GROWING INTO CLOTHES

To help children relate to the concept of clothes that are too big or too small, invite them to bring in an item of clothing that doesn't fit any more. You might also bring in dress-up clothes that will be too big. Have children try on the clothes and talk about how they feel.

READ ALOUD

You may want to read aloud "Something from Nothing," a Jewish folk tale on **pages 180E–180F.**

INTEGRATING

SPELLING AND GRAMMAR

SPELLING
You may want to present the spelling pretest of words with /ō/-*old*. See **pages 207Q– 207R** for the 5-Day Spelling Plan.

PHONICS AND DECODING CONNECTION
See lesson on Long Vowels and Phonograms: /ō/-*old* on **pages 207G–207I.**

GRAMMAR
See **pages 207O–207P** for Daily Language Activities. A 5-Day Grammar Plan is also presented.

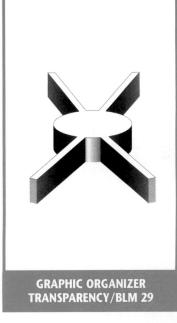

GRAPHIC ORGANIZER TRANSPARENCY/BLM 29

ORAL LANGUAGE ACTIVITIES

SURPRISES
To reinforce the selection theme, Surprises Along the Way, ask children to give examples of surprises. They might discuss surprise parties, presents they did not expect, or events that they did not anticipate.

Ask children with what they would most like to be surprised. Elicit that getting what you wish for is only a surprise if you are not expecting it.

PLANNING A SURPRISE
The class might enjoy planning a surprise for someone—an absent student, a visiting teacher, or the school principal. Discuss what surprises that person would enjoy and how children could make them the most surprising.

Children who don't speak English can be paired with English speakers to help them find the words to express themselves.

NONVERBAL RESPONSE
Encourage non-English speakers or limited-English speakers to illustrate a time when they were surprised with a party, a gift, or by an event. They might also act out situations in which they were surprised.

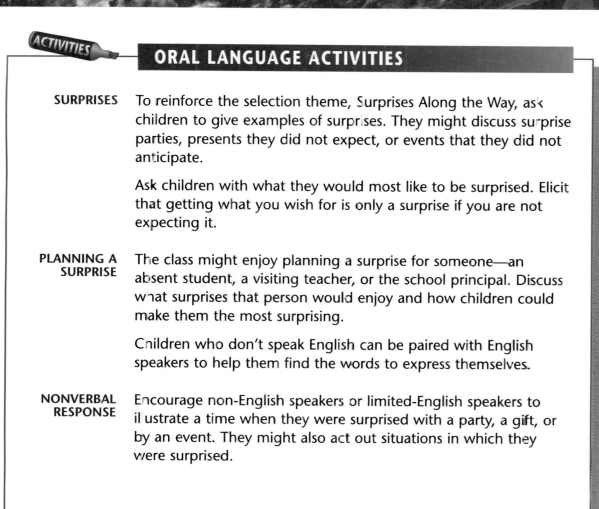

TEACHING
TIPS

Children may understand you even if they can't respond orally. Find alternate ways for them to respond, then model how they might put their responses into words.

LANGUAGE DEVELOPMENT

You may want to present the following words, idioms, and phrases to children who need language support:

grow into them, p. 180
a bit big, p. 184
brand-new, p. 195
there, p. 200
much too small, p. 204

ESL/Second-Language Teacher's Guide
A full teaching lesson for students acquiring English is available in the ESL/SECOND-LANGUAGE TEACHER'S GUIDE.

Vocabulary READ

INSTRUCTIONAL VOCABULARY

brother	a boy who has the same mother and father as you do
sister	a girl who has the same mother and father as you do
pants	clothes you wear on the bottom half of your body
pair	two things that go together or one thing with two parts
socks	soft covers for your feet, worn inside shoes
clothes	what you wear to cover your body

 ## VOCABULARY ACTIVITIES

WORD CLUES
GROUP

After you present the vocabulary, invite children to work in groups or as a class to answer the clues with the appropriate vocabulary word. Use **VOCABULARY STRATEGY TRANSPARENCY/BLM 6.**

> 1. I am a girl who may have the same mother and father as you do. Who am I?
> sister
>
> 2. I am a soft cover for your feet. What am I?
> socks
>
> 3. I am two things that go together. What am I?
> pair

PERSONAL EXPERIENCE
PARTNER

After discussing the vocabulary, have partners tell of their own experiences. They may describe favorite items of clothing or their relationships with people who are brothers and sisters. If necessary, they can check definitions in the glossary.

WORDS IN CONTEXT
ONE

For more vocabulary practice, assign **PRACTICE BOOK, page 208.**

VOCABULARY
Word Clues

brother	pair
sister	socks
pants	clothes

1. I am a girl who may have the same mother and father as you are I?
   sister
2. I am a soft cover for your feet. What am I?
   socks
3. I am two things that go together. What am I?
   pair
4. I am things you wear. What am I?
   clothes
5. You wear me over your legs. What am I?
   pants
6. I am a boy who may have the same mother and father as you do. Who am I?
   brother

6   Level 4 / Unit 2: You'll Soon Grow Into Them, Titch

VOCABULARY STRATEGY TRANSPARENCY/BLM 6

YOU'LL SOON GROW INTO THEM, TITCH

| brother sister pants pair socks clothes |

Circle the word that completes the sentence. Write the word.

1. I called my ___sister___. (sister) clothes
2. Sam is her ___brother___. pants (brother)
3. I have red ___socks___. sister (socks)
4. My ___clothes___ are clean. pair (clothes)
5. Where are my ___pants___? sister (pants)
6. This is an old ___pair___ (pair) shoes of shoes.

PRACTICE BOOK, page 208

Strategic Reading

SET PURPOSES

JOURNAL WRITING

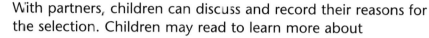

With partners, children can discuss and record their reasons for the selection. Children may read to learn more about

- brothers and sisters.
- new and old clothes.
- what Titch will grow into.

ENGAGE THE READER

Children will have the opportunity to role-play story characters as suggested in the Strategic Reading columns. You may also want children to list information about characters, plot, and setting in a story chart.

Characters	Plot	Setting

As they read, children can note in their journals any comments or questions they may want to explore. Invite children to refer to their journals and their charts in the discussion after reading. **(pages 207A–207B)**

SUGGESTIONS FOR READING

OPTIONS MANAGEMENT TIPS

Books for Meeting Individual Needs, **pages 207D–207E,** offer teaching suggestions for working with groups of children who have specific needs

READ INDEPENDENTLY

Have independent readers read silently, noting how the pictures help them follow the events in the plot.

READ ALOUD

Read the story aloud or play the **LISTENING LIBRARY AUDIOCASSETTE.** Children may use **Story Web™** to hear narration in English or Spanish as the selection appears on the monitor.

READ TOGETHER

Assign groups the roles of Titch, Pete, Mary, Mother, and the narrator. Encourage readers to say the dialog the way they think the characters would.

READ AND TEACH

☑ Character, Plot, Setting

Use comprehension strategies beginning on **page 180** as you and your children read the literature, or use the strategy after any other Suggestions for Reading Option.

Comprehension

STRATEGIC READING

☑ CHARACTER, PLOT, SETTING

Share the comprehension strategies that will be focused on.

When you read a story, it helps to notice who the characters are, what they do, how they feel, and where they are. The plot is what happens in a story. Often the characters must solve a problem. It's also important to pay attention to how characters are related to each other. In this story, understanding the relationship between Titch and his brother and sister will help you understand the problem in the story and why the characters act the way they do.

TEACHING
TIPS

Tell children that you will model how readers notice characters, plot, and setting as you read together. They will have a chance to use these strategies, too.

180

Titch needed new pants.

181

Skills in Context

Comprehension

STRATEGIC READING

1 **PLOT** Look at the pictures on this page and on the page before. What problem does Titch have? (His pants are too small.) How would you suggest that he solve it?

2 **CHARACTER** When I read a story, it helps to learn the names of characters and how they are related to each other. What word on this page tells me how Titch and a boy named Pete are related? (brother)

3 **CHARACTER** Sometimes I need to look at the pictures and see how characters react to each other. Then I can make a guess about their relationship. I think that the man and woman are the boys' parents. What do you think?

4 **SETTING** Where does this story take place? (in a home) How do you know? Look out the window. What time of year is it? (early spring)

PHONICS AND DECODING

/ō/-*old* as in *old*, **page 183**
See Phonics and Decoding lesson on Long Vowels and Phonograms: /ō/-*old* on **pages 207G–207I.**

182

His brother Pete said, /2/
"You can have my old pants,
they're too small for me."

/4/

183

Skills in Context

COMPREHENSION

✔ Problem and Solution

INTRODUCE Remind children that a story is often about a problem that a character has to solve.

DEVELOP/APPLY Invite children to discuss the problem that Titch has in this story. Encourage them to tell what his brother, Pete, suggests. Then have them brainstorm how else it might be solved.

After children finish reading the story, talk about all of the different solutions that story characters suggested to help Titch solve his problem. Have them identify the solution that finally worked.

CLOSE Invite children to look at the ending of the story. What problem does Titch think the new baby has? What solution does he offer?

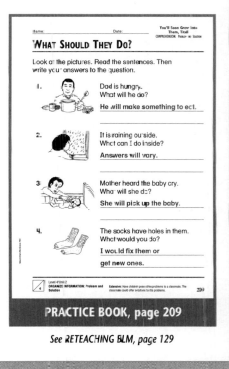

PRACTICE BOOK, page 209

See RETEACHING BLM, page 129

SKILLS ✕ TRACE

PROBLEM AND SOLUTION

Tested: Progress Assessment: Level 4 Unit 2

Introduce:	Level 4: 183
Review:	Level 4: 259, Level 5: 165
Practice Book:	209, 232, 299
Reteaching BLM:	129, 148, 203

Comprehension

STRATEGIC READING

5 **PLOT** Is Titch's problem solved now? (no) Why? (These pants are too big for him.) What does Pete tell him?

6 **CHARACTER** How do you think Titch feels in his big pants? Make a facial expression that shows how you would feel if you were Titch. **NONVERBAL RESPONSE**

7 **CHARACTER** Do you think Titch and Pete said anything more to each other than the story tells us? Who wants to volunteer to be Titch? Who will be Pete? Tell us what else they might say to each other. **ROLE-PLAY**

5 "They're still a bit big for me," said Titch.

184

"You'll soon grow into them," said Pete.

185

Skills in Context

✓ Short Vowels and Phonograms: /i/-ig

INTRODUCE Reread **page 184** together. Stress the *-ig* sound as you read the word *big*.

DEVELOP/APPLY Write the spelling pattern *ig* on the chalkboard or on chart paper. Ask children to point to a word on **page 184** that ends with the sound these letters make. Write the word and underline the letters *ig*. Invite children to suggest other words containing the phonogram *-ig*, such as *pig*, *dig*, and *jig*. Write their suggestions under the word *big*.

CLOSE Have children write the word *big* using very big letters. Then ask them to circle the letters that make the *-ig* sound.

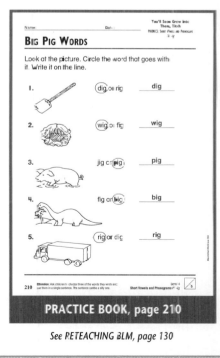

PRACTICE BOOK, page 210

See PETEACHING BLM, page 130

SHORT VOWELS AND PHONOGRAMS: /i/-*ig*

Tested: Progress Assessment: Level 4 Unit 2

Introduce:	Level 2: 146
Review:	Level 4: 21, 185
Practice Book:	93, 157, 210
Reteaching BLM:	53, 88, 130

Comprehension

8 **PLOT** Here's how I figure out a story's plot. First I identify the problem. Titch's pants were too small. Now his sweater is too small. I bet Titch's problem is that he has outgrown all his clothes. What do you think?

9 Do you expect Mary's sweater to fit Titch? Why or why not?

Observe if children notice the story's repetitive language pattern and use it to predict what Mary may also say to Titch.

And when Titch needed a new sweater,

186

his sister Mary said,
"You can have my old sweater,
it's too small for me."

Skills in Context

GRAMMAR REVIEW

Verbs

PAST TENSE VERBS Invite children to reread **pages 186–187.** Help them identify the verb *needed* in this sentence. Ask children when the action described by this verb took place. "Is it happening now? Has it already happened?" Guide children to identify the *-ed* ending as a clue that the action has already taken place.

RELATING TO PRESENT-TENSE VERBS Have children use the word *needed* in several sentences telling some of the things that Titch needed. Record these on the chalkboard under a column headed, "Yesterday." Begin a second column headed, "Today." Ask children to rewrite the sentences in the Yesterday column by changing the verb tense. Help children notice the way the verb changes when the action is happening now, not in the past.

For lessons on present and past tense verbs, see **TAKE A CLOSER LOOK. pages 69O–69P** and **133O–133P.**

Comprehension

STRATEGIC READING

10 Do you remember when you heard these words before? **(when Titch tried on Pete's pants)**

11 **CHARACTER** Mary said almost the same thing as Pete. Why do you think their words are so much alike?

12 **SETTING** Before we leave this scene, let's look out the window. What time of year is it? **(mid-spring)** How can you tell? **(Plants and leaves are starting to grow; the bird is sitting on her nest.)** Look back at **page 182.** What time of year was it then? **(early spring)** What do these pictures tell you? **(Time is passing.)**

13 **CHARACTER, PLOT, SETTING** Let's work on our story charts. We're going to write about who is in the story, what is happening, and where everything is taking place up to this point.

Characters	Plot	Setting
Titch	Titch's clothes are too small.	Inside the house, in the spring
Pete	Pete gives Titch his old pants.	
Mary	Mary gives Titch her old sweater. Pete and Mary give Titch their old clothes.	

 "It's still a bit big for me," said Titch.

188

/11/ "You'll soon grow into it," said Mary.

/12/

/13/

189

Skills in Context

PHONICS AND DECODING

☑ Consonant Blends: /st/ *st*

INTRODUCE Reread **page 188**, emphasizing the word *still* as you read.

DEVELOP/APPLY Write the word *still* on the chalkboard or chart paper. Tell children that this word begins with a consonant blend. Circle the *st,* saying the sound /st/ at the same time.

Invite volunteers to suggest other words that begin with this blend.

CLOSE Say the following words slowly, inviting children to *stomp* their feet each time they hear a word that begins with /st/: *stairs, sit, stamp, star, tip, stand, share, stick.*

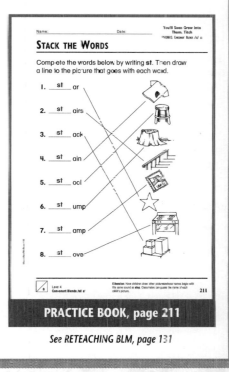

PRACTICE BOOK, page 211

See RETEACHING BLM, page 131

SKILLS ✦ TRACE

CONSONANT BLENDS: /st/ *st*

Tested: Progress Assessment: Level 4 Unit 2

Introduce:	Level 3: 51
Review:	Level 4: 189; Level 5: 91
Practice Book:	119, 211, 272
Reteaching BLM:	67, 131, 181

Comprehension

STRATEGIC READING

14 **CHARACTER** I see Pete and Mary offering their old socks to Titch. They see that he has a problem, and they are trying to help him solve it. How would you describe them?

MEETING INDIVIDUAL NEEDS

Second-Language Support

Help children identify the signs that show time is passing, including the change of seasons as seen through the window, the growing cat, the mother's knitting, and the growing plant on the coffee table.

And when Titch needed new socks,

190

they both said,
"You can have our old socks,
they're too small for us."

191

Skills in Context

Contractions

Read aloud what Pete and Mary say on **page 191.**

THINK ALOUD *When I read Pete and Mary's words, I see a special mark called an apostrophe in the word* they're. *The apostrophe may mean that the word is a contraction—a shortened word made from two other words. I look closer at the word* they're, *and I see the word* they *and the letters* re. *The* re *could stand for* are. *Let's see if that makes sense:* They are too small for us. *That sounds right! So* they're *must be a contraction—a shortened form, of* they are.

Invite children to find other contractions in the selection and identify the two words each contraction was made from.

MEETING INDIVIDUAL NEEDS

Second-Language Support
Write pairs of sentences on the chalkboard. Use a contraction in the first sentence of each pair, and the two words that make up the contraction in the second sentence. Ask children to read the two sentences and find the contraction and the two words that form it.

Comprehension

STRATEGIC READING

15 **PLOT** Do you remember what Titch has said every time he got some clothes that were too big? What did Mother say each time? **(nothing)** What is she saying now? **(Titch needs some new clothes.)** Why do you think she has changed her mind?

16 I was so glad when Mother said Titch needed new clothes! How do you think Titch would have felt if he had had to wear those big clothes? Who wants to show us? Pretend you're Titch and tell us how you feel. **ROLE-PLAY**

SELF ASSESSMENT

Ask children to think about their reading by asking themselves questions such as the following:

- Is there anything I haven't understood about Titch or his family so far?

- Am I using the illustrations to help me understand this story?

- Am I stopping to summarize Titch's problem and the way his family has tried to help him solve it?

To help children Analyze Character, Plot, and Setting, see Reteaching lesson on **page 203**.

"And I'll soon grow into them," said Titch.

192

"I think," said Mother, "that Titch should have some new clothes." 15

193

Skills in Context

COMPREHENSION

✐ Sequence of Events

INTRODUCE Remind children that recalling story events in the order in which they occurred can help them understand the story better.

DEVELOP/APPLY Work with them to list the story events in a cumulative story staircase chart. Help children to list the events in the right order. Then talk with children about the order of events in the story.

CLOSE Have children use the list to talk about favorite parts of the story with partners.

PRACTICE BOOK, page 212

See RETEACHING BLM, page 132

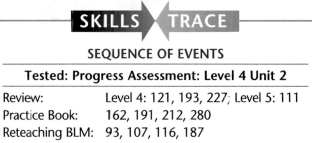

SKILLS TRACE

SEQUENCE OF EVENTS

Tested: Progress Assessment: Level 4 Unit 2

Review: Level 4: 121, 193, 227; Level 5: 111
Practice Book: 162, 191, 212, 280
Reteaching BLM: 93, 107, 116, 187

Comprehension

STRATEGIC READING

17 **PLOT** What did Dad and Titch do to solve Titch's problem? **(They went shopping.)**

18 **SETTING** Where is the story taking place now? **(store)** Point to what Dad and Titch bought first. **NONVERBAL RESPONSE**

MATH CONNECTION

Encourage children to comment on how the clothes in the store are organized. Have them count the number of articles of clothing in each stack. Make comparisons by asking questions such as:

• What does the store owner stock the most of? Least of?

17 So Dad and Titch went shopping.

194

They bought a brand-new pair of pants,

COMPREHENSION

✔ Summarize

INTRODUCE Remind children that a summary is a retelling of something using only the most important details.

DEVELOP/APPLY Reread **page 181** with children. Ask them to tell what happened in the story up to the part where Titch goes to the store with Dad. Encourage children to use as few words as possible. Point out that they have just given a summary of the story. Invite them to identify details they have not included in their summaries and then explain why they left this information out.

CLOSE Have children summarize the rest of the story after Titch and Dad leave the store.

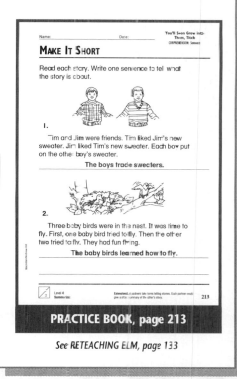

PRACTICE BOOK, page 213

See RETEACHING ELM, page 133

SKILLS ✕ TRACE

SUMMARIZE

Tested: Progress Assessment: Level 4 Unit 2

Review:	Level 4: 127, 195, 279; Level 5: 129
Practice Book:	213, 237, 286, 297
Reteaching BLM:	133, 153, 193, 201

Comprehension

STRATEGIC READING

19 **PLOT** What else did Titch get? (sweater and socks) Let's record the events that are happening now on our Story Charts.

Characters	Plot	Setting
Titch	Titch's clothes are too small.	Inside the house, in the spring
Pete	Pete gives Titch his old pants.	
Mary	Mary gives Titch her old sweater. Pete and Mary give Titch their old clothes.	
Mother	Mother says Titch should have new clothes.	
Dad	Dad and Titch go shopping. Titch gets new clothes.	A clothing store
Store Clerk		

20 **CHARACTER** How do you think Titch is feeling now?

INFORMAL ASSESSMENT

Observe if children are tracking print from the beginning of the sentence on **page 195** to the end of the sentence on **page 197.**

a brand-new sweater,

196

and a brand-new pair of socks.

Skills in Context

COMPREHENSION

☑ Use Illustrations

INTRODUCE Reread with children **pages 196–197.** Invite children to discuss what is happening in the illustrations that the words don't mention.

DEVELOP/APPLY Ask children to look at **page 193** and identify what Mother is knitting. Have them look back through the pictures and identify something else that she knitted. What clues do the tiny clothes give about what may happen in this story?

CLOSE Encourage children to look through the illustrations again and track the parts of this story told only by the pictures: the bird's egg-laying, the flowering plants, and the cat's playfulness.

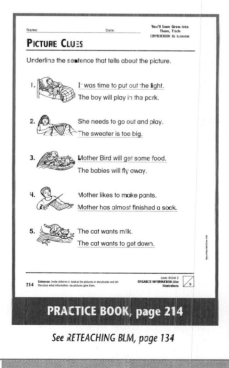

PRACTICE BOOK, page 214

See RETEACHING BLM, page 134

SKILLS TRACE

USE ILLUSTRATIONS

Tested: Progress Assessment: Level 4 Unit 2

Review:	Level 4: 105B, 197, 219
Practice Book:	214, 222
Reteaching BLM:	134, 140

Comprehension

STRATEGIC READING

21 What is Titch holding behind his back? (**his old clothes**) Why do you think he's holding them? (**Maybe he plans to give them to the baby.**)

22 **CHARACTERS** What do you think Titch and his brother and sister are thinking right now? What will they say? Who would like to volunteer to be Titch, Mary, and Pete and show and tell us what they might do and say? **ROLE-PLAY**

23 **PLOT** Let's add this new event to our story charts.

Characters	Plot	Setting
Titch	Titch's clothes are too small.	Inside the house, in the Spring
Pete	Pete gives Titch his old pants.	
Mary	Mary gives Titch her old sweater. Pete and Mary give Titch their old clothes.	
Mother	Mother says Titch should have new clothes.	
Dad	Dad and Titch go shopping. Titch gets new clothes.	A clothing store
Store Clerk		
Baby	A new baby is added to the family.	Home

198

SECOND-LANGUAGE SUPPORT

Invite volunteers to explain what *brand-new* means, and how it could apply to both a sweater and a baby.

And when Mother brought their brand-new baby home, Titch wore the new clothes.

23

199

Skills in Context

PHONICS AND DECODING

☑ Consonant Blend: /kl/*cl*

INTRODUCE Reread **page 199** with children. Emphasize the *cl* in *clothes*.

DEVELOP/APPLY On chart paper or on the chalkboard, write the letters *cl*. Invite children to point to the word on **page 199** that starts with these letters. Write the word, underlining the *cl*. Ask children to name other words that start with that sound, such as *clap, climb,* and *close.* Write these words as well.

CLOSE Encourage children to create a page listing words that begin with the letters *cl* and make the /kl/ sound. They may display it and add words whenever they wish.

CLEAN CLOTHES WORDS

Name: _____ Date: _____

You'll Soon Grow Into Them, Titch
PHONIC: Consonant Blends /cl/ cl

Make the word. Circle the picture that goes with the word.

1. cl + ip = __clip__
2. cl + ock = __clock__
3. cl + aw = __claw__
4. cl + oud = __cloud__
5. cl + own = __clown__
6. cl + ay = __clay__
7. cl + ap = __clap__
8. cl + ub = __club__

Level 4
Consonant Blends /cl/ cl

Extension: Invite children to write bonus holders using several CCVC all-word list help words.

215

PRACTICE BOOK, page 215

See RETEACHING BLM, page 135

SKILLS ✶ TRACE

CONSONANT BLENDS: /kl/*cl*

Tested: Progress Assessment: Level 4 Unit 2

Review: Level 4: 199
Practice Book: 215
Reteaching BLM: 135

Comprehension

STRATEGIC READING

24 **CHARACTER** How do you think Titch feels now that he finally has somebody to give his old clothes to? What else do you think he might give the baby?

25 **CHARACTER** How do you think Pete and Mary feel about the new baby? What makes you think so?

INFORMAL ASSESSMENT

Observe if children are using clues from illustrations to understand characters' feelings. See if children can identify the new features—the baby birds and the blooming tulips.

To help children Analyze Character, Plot, and Setting, see Reteaching lesson on **page 203**.

24 "There," said Titch,
"he can have my old pants,

200

25

201

Skills in Context

MULTICULTURAL PERSPECTIVES

Birthdays

Discuss with children the different ways that various cultures celebrate the birth of a baby. Point out that in many places in the United States, relatives and friends give a mother presents for her baby. These gifts are often given at a party called a baby shower, or guests may bring gifts when they come to visit the newborn. Explain that in some cultures, the custom is different—the family gives gifts to the guests! For example:

- In China, the family of a newborn dyes eggs red and gives them to visitors. The eggs symbolize good luck and a good life.

- Traditionally, the Blackfoot hold a feast when a baby is one month old. Guests at the feast receive gifts.

- Among the Samburu people of East Africa, the custom is for rich people to celebrate the birth of a son by giving their guests cattle.

Comprehension

STRATEGIC READING

27 **CHARACTER** How do you think Titch feels about saying that his old clothes are too small for him? **(proud, happy)** How can you tell?

28 Now Pete and Mary are saying the same words that Titch was saying before. Can you guess what Titch's answer will be?

and my old socks. They're much too small for me!"

204

"They're a bit big for him," /28/
said Pete and Mary.

205

Skills in Context

CONCEPTS OF PRINT

Quotations

Reread **page 205** to children, emphasizing the words spoken by Pete and Mary. Point out the quotation marks, reminding children that when an author tells a speaker's exact words, those words have special marks around them called quotation marks.

Encourage children to take the parts of Titch, Pete, and Mary and read only the words inside quotation marks on **pages 199–206.** Then have another set of volunteers reread the scene, with a fourth child reading the narration. Encourage children to explain the difference between the words inside quotation marks and those outside quotation marks.

Model for children how to write something Titch could have said at the end of the story. (For example, "I like our baby!" said Titch.) Then invite them to write their own sentence for Titch to say.

Comprehension

STRATEGIC READING

29 Did you expect this ending? What clues in the story helped you guess that this is what Titch would say? **(The conversation followed a repetitive language pattern, into which the sentence fit.)**

MEETING INDIVIDUAL NEEDS

Challenge
Pairs of children can think of things other than clothing that children need to "grow into." Invite children to suggest ways to continue the story with some of these examples.

☑ CHARACTER, PLOT, SETTING

Encourage children to personalize the strategies and their possible transfer to other situations by discussing these questions:

• Suppose a story takes place inside a house. What kinds of events might happen in that story? What kinds of people might be in the story?

• How can paying attention to characters, plot, and setting help you understand stories?

FOR RESPONSE AND ASSESSMENT OPPORTUNITIES
see page 207A–207B

"He'll soon grow into them," said Titch.

206

Meet
Pat Hutchins

Pat Hutchins says, "I wrote *You'll Soon Grow into Them, Titch* for my son Sam. He has an older brother, Morgan. When Morgan grew out of his clothes, he gave them to Sam. Suddenly, we realized that Sam never had any new clothes of his own. So we went out and bought him his own new set of clothes."

About the pictures, Ms. Hutchins tells children, "The story is all about growing, so I put a bird's nest in the pictures. When Mother's baby is born, the baby birds have hatched."

Skills in Context

WRITING

Characterization

Help children recall that we learn about characters from what they do and say. Model how to understand the character of Titch.

THINK ALOUD *When the baby comes home, Titch brings his new brother the old clothes that Pete and Mary gave to him. Then Titch says the baby will grow into the old clothes. These words and actions tell me that Titch is generous and proud of being an older brother.*

STRATEGY: MAKE A LIST Create a list of the things that Titch does and says. Then discuss with children what each item on the list tells about Titch.

Tell children that brainstorming a list that tells about a character can help readers come up with ideas when they want to write about a character. This strategy will help to prepare them for the writing process lesson on **pages 207M–207N**.

Have children make a list for another character from the story. Ask them to write a paragraph to tell what that person is like.

Respond to the Literature

ACTIVITIES

PERSONAL RESPONSE

JOURNAL WRITING

Children may use their journals to express their thoughts and questions about the story. The following questions may help get them started:

- What part of the story surprised you most? Why?
- Which picture was your favorite? Why?
- Have you ever been in a situation similar to Titch? What did it feel like?

ACTIVITIES

SMALL GROUP RESPONSE

JOURNAL ENTRIES

Children may work in small groups to discuss the selection. Encourage them to share thoughts from their journals with other group members.

READER RESPONSE CARD 2 is available to help guide the discussion.

To check story comprehension, you may want to assign **PRACTICE BOOK, page 217.**

ACTIVITIES

WRITING ABOUT THE THEME

CRITICAL THINKING

How does **"You'll Soon Grow into Them, Titch"** relate to the unit theme of Surprises Along the Way? Children may realize after discussions that Titch is surprised twice: first when he gets new clothes and second when he gets a new baby brother! Children may be surprised when Titch gives his old clothes to the baby just as his brother and sister gave theirs to him.

QUICK WRITE

Invite children to think of an idea for a new story about Titch. What problem will he have now? How will it be solved? Encourage them to write a few sentences to tell about their story idea.

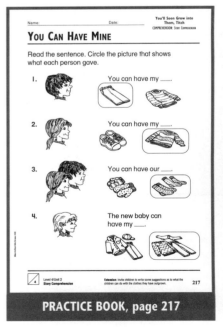

READER RESPONSE CARD 2

You'll Soon Grow Into Them, Titch
pages 180–207

With your partner or small group, share your responses to the selection. Discuss these questions or ideas of your own.

■ Which thoughts would you like to share from your journal?

■ Have you ever been in a situation similar to Titch? Describe what it was like.

■ Do you or does anyone you know have a new baby brother or sister? How does it feel?

■ How many brothers or sisters do you have in your family? Are you the youngest or oldest?

■ This unit is about surprises. What surprised you the most in this story?

READER RESPONSE CARD 2
page T3

PRACTICE BOOK, page 217

Comprehension Checkpoint

INFORMAL ASSESSMENT

☑ ANALYZE
CHARACTER
PLOT
SETTING

STORY CHARTS Display GRAPHIC ORGANIZER TRANSPARENCY/BLM 30 or copy the following chart onto the chalkboard. Help children complete their Story Charts by including information about the characters' feelings throughout the story.

Characters	Plot	How They Feel	Setting
Titch	Titch's clothes are too small.	Titch feels unhappy.	Inside the house, in the spring.
Pete	Pete gives Titch his old pants.		
Mary	Mary gives Titch her old sweater. Pete and Mary give Titch their old clothes.	Pete and Mary feel sorry for Titch and want to help him.	
Mother	Mother says Titch should have new clothes.	Mother and Dad feel happy to help Titch.	
Dad	Titch goes shopping. He gets new clothes.	Titch is surprised and happy to get new clothes.	A clothing store
Store Clerk			
Baby	A new baby is added to the family.	Titch is excited and happy to have a brother he can give his clothes to.	Home

COMPREHENSION

Assessment Checklist

• When you assess Story Charts, look for **Concepts** and **Comprehension**. Do children understand who the characters are, what happens in the story, and where events take place?

• Look for **Association** in identification of setting and details. Can children relate the baby birds and blooming flowers to the birth of a baby?

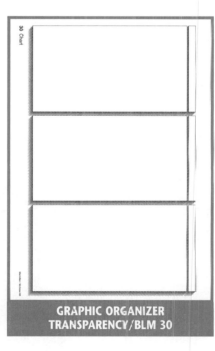

**GRAPHIC ORGANIZER
TRANSPARENCY/BLM 30**

FORMAL ASSESSMENT

ONGOING
ASSESSMENT

To check story comprehension and vocabulary, administer the multiple choice **Selection Assessment** for **"You'll Soon Grow into Them, Titch"** in **SELECTION AND UNIT TESTS** for Levels 4–5.

RETEACHING

ONGOING
ASSESSMENT

For additional work with analyzing character, plot, and setting, use the Reteaching lesson on **page 203** or the **RETEACHING BLM, page 136.**

Extend Skills In Context

Literature-Based Instruction

To provide skills and strategies instruction to meet the needs of your children, select from these lessons.

☑ These skills are tested in the Unit Progress Assessment.

Meeting Individual Needs

*To provide additional literacy experiences tailored to specific students' needs and interests, use this literature and these resources. Activities are provided on **pages 207E–207F**.*

MULTILEVEL RESOURCES FOR FLEXIBLE GROUPING

EASY

Sarah's SURPRISE

BY LAUREN RAY POLLARD
ILLUSTRATED BY DIANE PATERSON

SPOTLIGHT: LITERACY SUPPORT

EARLY INTERVENTION
COMPREHENSION:
Use Illustrations

PHONICS AND DECODING:
Short Vowels and
Phonograms: /a/-at

EASY AVERAGE

OLD JACK FOLD

By Mindy Menschell
Pictures by Randall Enos

SPOTLIGHT: PHONICS/
DECODING

PHONICS/DECODING
☑ LONG VOWELS AND
PHONOGRAMS: /ō/-old

'TRONIC PHONICS

⬤ Also available on CD-ROM

EASY

Good Idea Mikey!

Written by Susan McCloskey
Illustrated by Alexandra Wallner

SPOTLIGHT: VOCABULARY/
COMPREHENSION

VOCABULARY
• brother
• sister
• pants
• pair
• socks
• clothes
COMPREHENSION
☑ CHARACTER, PLOT, SETTING

Meeting Individual Needs
Multilevel Resources

| EASY | EARLY INTERVENTION |

SARAH'S SURPRISE

Sarah's SURPRISE

BY LAUREN RAY POLLARD
ILLUSTRATED BY DIANE PATERSON

REREAD A FAMILIAR BOOK — Reinforce successful reading experiences. Ask children to read a familiar book, such as the **LITERACY SUPPORT BOOK** *One Sunny Morning.*

READ A NEW BOOK — Preview the **LITERACY SUPPORT BOOK** *Sarah's Surprise.* Point out illustrations, using story vocabulary such as *attic* and *trunk.*

Read aloud the story, modeling how to use illustrations. As you read **page 7,** you might say, *"In the picture, Sarah is holding a brown teddy bear. The last word in the sentence begins with* b, *so the word must be* bear."

BUILD WORDS — Point out the word *hat* on **page 5.** Ask children to think of a word that rhymes with *hat.* Invite them to use the **Word Building Kit** to build rhyming words with the -*at* phonogram, such as *bat, fat, mat, pat, rat,* and *sat.*

For full lessons on short vowels and phonograms: /a/-*at,* see Read All About it! **pages 48–50.**

WRITE SENTENCES — Invite children to work together to write sentences about the things Sarah finds in the trunk in *Sarah's Surprise.* Write their sentences on the chalkboard and invite children to copy them on sentence strips. Have children point to each word as they reread the sentences.

Reinforce vocabulary by asking children to point out specific words in their sentences. Children can then illustrate their sentences.

READ INDEPENDENTLY — Have children reread *Sarah's Surprise* independently. Invite them to draw pictures of each surprise Sarah finds in the trunk.

Sarah finds teddy bear.

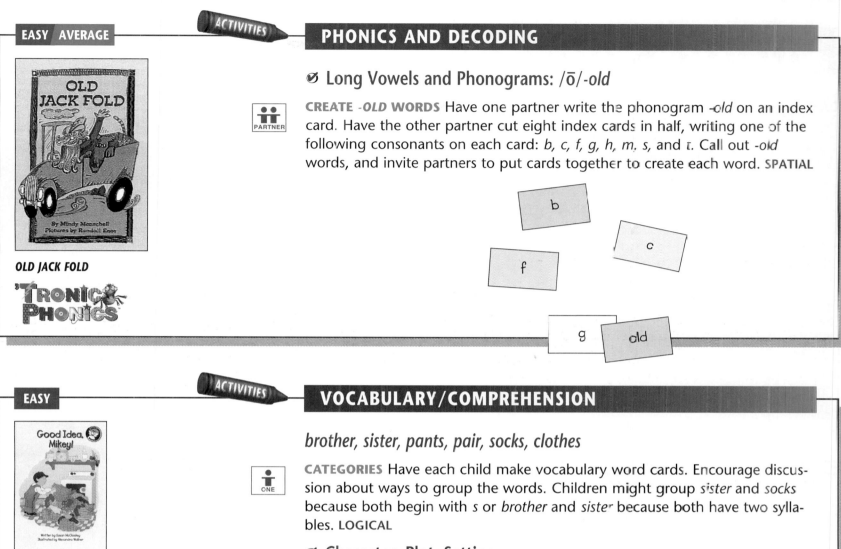

EASY | AVERAGE

OLD JACK FOLD

By Mindy Menschell
Pictures by Randall Enos

OLD JACK FOLD

'**TRONIC PHONICS**

PHONICS AND DECODING

✒ Long Vowels and Phonograms: /ō/-*old*

PARTNER

CREATE -OLD WORDS Have one partner write the phonogram -*old* on an index card. Have the other partner cut eight index cards in half, writing one of the following consonants on each card: *b, c, f, g, h, m, s,* and *t.* Call out -*old* words, and invite partners to put cards together to create each word. **SPATIAL**

EASY

Good Idea, Mikey!

Written by Susan McCloskey
Illustrated by Alexandra Wallner

GOOD IDEA, MIKEY

VOCABULARY/COMPREHENSION

brother, sister, pants, pair, socks, clothes

ONE

CATEGORIES Have each child make vocabulary word cards. Encourage discussion about ways to group the words. Children might group *sister* and *socks* because both begin with *s* or *brother* and *sister* because both have two syllables. **LOGICAL**

✒ Character, Plot, Setting

GROUP

PLOT STUDY Help children recall the people in Mikey's family. Write their names on chart paper. Talk about the piece of clothing each had trouble with and add it to the chart. Then discuss how Mikey solved the problem. **LINGUISTIC**

Phonics and Decoding /ā/ /el /ôr/

☑ Long Vowels and Phonograms: /ō/-old

1 DEVELOP PHONEMIC AWARENESS

READ THE LITERATURE
- Reread **page 183** of **"You'll Soon Grow into Them, Titch,"** emphasizing the word *old.* Then introduce the **BIG BOOK OF RHYMES AND CHIMES**, reading the rhyme on **page 21**.

SAY THE RHYME
- Repeat the rhyme, encouraging children to chime in.
- Say the words *old, told, fold,* and *gold.* Point out that these words rhyme.
- Ask children to listen as you read the following pairs of words and raise their hands if they rhyme.
  sold/gold   story/gold   hair/gold   fold/gold

2 DISCOVER THE SPELLING PATTERN

SHOW THE RHYME
- Display **page 21** of the **BIG BOOK OF RHYMES AND CHIMES**. Point out the word at the bottom of the page and direct children's attention to the underlined letters. Ask a volunteer to read the word aloud.
- On the chalkboard, write words that contain the phonogram *-old* along with words that do not. Ask volunteers to identify and spell the rhyming words.
- Read the rhyme aloud with children, asking them to wave both hands in the air every time they see and hear a word with *-old.*

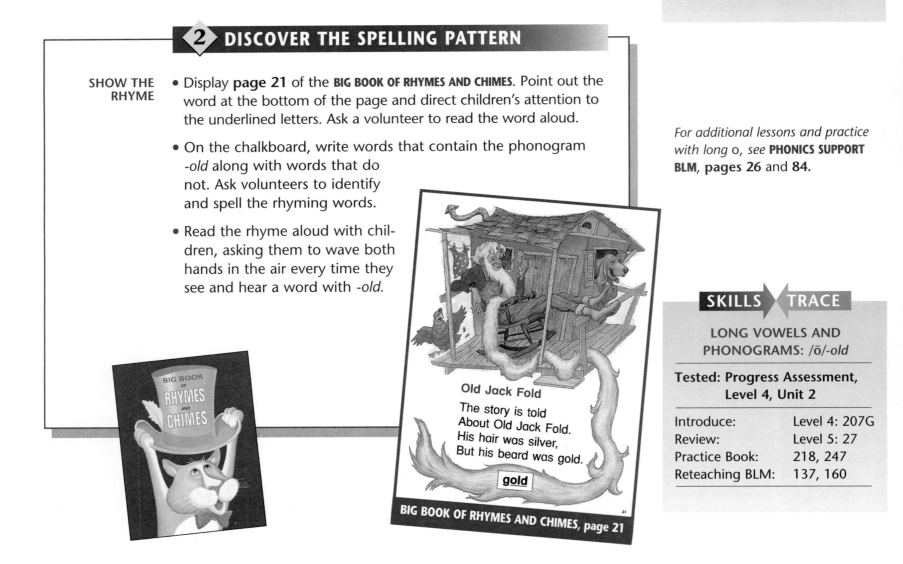

Old Jack Fold

The story is told
About Old Jack Fold.
His hair was silver,
But his beard was gold.

gold

BIG BOOK OF RHYMES AND CHIMES, page 21

5-STEP PLAN

DECODING STRATEGIES:
RHYMING, BLENDING

1 DEVELOP PHONEMIC AWARENESS

2 DISCOVER THE SPELLING PATTERN

3 USE DECODING STRATEGIES

4 WRITING

5 READING

CONSONANT BLENDS

For additional lessons and practice with long o, see **PHONICS SUPPORT BLM, pages 26** and **84.**

SKILLS TRACE

LONG VOWELS AND PHONOGRAMS: /ō/-old

Tested: Progress Assessment, Level 4, Unit 2

Introduce:	Level 4: 207G
Review:	Level 5: 27
Practice Book:	218, 247
Reteaching BLM:	137, 160

ACTIVITIES

3 DECODING STRATEGIES: BLENDING ACTIVITIES

MODEL THE STRATEGY
- Write the phonogram -old on chart paper or on the chalkboard. Model the blending strategy by blending the letter f and the phonogram -old.

THINK ALOUD *Now I'm going to build words with -old. Let's add f to make the word fold. Listen as I blend letters together: f-old. Let's try to think of more words that we can build.*

MAKE A WORD WALL
- Write the phonogram -old on a large piece of oak tag or construction paper. Display the piece on a wall, and invite children to add words containing the phonogram -old to the Word Wall. Suggest that they refer to the rhyme "Old Jack Fold" from the **BIG BOOK OF RHYMES AND CHIMES** to help them generate more words.
- Keep the Word Wall posted so that children can add to it.

MAKE A WORD SLIDE
- Draw a slide on the chalkboard and write the phonogram -old on the bottom of the slide.
- Have a volunteer write the letter t on a piece of paper, and bring it to the slide. Ask the class what happens when the letter t climbs up the stairs and slides into -old.
- The class can mimic the strategy with other letters.

USE THE WORD BUILDING KIT
- Continue to model the blending strategy by using the Word Building Kit. Insert cards containing the phonogram -old into each pocket of the mini-pocket chart.
- Let children experiment with placing different letters in front of the phonogram.
- Encourage children to use the blending strategy to build new words.

-OLD WORDS

Read the sentence and look at the picture. Write the word that completes the sentence.

1. Tim wants to ___hold___ a kitten.
   mold   hold   fold

2. The day is very ___cold___.
   told   sold   cold

3. Mother has a ring of ___gold___.
   gold   told   bold

4. The big house was ___sold___.
   told   sold   bold

5. There is ___mold___ on the old bread.
   mold   cold   sold

PRACTICE BOOK, page 218

See RETEACHING BLM, page 137

WORD BUILDING KIT

INTEGRATING SPELLING

OPTIONS

SPELLING
To work with spelling words that contain the -old phonogram, see the 5-Day Spelling Plan on **pages 207Q–207R.**

Phonics and Decoding

🖋 Long Vowels and Phonograms: /ō/ -old

ACTIVITIES

4 WRITING

USE THE PHONOGRAM

- Encourage children to write sentences about Old Jack Fold that include the -old phonogram. Then have children illustrate their sentences.

Old Jack Fold had a cold.

Old Jack Fold sold gold.

Old Jack Fold told me about the gold.

Name _____ Date _____

Read each sentence.
Circle the word that completes the sentence.
Then write the word on the line.

1. Come inside if you are **cold** — hold / mold / (cold)
2. **Fold** the paper. — (Fold) / Told / Sold
3. May I **hold** your toy bear? — told / (hold) / bold
4. We **sold** our house. — (sold) / cold / told
5. Dad **told** us a story. — hold / (told) / cold

109 Long Vowels and Phonograms: /ō/-old

PHONICS ACTIVITY BOOK, pages 109–110

ACTIVITIES

5 READING

READ "YOU'LL SOON GROW INTO THEM, TITCH"

Let children know that they will keep encountering words with the phonogram -old in their reading. Reread **"You'll Soon Grow into Them, Titch"** together, and ask children to point out words with the phonogram -old.

READ "OLD JACK FOLD"

Introduce small groups to "Old Jack Fold." Help children note that the book contains the rhyme from the **BIG BOOK OF RHYMES AND CHIMES, page 21**. Invite them to read the book with partners and to discuss the stories about Old Jack Fold that contain the -old words.

'TRONIC PHONICS

"Old Jack Fold" is also available in **'TRONIC PHONICS™** on CD-ROM. Children can work independently or in pairs to read the story, engage in blending activities, and write their story.

**SPOTLIGHT: PHONICS AND DECODING
Old Jack Fold**

✓ Consonant Blends: /sw/ *sw*

DEVELOP PHONEMIC AWARENESS FOR /sw/ *sw*

READ ALOUD
- Ask children to listen as you read **pages 186–187** of **"You'll Soon Grow into Them, Titch."** Emphasize the /sw/ sound in *sweater.*
- Have children identify the word that has the /sw/ sound.

DEVELOP PRINT AWARENESS FOR /sw/ *sw*

SHOW THE WORDS
- Write the following phrase on the chalkboard: *And when Titch needed a new sweater.* Read the phrase, emphasizing the /sw/ in *sweater.*
- Use a word mask to frame the blend *sw.* Ask children to identify both the letters and the sound they stand for.
- Ask children to explore classroom print for examples of words with the same beginning sound as *sweater.*
- List children's suggestions on the chalkboard.

ACTIVITIES

READ AND WRITE

FIND OTHER WORDS
- Invite children to choose a favorite story for you to read aloud. Ask them to clap their hands when they hear a word beginning with the same sound as *sweater.*

CREATE TONGUE TWISTERS
- Invite children to list as many words beginning with the /sw/ sound as they can. Encourage them to combine these words into one or two silly sentences to create tongue twisters; for example: Sweep the sweet sweater under the switch.
- Encourage children to share their tongue twisters with classmates.

SWELL SWEATER WORDS

Read each question. Circle the picture whose name begins with the same sound as **swell** and answers the question.

1. What do you put on when you are cold?
2. What could you play on in a park?
3. Which is a beautiful bird that swims?
4. What can you use to turn off lights?
5. What can you do in the water?

PRACTICE BOOK, page 219

See RETEACHING BLM, page 138
See PHONICS ACTIVITY BOOK, pages 111–112

SKILLS ✦ TRACE

CONSONANT BLENDS: /sw/ *sw*

Tested: Progress Assessment, Level 4, Unit 2

Introduce:	Level 4: 207J
Review:	Level 4: 275
Practice Book:	219, 236
Reteaching BLM:	138, 152

Vocabulary

VOCABULARY REVIEW

brother	sister	pants
pair	socks	clothes

WORD CARDS Have children write each vocabulary word on a separate index card. Then ask them to hold up the appropriate card(s) in response to your requests. Have volunteers name the word(s) and then illustrate the indicated words on the chalkboard.

1. Hold up the cards that tell about family members. (**brother, sister; draw a brother and sister stick figure**)

2. Hold up the cards that tell about pairs of things you wear over your legs. (**pants; draw pants on the brother and sister**)

3. Hold up the card that tells about what you wear on your feet under your shoes. (**socks; draw socks on the brother and sister**)

4. Hold up the cards that tell about things you wear. (**clothes, pants, socks; draw remaining clothes**)

5. Hold up the card that can mean one thing with two parts. (**pair; We've drawn a brother and sister pair.**)

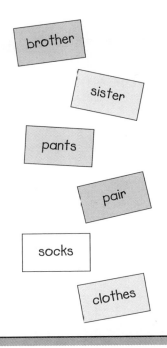

VOCABULARY STRATEGY   Antonyms: *big, small; new, old*

LINK TO LITERATURE Read **pages 183–184**, emphasizing the words *big* and *small*. Write the words on the chalkboard. Then read **pages 181** and **183**, emphasizing the words *new* and *old*. Write these words on the chalkboard, too.

Invite children to look at the words and identify the relationship between each pair. Elicit that they are opposites.

EXPLORE Invite children to work in pairs. Have one partner use the word *small* to describe something and then illustrate it, such as "a *small* house." The other partner can use the word *big* to describe and draw the same object, "a *big* house."

DISCUSS Children can suggest additional word pairs that are opposites. Talk about the meaning of each word. Ask volunteers to use each antonym in a sentence.

USE DIFFERENT MODALITIES Have children use gestures and body language to convey such antonyms as *small* and *big* or *mine* and *yours*.

Listening, Speaking, Viewing

DRAMATIZE A STORY

GROUP Invite groups of children to act out the story of **"You'll Soon Grow into Them, Titch."** Help children break the action into three scenes: Titch getting old clothes, Titch shopping, and Titch offering his clothes to the baby.

LISTENING AND SPEAKING TIPS Remind actors to speak loudly and clearly so everyone can understand them. Remind audience members to listen quietly so they can hear and enjoy the actors' words.

NOTICE PICTURE CLUES

PARTNER In the story, a bird is building a nest in which to lay eggs. Find some other examples of books in which the illustrations include action that is not described in the text. Invite partners to view the illustrations, identify the picture clues, and describe them in their own words.

VIEWING TIP Remind children to look closely at all the details in the illustrations.

PORTFOLIO

OPPORTUNITIES

Use a tape recorder or a video camera to record children's dramatizations.

ORAL LANGUAGE DEVELOPMENT

GROUP **CARTOON STORIES** Small groups can retell the story of Titch in the form of cartoon characters speaking in speech balloons. They can use dialog from the story or invent their own. Then pair up the small groups, letting each display its cartoons and trade comments. Encourage group members to read the cartoons orally. Model positive comments, such as: "I like what Titch says here. This is a great picture."

ADDITIONAL RESOURCES

GROUP **STORYTELLING** You may want to read aloud "The Emperor's New Clothes" from **READ ALOUDS, PLAYS, & CHORAL READINGS.**

ONE **LISTEN TO THE STORY** If children haven't already done so, they can listen to the **LISTENING LIBRARY AUDIOCASSETTE** for a dramatic reading of "You'll Soon Grow into Them, Titch."

PARTNER **LISTEN TO THE SONG** Invite children to listen to the song "Seeds" on the **SONGS AND STORIES AUDIOCASSETTE.**

Writing

Writing Process: Character Description

Ask children to think of a person they know, such as a brother, sister, cousin, new baby, or another family member, as they saw in **"You'll Soon Grow into Them, Titch."** Encourage them to imagine that they are describing that person to someone who has never met them. Have them write the description they would give.

PREWRITING

STRATEGY: MAKE A LIST Creating a list helps writers come up with ideas they can choose from when they write. Remind children that the point of making a list is to help them come up with many ideas. After children choose a person they want to describe, have them brainstorm a list of things that this person does and says. They might also list other details that help make this person special.

DRAFTING

Children can select details from their lists to draft their character descriptions. Remind them that they can worry about spelling and punctuation later. Now is the time to get their ideas down on paper.

REVISING

At this stage, children can reread their work and decide if words or phrases need to be changed, added, or deleted. Children might benefit from reading their drafts aloud to a partner. Partners can comment on whether or not they get a clear picture of the person described.

PROOFREADING

Once children are satisfied with their choice of words, they can focus on spelling, grammar, and punctuation. If you have presented the grammar lesson on **pages 207O–207P**, remind children to check their use of the verbs *say* and *said*.

PUBLISHING

Children might illustrate their sketches and post them on a bulletin board in a display called "Some Very Special People." Encourage them to comment on each other's work.

	RUBRIC FOR CHARACTER DESCRIPTION
4	**EXCELLENT** This description offers creative ideas and interesting details that tell about a special person. It is organized well.
3	**GOOD** This narrative describes a person well. Several descriptive details are presented in a logical way.
2	**FAIR** This narrative attempts to describe a particular person but details may be sparse and the organization confused.
1	**POOR** This paper is not a description or it meets the criteria only minimally.

WRITING ✕ TRACE

Descriptive Writing
177, 177M, 207, 207M, 211A–H
Strategies:
Cluster: 177, 177M, 211A–H
List: 207, 207M

Writing Projects

TRONIC PHONICS *The **Make a Book** section allows children to write and illustrate their own stories.*

PROJECT 1

FAMILY PORTRAITS Draw a picture of your family. Label each person and their relationship to you. Tell who is the mother, father, brother, and sister. Tell who is the oldest and youngest. **EASY**

PROJECT 2

SHARING LIST Make a list of things you might share with a new baby brother or sister. You can include foods, pets, toys, or even things in nature, such as a sunny day. **AVERAGE**

PROJECT 3

POEM OR STORY ABOUT GROWING How do things change when they grow? Write a short poem or story telling about something that grows. Describe how it looks and all the changes that happen. You could write about a plant, an animal, or even about yourself. **CHALLENGE**

GRAMMAR, MECHANICS, AND USAGE If you have already presented the grammar lesson on **pages 207O–207P** or in the **GRAMMAR MINILESSONS**, **page 21**, remind children to review their use of the verbs *say* and *said.*

SPELLING Encourage children to identify words that they want to learn to spell and to add these to their personal spelling lists. You might also refer to the spelling lesson on **pages 207Q–207R.**

POETFOLIO

OPPCRTUNITIES

Invite children to choose samples from their writing to include in their portfolios.

5-Day Plan
Grammar

SAY AND SAID

Second-Language Support
Some English learners may have trouble understanding how past and present tense are used in English. Model examples using pairs of sentences.

DAY 1

Daily Language Activity

Write the sentences on the chalkboard each day or use Transparency 6. Have children orally make each sentence tell about the past.

1. Titch says hello to the new baby yesterday. **said**
2. Mary says hello to the baby, too. **said**
3. They say hello to Mother. **said**

DAY 2

Daily Language Activity

Present these sentences and have children orally make each sentence tell about now.

1. Titch and Pete said goodnight to the baby now. **say**
2. Mom and Dad said goodnight, too. **say**
3. Mary said goodnight to everyone. **says**

TEACH *SAY* AND *SAID*

FROM THE LITERATURE

INTRODUCE Read the sentence on **page 183** of "**You'll Soon Grow Into Them, Titch.**" Invite children to identify the word that tells what Pete did. (said)

"His brother Pete said, 'You can have my old pants, they're too small for me.'"

IDENTIFY TENSE

DEVELOP/APPLY Read the following sentences, and write *say, says,* and *said* on the chalkboard. Ask children how the three verbs are alike and how they are different.

Pete *said* good-bye. Pete and Mary *say* hello. Titch *says* yes.

Say and *says* tell about actions that are happening now. *Says* tells about one person and *say* about more than one. *Said* tells about the past. Encourage children to suggest sentences using *say* and *said.*

SUMMARIZE

CLOSE Help children list rules for *say* and *said.*

SAY AND SAID

- Use *say* and *says* to tell about someone talking right now.
- Use *said* to tell about someone talking in the past.

USE SAY OR SAID

| Remember |

Use **say** to tell about someone talking right now.
Use **said** to tell about someone talking in the past.

Circle **say** or **said** to complete each sentence.

1. Dad _____ the baby cried all day yesterday.
   say   said

2. Now Ann and Andy _____ the baby is crying again.
   say   said

3. The baby _____ her first word last week.
   say   said

4. Now, Dad and the baby _____ the word together.
   say   said

5. Yesterday, Mom _____, "The baby is growing fast."
   say   said

DAY 1, GRAMMAR PRACTICE BOOK, page 96

USING SAY AND SAYS

| Remember |

Some verbs tell about actions that are happening now. Use **say** or **says** for actions that are happening now.

Write **say** or **says** to complete each sentence.

1. Dad _____ we can go skating with him.

2. Bill _____ that he needs help skating.

3. Kim and I _____ we need help, too.

4. Dad _____ he can help us all.

5. We _____ "Thanks, Dad!"

DAY 2, GRAMMAR PRACTICE BOOK, page 97

DAY 3

Daily Language Activity

Present these sentences and have children orally make each sentence tell about the past.

1. Yesterday Mary says, "What a cute baby!" said
2. Titch says, "What a small baby!" said
3. Pete says the baby was crying. said

WRITING APPLICATION

CONVERSATION

Invite children to work in pairs to write a short conversation between two family members. They may want to have the people talk about something surprising that happens to the family. Remind them to use *say* and *said* correctly.

GRAMMAR/MECHANICS CHECKLIST

As children evaluate their writing, they may check that
* they have used *say* and *says* correctly to tell about someone talking right now.
* they have used *said* to tell about someone talking in the past.
* they have used quotation marks to set off a speaker's exact words.

DAY 4

Daily Language Activity

Present these sentences and have children orally make each sentence tell about now.

1. Titch said he will help with the baby. says
2. Mom said, "Good job!" says
3. Pete and Mary said they will help, too. say

QUICK WRITE

CREATING DIALOG

Invite children to write a few sentences of dialog between Titch and Pete or Mary as they talk about the new baby. Afterwards, have children check their use of *say* and *said.*

DAY 5

Daily Language Activity

Present these sentences and have children orally make each sentence tell about the past.

1. Last week Dad says, "Look at the birds outside." said
2. Yesterday Pete says, "Have they hatched yet?" said
3. This morning Titch says, "Look at the baby birds." said

See page 21 of the GRAMMAR MINILESSONS *for more information on the verbs* say *and* said.

USING SAID

Remember

Some verbs have special forms to show an action in the past.
Use **said** to show an action in the past.

Read each sentence.
If the action happened in the past, write the word **said** on the line.
If it is happening now, do not write anything.

1. Barb _____ she was sick yesterday.
2. Now she _____ she feels well.
3. Tony _____ he had a cold last week.
4. He _____ he had to stay home from school.
5. Now he _____ he still has a cough.

DAY 3, GRAMMAR PRACTICE BOOK, page 98

SAY OR SAID

Remember

Use **say** to tell about someone talking now.
Use **said** to tell about someone talking in the past.

Write **say**, **says** or **said** to complete each sentence.

1. I wake up when Mom _____, "Rise and shine!"
2. I close my eyes and _____, "Just a little longer, please."
3. But yesterday, I _____, "Rise and shine."
4. Mom _____ "Just a little longer, please."
5. Then I _____, "Mom, you are silly!"

DAY 4, GRAMMAR PRACTICE BOOK, page 99

USING SAID IN STORIES

Remember

Said shows an action that happened in the past.
Most stories use **said** when people speak.
Mother **said**   Little Red Riding Hood **said**

Read the story.
Write **said** on each line.

Mother _____, "Take this basket to Grandmother."

Little Red Riding Hood _____, "I love to visit Grandmother. I can walk through the woods."

Big Bad Wolf _____, "Hello, Red Riding Hood."

Little Red Riding Hood _____, "Grandmother, what big teeth you have!"

DAY 5, GRAMMAR PRACTICE BOOK, page 100

5-Day Plan
Spelling

DAY 1

BEGIN WITH A PRETEST

ASSESS PRIOR KNOWLEDGE: WORDS WITH /ō/-old

Use the dictation sentences below and **page 96** of the SPELLING ACTIVITY BOOK for the pretest. A Student Record form is provided.

Allow children to correct their own papers. Ask them to pay special attention to the words they misspelled.

SPELLING WORDS /ō/-old			CHALLENGE WORDS	
old	told	cold	**him**	new
gold	sold			

Note: Words in **dark type** are from the story.

DICTATION SENTENCES

SPELLING WORDS
1. Titch's socks were <u>old</u>.
2. The cat's eyes are <u>gold</u>.
3. Mary <u>told</u> Titch to take her sweater.
4. The man <u>sold</u> Titch a shirt.
5. Titch needs a sweater for <u>cold</u> weather.

CHALLENGE WORDS
6. Dad took <u>him</u> to a store.
7. Titch wanted some <u>new</u> clothes.

DAY 2

EXPLORE THE SPELLING PATTERN

IDENTIFY THE PHONOGRAM -old

Write the spelling words on the chalkboard. Read them with children, underlining the *old* phonogram as you read each word. Have children write each word on a piece of paper and circle the *old* phonogram with a crayon. As they circle each phonogram, they should say the word and then identify the phonogram and its sound.

DAY 1, SPELLING ACTIVITY BOOK, page 96

DAY 2, SPELLING ACTIVITY BOOK, page 97

DAY 3

CONSTRUCTING WORDS

MAKE A WORD WHEEL

Provide each child with a paper plate of 6" diameter and one of 4" diameter along with a brad. Center the smaller plate on top of the larger one and connect them by pushing the brad through their centers. Have children write the following letters on the space between the edges of the two plates: *g, t, s,* and *c.* Invite them to write *old* on the left side of the small plate. Encourage them to record the different words that are spelled by turning their wheels. Challenge children to tell how to turn the wheel to get the word *old.*

WORK WITH MEANING

MAKE A DICTIONARY

Distribute 2" x 3" cards and have children write a Spelling Word along the bottom of each one. Invite children to draw pictures illustrating the words. When they are finished, they can alphabetize the words and take home a spelling dictionary.

The optional extension activity for the Challenge Word on **page 98** of the **SPELLING ACTIVITY BOOK** may be assigned on Day 3.

DAY 4

SPELLING AND WRITING

RHYMING PHRASES

Children will probably notice that the Spelling Words rhyme. To reinforce awareness of the spelling pattern among the words, encourage children to fill in the blanks in the following phrases with a Spelling Word. They can then illustrate the phrases: *an old _____ watch; a story that was _____ about gold; a gold ring was _____ for $20, a _____ gold igloo*

an old gold watch

DAY 5

END WITH A POSTTEST

REASSESS CHILDREN'S KNOWLEDGE

Use **page 100** of the **SPELLING ACTIVITY BOOK** or the dictation sentences on **page 207Q** for the posttest. A Student Record form is also provided so that children can record their scores.

DAY 3, SPELLING ACTIVITY BOOK, page 98

DAY 4, SPELLING ACTIVITY BOOK, page 99

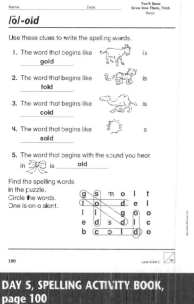

DAY 5, SPELLING ACTIVITY BOOK, page 100

Across the Curriculum

ART

SILLY SELF-PORTRAITS
30 minutes

Materials: drawing paper; crayons

DRAWING

Children can draw themselves wearing clothes that are too big for them.

- Invite children to think of how they would look if their clothes were too big for them. Have they ever worn their parents' shoes or boots? Have they ever tried on a sweater that reached the floor?

- Guide children to imagine themselves wearing clothes so big that they can barely walk. Suggest they make a silly drawing or painting of what they would look like.

SPATIAL

SOCIAL STUDIES

WHAT IS COTTON?
2 days

Materials: cotton balls; cotton clothing; children's encyclopedias; butcher paper; markers

FACT FINDING

Children can make a mural about cotton.

- Explain to children that many clothes are made from a plant called cotton.

- Show children cotton balls and examples of cotton clothing, then ask them to work in groups to find out more about using children's encyclopedias.

- Groups can make small murals about cotton which include text and pieces of fabric.

INTERPERSONAL/SPATIAL

Some clothes are made of cotton.

MATH

A CLASSROOM STORE

1 day

GROUP

Materials: clothing or cutouts of clothing; labels; "display table"; paper; markers

ROLE-PLAYING AND COUNTING

Children can get hands-on experience with story concepts by creating a classroom "store."

- Bring in clothing for the store or make large paper cutouts of clothing.

- Work with children to choose prices for the merchandise. Ask them to write the prices on labels to make price tags for each item. Then display the clothes on shelves or a table.

- Encourage children to make play money and then shop at the store. Children can take turns playing cashier, manager, and shoppers.

LOGICAL/MATHEMATICAL/INTERPERSONAL

SCIENCE/ART

THROUGH A WINDOW

1 hour

ONE

Materials: drawing paper; art supplies

ILLUSTRATING SEASONS

Children can make drawings of the different seasons outside a window.

- Work with children to track the window throughout the story, identifying the clues that tell what season it is.

- Invite children to draw their own window showing a season outside. Encourage them to include objects and animals that reflect the season, such as a snowman for winter or a pile of leaves for autumn.

- Display children's work on a bulletin board divided into seasons. Invite children to place their drawings in the correct season. Together, discuss the ways plants and animals grow and change throughout the seasons.

SPATIAL

Spotlight on Inquiry

EXPLORE MULTIPLE SOURCES

Encourage children to use various resources, including this selection, to pursue ideas related to **"You'll Soon Grow into Them, Titch."** Use the questions below as well as children's questions to generate interest and inquiry.

- In what ways are clothes passed along in families?

- What is it like to have lots of sisters and brothers?

FAMILY CIRCUS

PREVIEW/QUESTIONS Introduce the selection to answer the first inquiry above. Then ask:

- What do you think the reading will be about?

- What do you notice about the pictures?

STRATEGIC READING Have children look at the pictures and determine the relationship of the people shown: father, mother, and three sons. Discuss the differences between the speech balloon and the thought balloons. Read each aloud. Notice that the father's words direct our attention to the boy's shirt. Ask what children notice about each boy's shirt. How does the cartoon show which boy wore the shirt when it was new? How does it show the shirt getting older? Why isn't the father sure if he's seen the shirt before? Discuss the humor of the cartoon. **USE ILLUSTRATIONS**

RESOURCES

- *Ragsale.* Artie Ann Bates, Boston: Houghton Mifflin Company, 1995. Driving to various sales, a family looks for used clothes and other things they need.
- *Just My Size.* Mary Garelick, New York: Harper & Row Publishers, 1990. When a little girl outgrows her coat it is remade into other clothes and finally a coat for her doll.
- *Brothers and Sisters.* Maxine B. Rosenberg, New York: Clarion Books. 1991. Three stories about real families told from the point of view of a sibling.

LINKS ACROSS THE LITERATURE

Invite children to put together a list that describes some events associated with passing down clothes among children. They may include their own ideas, as well as ideas from **"You'll Soon Grow into Them, Titch"** and "Family Circus." Encourage them to consider the appearance of the clothing, the children's feelings, where the clothes may have come from, and how parents might be involved. Use a chart like the one below to help children categorize their ideas. **(GRAPHIC ORGANIZER TRANSPARENCY/BLM 30)**

ORGANIZE INFORMATION

MAKE IT REAL!

Have groups create and dramatize a skit about how an item of clothing gets passed down in a family. Group members should decide which roles they will play and brainstorm a simple plot. What will be passed down? Who will give the clothing? Who will receive it? Provide time for children to practice their skits before performing for the class.

209

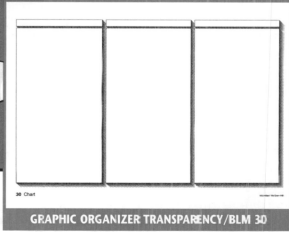

GRAPHIC ORGANIZER TRANSPARENCY/BLM 30

CLOTHING	CHILD	ADULT
• may be too big	• wants something new	• remembers clothing from when older child was little
• may look worn out	• feels sad	

Poetry

READING THE POEM

TEACHER READ ALOUD Invite children to look at the illustration while you read the title of the poem. Then read the entire poem aloud. Encourage them to imagine what the poet could be describing in this poem. If you wish, refer to the illustration. You can play **"Something Big Has Been Here"** on the **LISTENING LIBRARY AUDIOCASSETTE** for a reading of the poem.

GROUP READING This poem invites group choral reading because of its short length and natural language. You may wish to model fluent reading for children before reading aloud with them several times, urging them to speed up by their last reading.

LITERARY DEVICES AND TECHNIQUES

USING READER'S IMAGINATION Call children's attention to the way the poem never tells them what the something big might be. Explain that poets often rely on the readers' imagination. They use poetry to get readers to think about a subject in a new way. Discuss with children how using their own imagination adds to the fun of the poem.

Something BIG Has Been Here

Something big has been here,
what it was, I do not know,
for I did not see it coming,
and I did not see it go,
but I hope I never meet it,
if I do, I'm in a fix,
for it left behind its footprints,
they are size nine-fifty-six.

Jack Prelutsky

210

211

POETRY TALK

Children can discuss their personal responses to the poem and talk about these and other questions in small groups.

- What do you think the big thing was? Describe it.

- Would you want to meet the big thing in the poem? Why or why not?

- How would you feel if you saw size nine-fifty-six footprints?

MEET THE POET

ABOUT JACK PRELUTSKY Children may be interested to learn that Jack Prelutsky is also a singer, a guitar player, and an actor. He says his poems are all about the people he knows, and about himself. Prelutsky lives in the state of Washington and sometimes sings with a local opera company. He also enjoys making up word games, making wooden toys, playing tennis, and riding his bike.

Writing Process
DESCRIPTIVE WRITING

LINK TO LITERATURE

In **"One Monday Morning,"** the little boy's neighborhood is pictured with many interesting details. Children can tell what details they see in the story illustrations. They can then brainstorm words that a writer might use to describe places that are familiar to them.

PORTFOLIO

OPPORTUNITIES

Children will write detailed descriptions of subjects of their own choosing. Their portfolios can be used to collect and review their process work.

IN THE WRITING CENTER

GROUP Display samples of descriptive writing to help children find ideas for their writing projects, such as travel posters, animal books, and picture postcards.

FEATURES OF DESCRIPTIVE WRITING

Students will use brainstorming, drafts, and revisions to help them write descriptions. To begin, use samples you have collected in the Writing Center for discussion, asking children:

- What is the subject of the description?
- Which words help you picture the subject?

Before they begin brainstorming you may want to talk about the features of good descriptive writing, such as using the five senses to find clear, vivid words that depict a person, place, or thing.

ASSESSMENT The self-evaluation and rubrics on **page 211H** tie into these features.

Suzy the Elephant has large ears and a long, strong trunk. She has thick, gray skin. Suzy enjoys the water. She fills her trunk with water and gives herself a bath.

My baby brother Joey is three months old. He has tiny fingers and toes. His hair is dark and soft and smells very sweet. He wiggles a lot. He loves to eat and sleep and laugh.

The beach is full of white sand and pink shells. Seagulls fly over the water. The waves are blue and green. The air smells clean and fresh. Often there are sailboats shining in the sunlight.

RESOURCES

- Writing Process Transparencies Descriptive Writing
- Writing and Language Handbook: Model for Descriptive Writing, **pages 40–41**

  For help with checklist items in Revising stage: **page 9.**
- Graphic Organizers for Reading and Writing
- Spelling Activity Book
- ESL/Second Language Teacher's Guide: **pages 187–195**

TECHNOLOGY

- WordBook from Story Web™
- Certificate Maker

WRITING TRACE

Descriptive Writing
177, 177M, 207, 207M, 211A–H
Strategies:
Cluster: 177, 177M, 211A–H
List: 207, 207M

Writing Process
DESCRIPTIVE WRITING

PREWRITING

THINK ALOUD

First, I need to picture in my mind the subject I want to describe. Then I want to find the best words to tell about my subject. To begin, I'm going to make a special kind of list called a cluster. In the cluster, I'll write details about my subject—how it feels and sounds, its colors, shapes, and so on.

▦ STRATEGY: MAKE A CLUSTER
GROUP Have children brainstorm their purposes and subjects of description. Then you might use an object in the classroom to demonstrate how to make a cluster on the board. Children can think of words to fill in the cluster.

Some children may benefit from using photographs or their own drawings to inspire their writing process.

Clocks Have:

• Hands

• Numbers 1–12

• A Dial

Birds Have:

• Wings

• Feathers

• Beaks

• They Sing

PLAN

After children have brainstormed the purposes and subjects for their descriptions, reinforce the value of a writing plan. Use **WRITING PROCESS TRANSPARENCY 2A** to model a cluster. Questions at the bottom of the transparency are offered to stimulate discussion and help children get ideas for their own clusters.

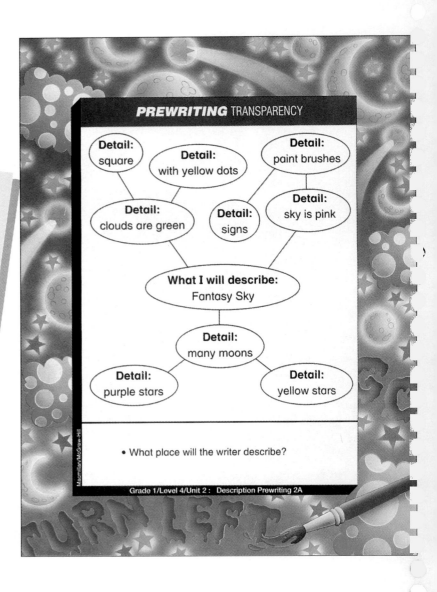

PREWRITING TRANSPARENCY

Detail: square

Detail: with yellow dots

Detail: paint brushes

Detail: clouds are green

Detail: signs

Detail: sky is pink

What I will describe: Fantasy Sky

Detail: many moons

Detail: purple stars

Detail: yellow stars

• What place will the writer describe?

Grade 1/Level 4/Unit 2 : Description Prewriting 2A

DRAFTING

THINK ALOUD

I want to begin with a sentence that tells the subject of my description. Then I can look at my cluster and turn my detail ideas into complete sentences.

Before children begin drafting, you may want to review key features of descriptive writing.

STRATEGY: FREEWRITING

Drafting is the time to capture ideas. Remind children that they should not worry about spelling or punctuation at this stage. Encourage them to jot down their ideas as quickly as possible and allow their thoughts to flow freely onto the page. Use **WRITING PROCESS TRANSPARENCY 2B**, a draft of a description, as a model for discussion.

KEY FEATURES

- begins with a sentence telling what is to be described
- gives a picture in words of a particular person, place, or thing
- uses the five senses to find clear, vivid words that tell what something looks, sounds, feels, tastes, and even smells like

---

DRAFTING TRANSPARENCY

Fantasy Sky

Fantasy Sky is pink. There are signs painted on the sky. The signs are made with paint brushes The signs give travelers directions. The clouds in the pink sky are green. All clouds are square with yellow dots. In Fantasy Sky there are hundreds of moons. At night you can see the yellow and purple stars. Don't you wish you could see Fantasy Sky

- Is this writer describing a real or an imaginary place? How do you know?

Grade 1/Level 4/Unit 2 : Description Drafting 2B

Writing Process

DESCRIPTIVE WRITING

REVISING

THINK ALOUD

I want to look again at the description I've written. I want to be sure the words describe my subject as I see it in my mind. I might want to add or change words to make the description even clearer.

Invite children to look at a revised model. Use **WRITING PROCESS TRANSPARENCY 2C** for discussion.

Children can "rethink" their writing, referring back to their clusters. Encourage children to ask themselves these questions:

CHECKLIST

- Do my words express my ideas?
- Have I used colorful words?
- Will my readers see what I see?

After sharing their drafts, partners can comment on each others' work. Children can describe their partners' subjects from memory. Help them focus on the following questions:

PEER CONFERENCING CHECKLIST

- What part of my description did my partner most remember?
- What could I add to make the description clearer or more interesting?

REVISING TRANSPARENCY

Fantasy Sky

Fantasy Sky is pink. There are signs painted on the sky. The signs are made with paint brushes The signs give travelers directions. The clouds in the pink sky are green. All clouds are square with yellow dots. In Fantasy Sky there are hundreds of moons. At night you can see the yellow and purple stars. Don't you wish you could see Fantasy Sky

- Look at the words the writer added. Do you like them?

Macmillan/McGraw-Hill

Grade 1/Level 4/Unit 2 : Description Revising 2C

PROOFREADING

THINK ALOUD

It's time to proofread. I'll pay special attention to punctuation, and be sure I've ended my sentences with periods or question marks. I need to check my verbs for past and present tense.

Use **WRITING PROCESS TRANSPARENCY 2D** to discuss:

Proofreader's Marks

- ∧ Add.
- Take out.
- ≡ Make a capital letter.
- ¶ Indent the paragraph.

GRAMMAR, MECHANICS, USAGE

- capital letter to begin a sentence
- period or question mark to end a sentence
- correct verb tense usage

Review punctuation and verb tense usage in the **WRITING AND LANGUAGE HANDBOOK.**

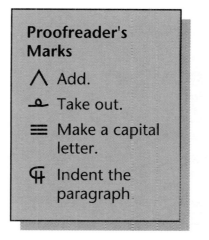

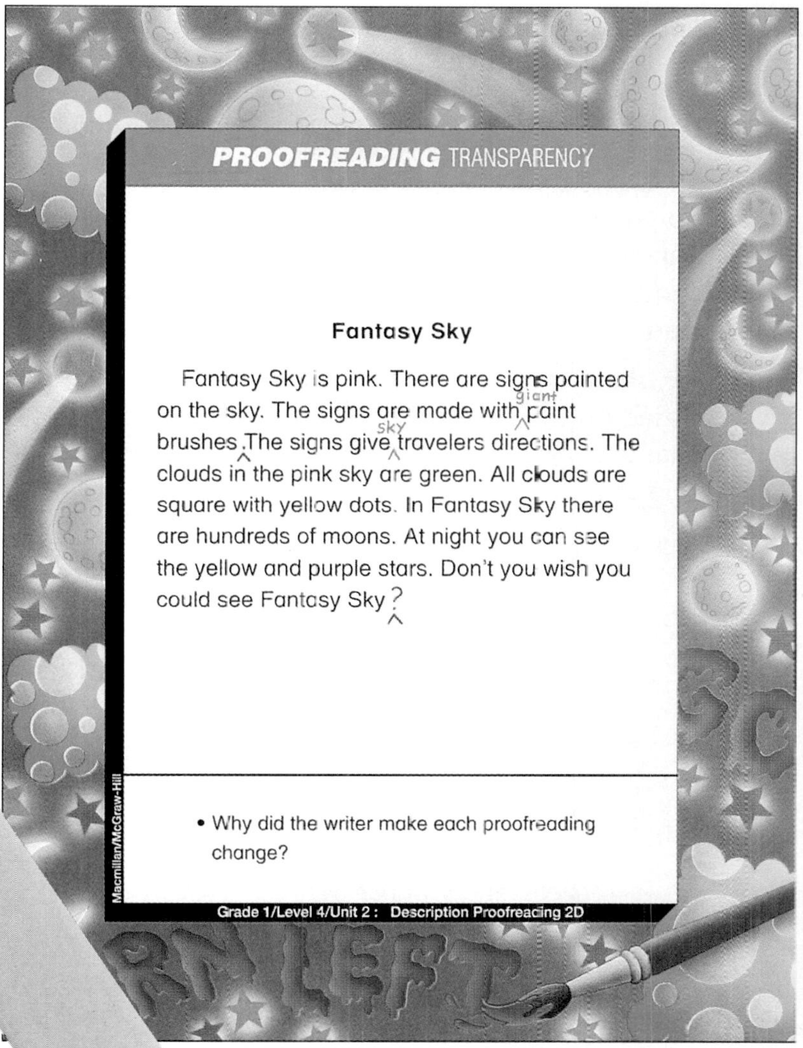
PROOFREADING TRANSPARENCY

Fantasy Sky

Fantasy Sky is pink. There are signs painted on the sky. The signs are made with giant paint brushes. The signs give sky travelers directions. The clouds in the pink sky are green. All clouds are square with yellow dots. In Fantasy Sky there are hundreds of moons. At night you can see the yellow and purple stars. Don't you wish you could see Fantasy Sky?

- Why did the writer make each proofreading change?

Macmillan/McGraw-Hill

Grade 1/Level 4/Unit 2 : Description Proofreading 2D

PUBLISHING

THINK ALOUD

I'm ready to publish my description. First, I'll draw a picture to go with my writing. Then, perhaps we can make a class display of everyone's work on the bulletin board.

Use **WRITING PROCESS TRANSPARENCY 2E** as a model to discuss the following questions.

CHECKLIST

- What do you notice that is special about this published description?
- How is it different from the other drafts?

ASSESSMENT OPPORTUNITY

To self-assess their published writing, children can compare their descriptions to the annotated model in the **WRITING AND LANGUAGE HANDBOOK** on **pages 40–41**.

Or, share these points with children. These are based on the Features of Descriptive Writing that occurred at the beginning of the lesson and during Drafting.

SELF ASSESSMENT

- Have I begun by clearly naming my subject?
- Have I used vivid words which tell how my subject looks, feels, smells, tastes, and sounds?

Publishing Ideas

- Make a display of children's written descriptions and drawings.
- Gather children's descriptions into a booklet.

PUBLISHING TRANSPARENCY

Fantasy Sky

Fantasy Sky is pink. There are signs painted on the sky. The signs are made with giant paint brushes. The signs give sky travelers directions. The clouds in the pink sky are green. All clouds are square with yellow dots. In Fantasy Sky there are hundreds of moons. At night you can see the yellow and purple stars. Don't you wish you could see Fantasy Sky?

- What do you like best about this description?

Macmillan/McGraw-Hill

Grade 1/Level 4/Unit 2 : Description Publishing 2E

SCORING RUBRIC: DESCRIPTIVE WRITING

When using this rubric, please consider children's creative efforts, adding a plus (+) for originality, wit, and imagination.

4 Excellent	3 Good	2 Fair	1 Poor
The paper begins with a sentence telling what will be described. The writer has used precise and vivid sensory words to describe the subject. The description is presented in an organized way. There s an awareness of audience in the picture this writer paints.	The paper informs the reader of what is to be described. The author uses some sensory descriptive words and phrases to paint a picture for an audience. The description is not as rich or full as in an excellent paper. It may not be as well or logically organized.	An attempt has been made to identify and describe something. There may be very few descriptive words or phrases. The details may be presented in an unorganized way. Parts of the paper may be only remotely related to the subject.	The purpose of the writing task has not been met. A topic may or may not be mentioned, but there is no real attempt to create a picture with words.

WRITING/LISTENING/SPEAKING CONNECTION

The following suggestions provide an opportunity for children to engage in formal listening and speaking activities.

WRITE A DESCRIPTION

GROUP Children can choose a person or animal to describe. They can make a cluster of details for their subject.

PRESENT THE DESCRIPTION

GROUP Volunteers can read their detail clusters to the class. They can act out sound and movement details, so classmates can guess the subjects of their descriptions.

SPEAKING GUIDELINES

1. Speak clearly.
2. Look at your audience.
3. Exaggerate words for special emphasis.

LISTENING/VIEWING GUIDELINES

1. Can I picture the subject clearly?
2. Which words and actions tell me about the subject?
3. Am I listening and watching carefully for details?

Seven Blind Mice

Selection Summary

Seven blind mice, each one a different color, live near a pond that has been visited by a great big "Something." One by one they take turns on a different day of the week to determine the stranger's identity. As each guesses, readers add another clue to their own solution of the mystery. Finally, the white mouse determines the stranger's identity, stating that each mouse's answer helped to fit together the puzzle pieces.

Linking Skills to Literature

Key Comprehension Strategies/Skills

☑ **MAKE, CONFIRM, REVISE PREDICTIONS**

MAKING, CONFIRMING, REVISING PREDICTIONS As the characters in this selection make educated guesses based on an accumulation of clues, children can see how cooperation can help in making predictions.

INTERACTING WITH THE TEXT

ENGAGE THE READER Children will have an opportunity to interact with the text by making, confirming and revising their predictions of what each mouse will do next. Discussion of their predictions and role-playing also build comprehension skills.

See **pages 212H** and **212**, where the story pages begin.

WRITER   **ED YOUNG**   ILLUSTRATOR

When he was a boy in China, Ed Young daydreamed. His dreams often took on the shape of plays and drawings. Since then, he has loved to read picture books, tell stories, and draw pictures. Mr. Young illustrated his first book, *The Mean Mouse and Other Stories* in 1962, after friends urged him to pursue a career illustrating children's books. Since then he has illustrated more than 30 stories.

"Seven Blind Mice" received several awards including the 1993 Caldecott Honor Medal. "I have never lost the child in me. I think everyone has a child in him that responds to anything that has true meaning."

Other Books by Ed Young
• *Little Plum* (Putnam, 1994)
• *Red Thread* (Putnam, 1993)
• *Moon Mother: A Native American Creation Tale* (HarperCollins, 1993)

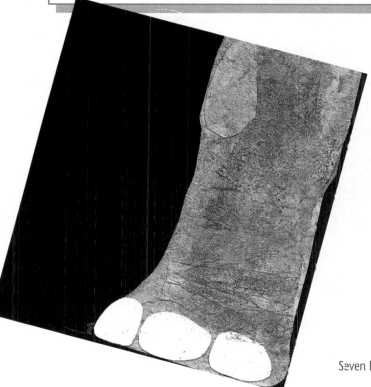

Suggested Lesson Planner
With Flexible Grouping Options

WEEK AT A GLANCE	PART 1 — DAY 1 FOCUS ON READING	PART 2 — DAY 2 READ THE LITERATURE

Seven Blind Mice
 	
◆ **Reading**
 	
◆ **Writing**
 	
◆ **Listening, Speaking, Viewing**
	Preview the Selection, 212E
	● Build Background, 212E
	Graphic Organizer Transparency/BLM 31
	● Oral Language Activities, 212F
	See also ESL/Second-Language Teacher's Guide, 206–214
	Vocabulary, 212G
	  Instructional Vocabulary
	    great
	    strange
	    agree
	    elephant
	    whole
	    turn
	Vocabulary Transparency/BLM 7
	Practice Book, 220
	
	If you wish to have children begin reading the selection at this point, see page 212H.
		Set Purposes, 212H
		  Journal Writing
		Suggestions for Reading, 212H
		● Read Independently
		● Read Aloud
		● Read Together
		  Read and Teach
		Teach Strategic Reading, 212H–249
		☑ Make, Confirm, Revise Predictions

◆ **Phonics and Decoding**	☑ Develop Phonemic Awareness for *-ide*, 249G Long *i*: Lessons and Practice ● Phonics Support BLM 25, 82	☑ Discover the Spelling Patterns *-ide* 249Q

◆ **Spelling**	For a detailed 5-day lesson plan for spelling, see pages 249Q-249R.
	Pretest (long *i*), 249Q
	Words in dark type appear in the story.
	  side **wide** slide ride hide
	Spelling Activity Book, 101
		● Challenge Words
		  first *find*
		Explore the Pattern, 249Q–249R
		Spelling Activity Book, 102

◆ **Grammar, Mechanics, and Usage**	Daily Language Activity: *Go* and *Went* 1. One day the mice go to the pond. (went) 2. They go last week. (went) 3. Then they all go home. (went) Grammar Practice Book: *Go* and *Went*, 101 ● Grammar Minilessons, 22 See pages 249O–249P	Daily Language Activity: *Go* and *Went* 1. Now the mice went one at a time. (go) 2. Red Mouse went to look first. (goes) 3. Green mouse went next. (goes) 5-Day Grammar Plan: *Go* and *Went*, 249O–249P Grammar Practice Book: *Go* and *Went*, 102

Flexible Grouping Options
● Extra Support
● Challenge
● Second-Language Support
☑ These core skills are tested in Unit Progress Assessment.

DAY 3 *READ THE LITERATURE*	**PART 3** **DAY 4** *EXTEND SKILLS IN CONTEXT*	**DAY 5** *EXTEND SKILLS IN CONTEXT*
Respond to the Literature Journal Writing, 249A ● Writing About the Theme, 249A Practice Book, 227 Comprehension Checkpoint, 249B ☑ Make, Confirm, Revise Predictions Practice Book, 223 Graphic Organizer Transparency/BLM 19 ● Reteaching ☑ Make, Confirm, Revise Predictions, 221 Practice Book, 223 Vocabulary Selection Assessment Selection Assessment/Unit Progress Assessment, Levels 4/5	Skills in Context ● Long Vowels and Phonograms: /ī/-*ice*, 215 Practice Book, 221 Capital Letters, 217 ☑ Use Illustrations, 219 Practice Book, 222 ● ☑ Make, Confirm, Revise Predictions, 221 Practice Book, 223 Quotation Marks, 223 Modeling and Phrasing, 225 ☑ Sequence of Events, 227 Practice Book, 224 Technique, 229 Visualize, 231 ● ● ● Multilevel Resources, 249D–249F ● ● Vocabulary, 249K Listening, Speaking, Viewing, 249L Across the Curriculum, 249U	Skills in Context Elephants, 233 Draw Conclusions, 235 Relate to Personal Experience, 237 Choral Reading, 239 ● ☑ Consonant Blends: /hw/*wh*, 241 Practice Book, 225 ☑ Spatial Relationships, 243 Practice Book, 226 ● Verbs, 245 Writing Fable, 249 Writing Process: Explanation, 249M ● ● Writing Projects, 249N Study Skills/Reading Resources: ☑ Use Parts of a Book, 249S Practice Book, 230 Multicultural Perspectives Fables, 249T Across The Curriculum, 249V
☑ Decoding Strategies: Blending Activities, 249I Practice Book, 228 w|ide sl|ide h|ide	Writing with the Phonogram, 249I ● Phonics Activity Book, 113–114	Reading with the Phonogram, 249I ☑ Consonant Digraphs: /th/*th*, 249J ● Phonics Activity Book, 115–116 Practice Book, 229 'TRONIC PHONICS™
Constructing Words, 249R Work with Meaning, 249R Spelling Activity Book, 103	Spelling and Writing, 249R Spelling Activity Book, 104	Posttest, 249R Spelling Activity Book, 105
Daily Language Activity: *Go* and *Went* 1. Yellow Mouse goes to the pond on Wednesday. (went) 2. Purple Mouse goes on Thursday. (went) 3. Orange Mouse goes on Friday. (went) Writing Application: Describing a Place, 249P Grammar Practice Book: *Go* and *Went*, 103	Daily Language Activity: *Go* and *Went* 1. All the mice went to see the strange Something. (go) 2. Each mouse went right up to it. (goes) 3. Purple Mouse went up a cliff. (goes) Quick Write: Evaluation, 249P Grammar Practice Book: *Go* and *Went*, 104	Daily Language Activity: *Go* and *Went* 1. Finally White Mouse goes to the pond. (went) 2. The mice go up and down the elephant. (went) 3. They go from end to end. (went) Grammar Practice Book: *Go* and *Went*, 105; Answer Key and Grammar Assessment, 24

Prepare to Read

PREVIEW THE SELECTION

AUTHOR, ILLUSTRATOR
Read **page 212**. Scan the illustrations and discuss them with the class. How do children think Ed Young created these illustrations? Explain that he used a form of paper collage.

GENRE: FOLK TALE
Ask children to read the title and predict what the story is about. Will the characters act like animals or people? Will they talk? Let children know that "**Seven Blind Mice**" is a *fable*—a story with a moral or lesson at the end.

EVALUATE PRIOR KNOWLEDGE

ANIMAL SURPRISES
Invite children to brainstorm facts about elephants that might surprise a person who has never seen one. Create a chart or use **GRAPHIC ORGANIZER TRANSPARENCY/BLM 31**.

Elephant Surprises

Size	Features
great	long trunk
huge	thick, round legs
enormous	huge ears
	strange tusks

ACTIVITIES FOR BUILDING BACKGROUND

MAKE IT REAL: SURPRISING SHAPES
Have children tear a sheet of construction paper into the shape of a zoo animal or part of an animal. Before children explain their animal shapes, call on several others to predict what they think the shape is. What is surprising about their predictions?

READ ALOUD
Children may enjoy hearing "Test of a Friendship," a Nigerian folk tale retold by Margery Bernstein, on **page 99** of **READ ALOUDS, PLAYS, AND CHORAL READINGS**.

INTEGRATING
SPELLING AND GRAMMAR

SPELLING
You may want to present the spelling pretest of words with *-ide*. See **pages 249Q–249R** for the 5-Day Spelling Plan.

PHONICS AND DECODING CONNECTION
See lesson on Long Vowels and Phonograms: /ī/-*ide* on **pages 249G–249I**.

GRAMMAR
See **pages 249O–249P** for Daily Language Activities. A 5-Day Grammar Plan is also presented.

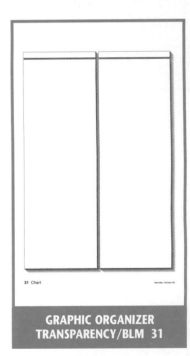

31 Chart

GRAPHIC ORGANIZER TRANSPARENCY/BLM 31

ACTIVITIES

ORAL LANGUAGE ACTIVITIES

PAINT BLOT PICTURES

Reinforce the theme of Surprises Along the Way by helping children make paint blot pictures. Have them drip tempera paint onto the center of a sheet of paper. Then have them fold the paper in half, press on it lightly, and open it again.

Children can use their imagination as they look at the shape of the paint blot. Have them tell a partner what familiar object it reminds them of.

DISCUSS SURPRISES

Have each child describe what they see in their partner's paint blot picture. Children may be surprised to discover their partner sees the same picture differently. Encourage children to discuss how the paint blot reminds them of something else familiar.

You may want to pair non-English speaking children with a bilingual child who knows their language.

NONVERBAL RESPONSES

Children with limited English capabilities can draw a picture of the item they see in the paint blot. Encourage them to label their picture in their native language as well as the English translation.

TEACHING
T I P S

Look at several paint blot pictures and model your own response to what you see in the picture.

LANGUAGE DEVELOPMENT

You may want to present the following words, idioms, and phrases to children who need language support.

pillar, p. 218
set out, p. 220
in turn, p. 226
up one side, p. 242
end to end, p. 242
moral, p. 249

ESL/SECOND-LANGUAGE TEACHER'S GUIDE
A full teaching lesson for students acquiring English is available in the ESL/ SECOND-LANGUAGE TEACHER'S GUIDE.

Vocabulary

INSTRUCTIONAL VOCABULARY

great	large
strange	very different from what is expected
agree	feel the same way as someone else
elephant	big, strong animal with gray skin and a trunk
whole	something with no missing parts
turn	a person's time to do something

 ## VOCABULARY ACTIVITIES

SENTENCE COMPLETION
GROUP

After you present the vocabulary, have children work in small groups or as a class to complete the following sentences. Use **VOCABULARY STRATEGY TRANSPARENCY/BLM 7.**

1. An elephant is not small. It is _____great_____.
2. A piece of an apple is not as big as the _____whole_____.
3. It is your time to do something. It is your _____turn_____.
4. A small gray animal is a mouse.
   A large gray animal is an _____elephant_____.
5. A thing you see every day is not _____strange_____.

PERSONAL EXPERIENCE
PARTNER

After presenting the vocabulary, have partners use the words to draw pictures that relate to their own experiences. For example, they could draw something strange they may have seen or illustrate a time when they did or did not agree with someone. Allow them to use their glossary.

WORDS IN CONTEXT
ONE

For more vocabulary practice, assign **PRACTICE BOOK, page 220.**

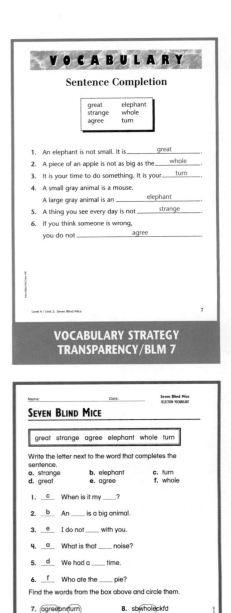

VOCABULARY

Sentence Completion

great	elephant
strange	whole
agree	turn

1. An elephant is not small. It is _____great_____.
2. A piece of an apple is not as big as the _____whole_____.
3. It is your time to do something. It is your_____turn_____.
4. A small gray animal is a mouse.
   A large gray animal is an _____elephant_____.
5. A thing you see every day is not _____strange_____.
6. If you think someone is wrong,
   you do not _____agree_____.

Level 4 / Unit 2: Seven Blind Mice   7

VOCABULARY STRATEGY TRANSPARENCY/BLM 7

Name: _____ Date: _____   **Seven Blind Mice** SELECTION VOCABULARY

SEVEN BLIND MICE

| great strange agree elephant whole turn |

Write the letter next to the word that completes the sentence.
a. strange	b. elephant	c. turn
d. great	e. agree	f. whole

1. _c_ When is it my ____?
2. _b_ An ____ is a big animal.
3. _e_ I do not ____ with you.
4. _a_ What is that ____ noise?
5. _d_ We had a ____ time.
6. _f_ Who ate the ____ pie?

Find the words from the box above and circle them.

7. (agree)bnrturn
8. sbwhole)ckfd
9. celephant)dhs
10. great)(strange)

220   **Extension:** Invite children to make their own word search puzzle, using own words of their own choosing.   Level 4/Unit 2 **Selection Vocabulary**

PRACTICE BOOK, page 220

Strategic Reading

SET PURPOSES

JOURNAL WRITING With partners, children can discuss and record their reasons for reading the selection. Children may read to discover

- what the mice are trying to identify.

- what the mice are going to guess next.

- how the seven blind mice finally figure out what the Something is.

ENGAGE THE READER Children might enjoy dramatizing parts of this story, so opportunities for **role-play** are included in the Strategic Reading suggestions. As they read, you may also want to encourage them to list their predictions about what they expect each mouse to say on a Prediction Chart. Draw the following chart on the chalkboard:

Day	Mouse	I Predict Mouse Will Think It's	Was Prediction Right?
Monday	Red Mouse		

As they read, children can note in their journals any reactions or questions they may want to explore.

SUGGESTIONS FOR READING

MANAGEMENT TIPS

Books for Meeting Individual Needs, **pages 249D–249F**, offer teaching suggestions for working with groups of children who have specific needs.

READ INDEPENDENTLY

Independent readers can read silently to discover what the strange Something is. Encourage them to pay attention to the repetitive language pattern and picture clues to help them understand the story.

READ ALOUD

Children may follow along as they listen to "**Seven Blind Mice**" on the **LISTENING LIBRARY AUDIOCASSETTE.** Suggest that they use the pictures to help them make predictions.

READ TOGETHER

Assign groups the roles of the narrator and the seven mice. Have them take turns reading. Encourage them to try using different voices to help give the mice different personalities.

READ AND TEACH

☑ Make, Confirm, or Revise Predictions

Use the comprehension strategy beginning on **page 212** as you and your children read the literature, or use the strategy after any other Suggestion for Reading option.

Comprehension

STRATEGIC READING

☑ MAKE, CONFIRM, OR REVISE PREDICTIONS

Explain the comprehension strategy that will be focused on.

When you read, it's fun to try to guess what will happen next. Use what you know from past events in the story to help you. Also use what you know from your own experience to make predictions. As you read, you will find out if you were right, almost right, or if you were off-track. You might need to revise your predictions. Rereading the story clues may help you do this. Predicting what will happen next will certainly keep you involved in the story!

TEACHING
TIPS

Tell children that, as they read, you will model how readers use the strategy, and they will have a chance to use the strategy, too.

MEET ED YOUNG

Ed Young was born in China in 1931. While he was growing up, China was at war. So his family had to move around a lot. Wherever he went he drew pictures. He also made up plays. Mr. Young always wanted to be an artist. When he was a young man, he moved to the United States. He did a lot of drawing for his job. His friends liked his drawings very much. They thought it would be great for him to draw children's books. So did he.

Today Ed Young has written and drawn more than forty books. He still loves to draw and make up stories. "I have never lost the child in me," he says.

212

Seven Blind Mice

BY ED YOUNG

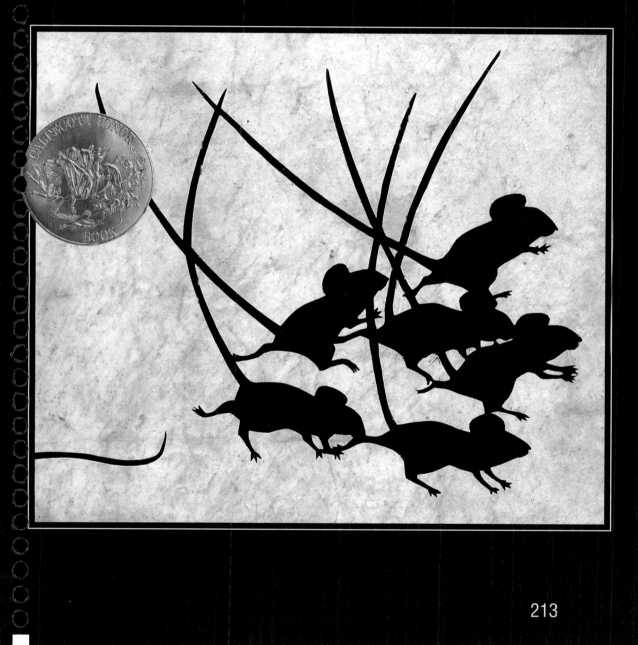

213

Skills in Context

To provide Skills and Strategies instruction, select from these lessons

☑ These core skills are tested in the Unit Progress Assessment.

Comprehension

STRATEGIC READING

1 Why did the seven blind mice run home? **(They found a strange Something by their pond and they were surprised.)** How else might they have felt? **(scared)**

TEACHING
TIPS

Point out to children that there is nothing wrong with making predictions that are not correct. Explain that it is important to confirm predictions based on events and clues in the story and to revise predictions when necessary throughout a story.

214

One day seven blind mice were surprised to find a strange Something by their pond. "What is it?" they cried, and they all ran home. *1*

215

PHONICS AND DECODING

☑ Long Vowels and Phonograms: /ī/-*ice*

INTRODUCE Ask children how they might use the phonogram -*ice* to read an unfamiliar word.

DEVELOP/APPLY Reread **page 215** to find a word with the phonogram -*ice*. Write *mice* on chart paper. Have children brainstorm a list of words that contain the phonogram -*ice*.

CLOSE Invite partners to write a sentence using words with the phonogram -*ice*.

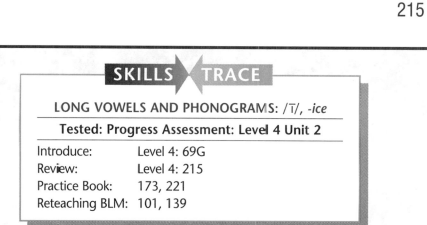

PRACTICE BOOK, page 221

See RETEACHING BLM, page 139

SKILLS ✭ TRACE

LONG VOWELS AND PHONOGRAMS: /ī/, -*ice*

Tested: Progress Assessment: Level 4 Unit 2

Introduce:	Level 4: 69G
Review:	Level 4: 215
Practice Book:	173, 221
Reteaching BLM:	101, 139

Comprehension

STRATEGIC READING

2 The mice have come back! Why do you think they returned? **(to find out what the strange Something is)** Who goes first to find out what the strange Something is? **(Red Mouse)** What day is it? **(Monday)**

3 **MAKE PREDICTIONS** I wonder if Red Mouse can figure out what the strange Something is. I think it might be a tree trunk. What do you think it looks like?

Let's record our predictions on our chart.

Day	Mouse	I Predict Mouse Will Think It's:	Was Prediction Right?
Monday	Red	tree trunk	

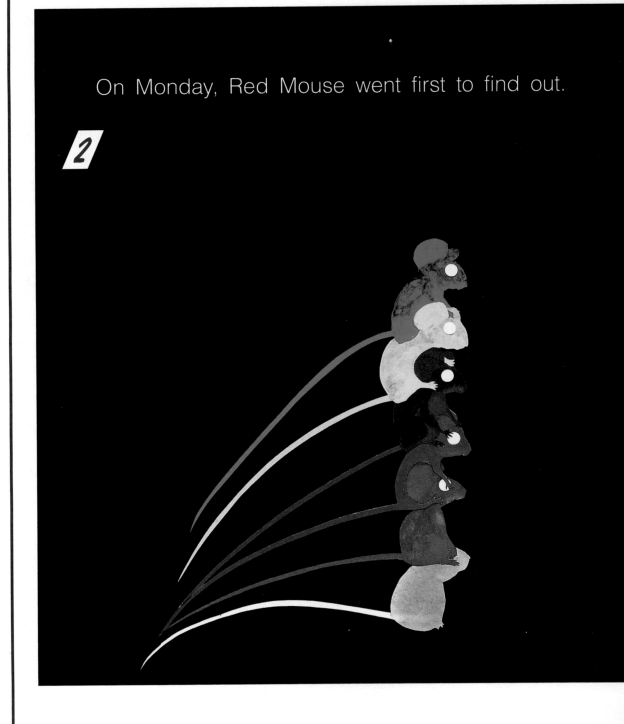

On Monday, Red Mouse went first to find out.

2

216

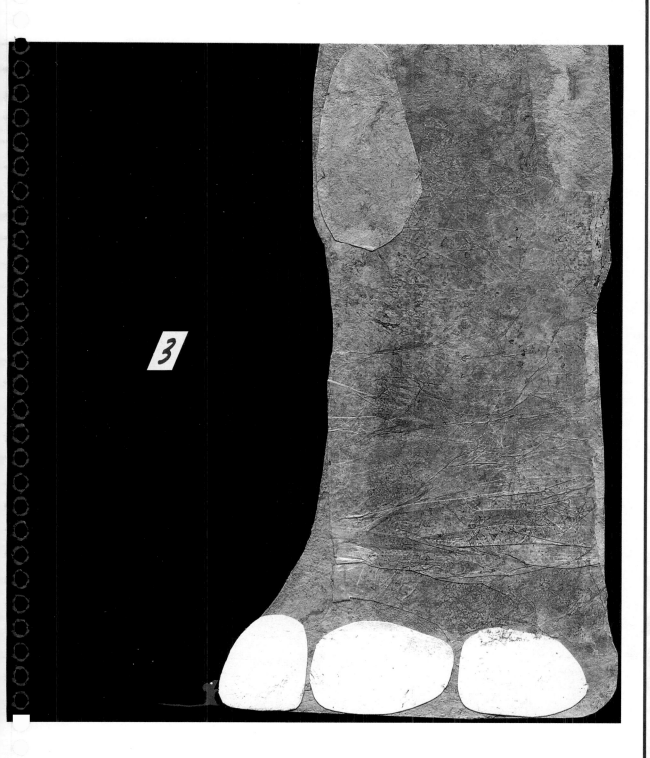

217

Skills in Context

Capital Letters

Invite children to find words on **page 216** that begin with capital letters.

- Write *Monday* on the chalkboard and explain that words that name the days of the week are always capitalized.

- Write *Red Mouse* on the chalkboard, and elicit from children that names always begin with capital letters.

Encourage children to work in small groups to make a list of days of the week and names that appear in the story.

MEETING INDIVIDUAL NEEDS

Second Language Support Encourage children to help you list the days of the week in other languages. Compare similarities and differences among the languages.

Comprehension

STRATEGIC READING

4 **CONFIRM PREDICTIONS** Let's check my prediction. I predicted that Red Mouse would tell the others that the strange Something was a tree trunk, but my guess was wrong. Red Mouse told them it was a pillar. Why do you think Red Mouse thought it was a pillar?

"It's a pillar," he said. No one believed him.

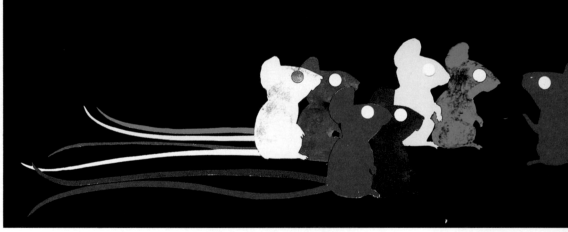

218

219

Skills in Context

COMPREHENSION

☑ Use Illustrations

INTRODUCE Ask children how using the illustrations can help them when they read.

DEVELOP/APPLY Look at the picture on **page 219** and ask children:

• How is this picture similar to the picture shown on **page 217?**

• How do these pictures help you understand what Red Mouse is thinking?

• What did you expect Red Mouse to say the Something was? Were you surprised?

CLOSE Ask children why they think the illustrator made the pillar on **page 219** red.

PRACTICE BOOK, page 222

See RETEACHING BLM, page 140

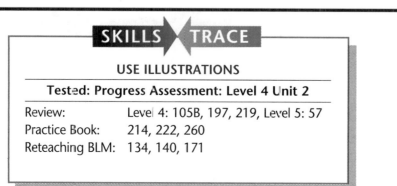

SKILLS TRACE

USE ILLUSTRATIONS

Tested: Progress Assessment: Level 4 Unit 2

Review:	Level 4: 105B, 197, 219, Level 5: 57
Practice Book:	214, 222, 260
Reteaching BLM:	134, 140, 171

Comprehension

STRATEGIC READING

5 **MAKE PREDICTIONS** On Monday, Red Mouse went off to find out what the strange Something was. Now it is Tuesday, and Green Mouse is going to try to figure out the mystery. What do you think he will tell the others? I think he is going to say it's a hose. What do you think?

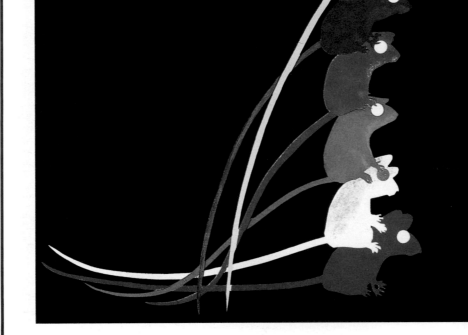

On Tuesday, Green Mouse set out.
He was the second to go.

220

SECOND-LANGUAGE SUPPORT

Explain the ordinal numbers to children by engaging them in activities that require them to stand in a line. Ask the second child to do something; the fourth child, etc.

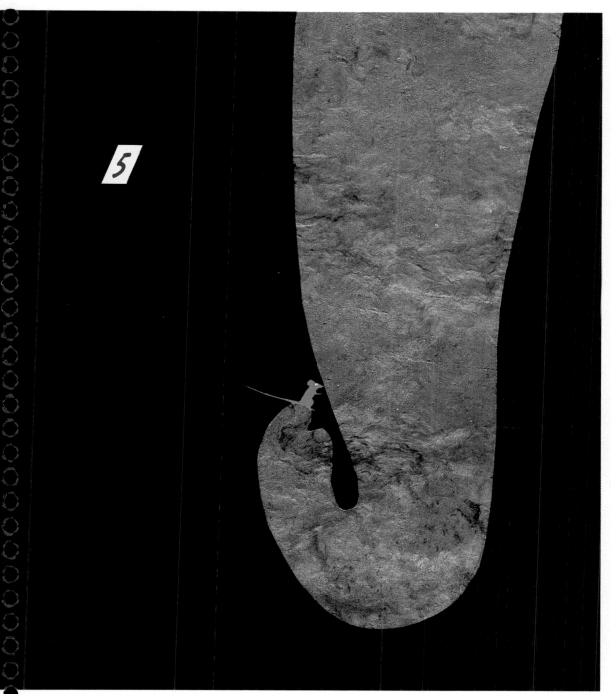

5

221

Skills in Context

RETEACHING

COMPREHENSION

✒ Make, Confirm, or Revise Predictions

INTRODUCE Ask children how making predictions can help them enjoy reading the story.

DEVELOP/APPLY Guide children to recognize patterns that will help them make predictions.

• Remind children that when Red Mouse left, Green Mouse was sitting on top. Ask who is leaving now. Who is sitting on top?

• Remind children that Red Mouse went to inspect the Something on Monday. Ask on what day Green Mouse is going to inspect the Something.

CLOSE Encourage children to write a prediction in their journal about who will be the third mouse to go and on what day that mouse will go.

PRACTICE BOOK, page 223

See RETEACHING BLM, page 141

SKILLS ✕ TRACE

MAKE, CONFIRM, REVISE PREDICTIONS

Tested: Progress Assessment: Level 4 Unit 2

Review:	Level 4: 212, 221, 249B, Level 5: 170, 197
Practice Book:	201, 310
Reteaching BLM:	123, 212

Comprehension

STRATEGIC READING

6 **CONFIRM PREDICTIONS** What did Green Mouse think the strange Something was? **(a snake!)** Let's check this against our prediction. How does Green Mouse look?

🔬 SCIENCE CONNECTION

Mice live everywhere—in fields, mountains, swamps, and deserts. Why do mice appear so often in stories? Perhaps it is because mice are charming and they love to eat food. They also like to snack on glue, soap, leather, and paste. Mice have many enemies, including people, cats, birds, and other animals.

"It's a snake," he said. **6**

222

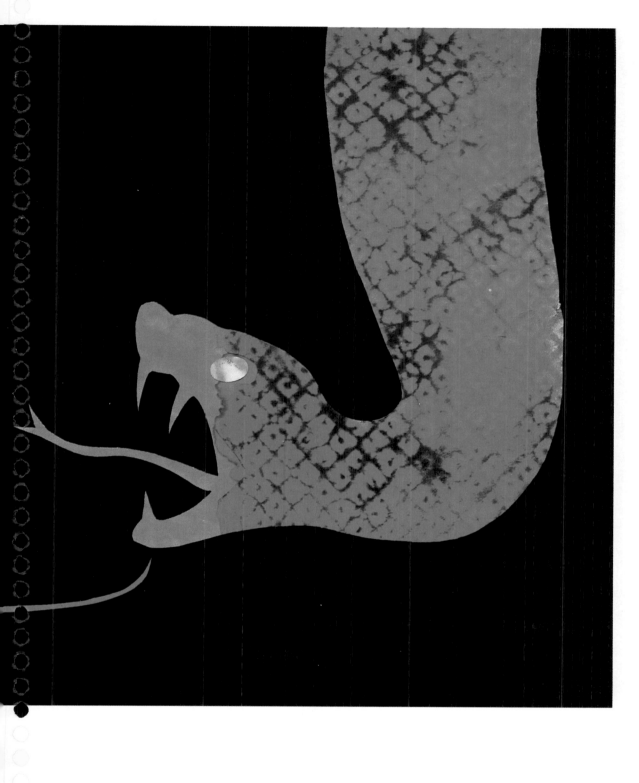

223

Skills in Context

CONCEPTS OF PRINT

Quotation Marks

Read the text on **page 222**, emphasizing the words spoken by Green Mouse. Point out the quotation marks. Explain that these marks tell the exact words a character is saying. The marks come just before and just after the character's words.

Invite children to identify other examples of quotes in the selection, and read them with expression.

Ask children to write what the other mice might be saying about the strange Something. Remind them to use quotation marks to enclose the speaker's exact words.

Comprehension

STRATEGIC READING

7 **MAKE PREDICTIONS** None of the other mice have been right about the strange Something. Do you think Yellow Mouse will know what it is? What do you expect him to say? Look at the picture to help you decide. I think he will say it's a big slide. Whee!

INFORMAL ASSESSMENT

Observe if children are using the pictures and the repetitive language pattern to help them make predictions about the story. You may use the Reteaching lesson on **page 221** to help children who have difficulty making predictions.

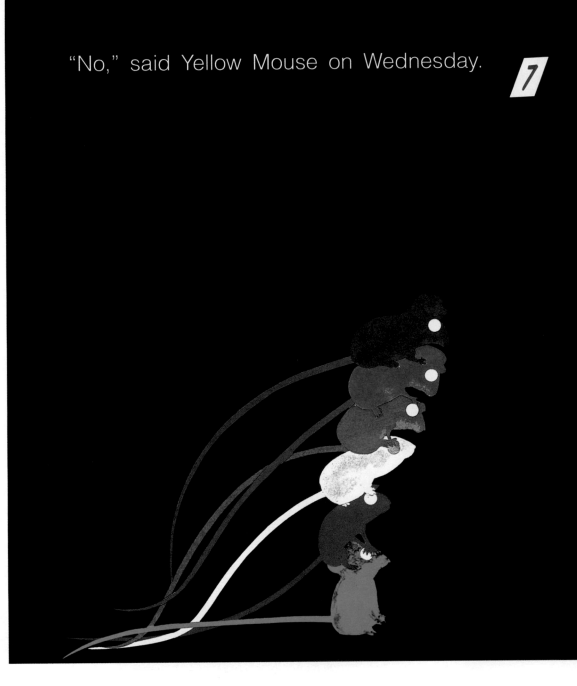

"No," said Yellow Mouse on Wednesday.

7

224

225

Skills in Context

Modeling and Phrasing

The comma within the text on **page 224** provides an opportunity for children to practice phrasing. The dialog within the quotation marks offers an opportunity for children to use emotion as they read aloud.

Model fluent reading by

- reading the dialog within the quotation marks with expression.

- pausing after the comma.

Invite children to suggest feelings the animals might be expressing through the dialog. Record these on a chart. Then have children reread sentences orally with feeling.

Comprehension

STRATEGIC READING

8 **CONFIRM PREDICTIONS** What did Yellow Mouse think the strange Something was? (a spear) Why does he think it's a spear? (He touched only the part that felt like a spear.) Did you predict that he would think the strange Something was a spear?

9 **MAKE PREDICTIONS** The first three mice set out on Monday, Tuesday, and Wednesday. When do you think the next mouse will set out? (Thursday) What makes you think so? (The story's pattern of events follows the days of the week.)

MEETING INDIVIDUAL NEEDS

Challenge

You may want to use this page to point out the difference between the ordinal number third, and the cardinal number three.

"It's a spear."
He was the third in turn.

226

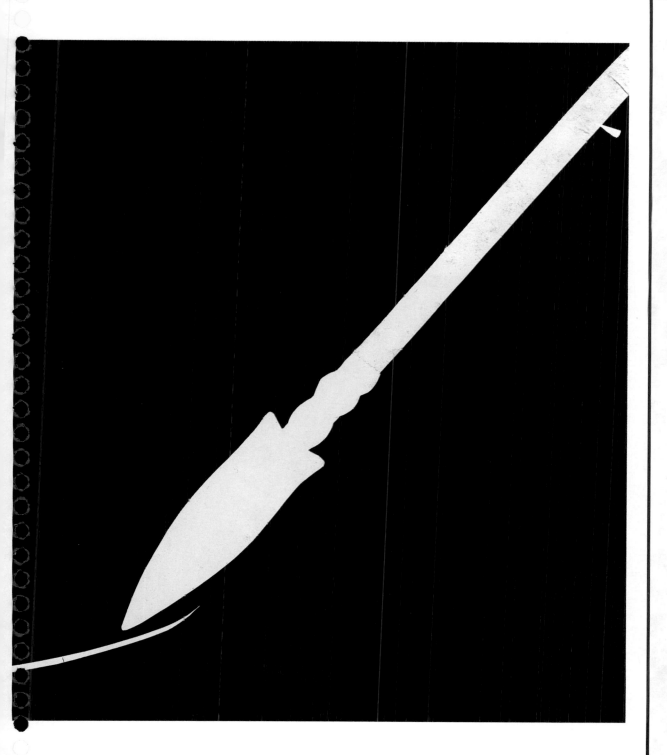

227

Skills in Context

COMPREHENSION

☑ **Sequence of Events**

INTRODUCE Ask children how many mice have examined the strange Something so far.

DEVELOP/APPLY Point out the word *third* on **page 226.**

- Help children recall other number words that were used in this story.

- Write *first, second, third* on the chalkboard.

- How can number words help you understand what has happened in a story?

CLOSE Have children work with a partner to retell the story up to this point. Encourage them to use the words *first, second,* and *third* in their retellings.

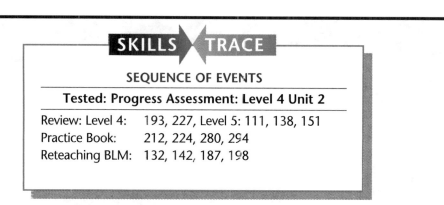

PRACTICE BOOK, page 224

See RETEACHING BLM, page 142

SKILLS TRACE

SEQUENCE OF EVENTS

Tested: Progress Assessment: Level 4 Unit 2

Review: Level 4:   193, 227, Level 5: 111, 138, 151
Practice Book: 212, 224, 280, 294
Reteaching BLM: 132, 142, 187, 198

Comprehension

STRATEGIC READING

10 **MAKE PREDICTIONS** Look at the picture carefully. What do you think Purple Mouse will say the strange Something is? It looks to me like a stone wall. Who would like to pretend to be Purple Mouse? What might you say the strange Something is? **ROLE-PLAY**

TEACHING
TIPS

You may want to have children work with a partner to use colored cutouts of mice to retell what has happened in the story so far.

The fourth was Purple Mouse.
He went on Thursday.

228

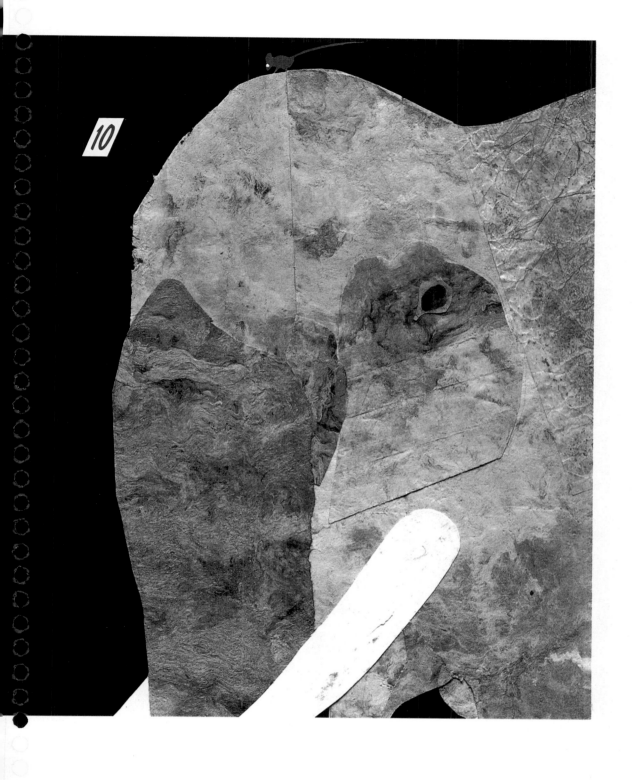

229

Skills in Context

Technique

Focus on the illustrations on **pages 228-229**. Discuss how the artist used a combination of paint and collage to illustrate this story.

Help children look closely at the illustrations throughout the selection:

- How does this artist show texture—roughness and smoothness?

- What materials does the artist use to show color?

MEETING INDIVIDUAL NEEDS

Challenge
Invite children to create an animal using the collage technique. Provide an assortment of paper with different colors and textures.

Comprehension

11 **CONFIRM PREDICTIONS** What did Purple Mouse think that he felt? **(a cliff)** Why might he think that? Is this what you predicted? How many mice have gone to see the strange Something now? **(four)**

Let's add our new predictions to our chart. Then let's check to see if they're right.

Day	Mouse	I Predict Mouse Will Think It's:	Was Prediction Right?
Mon.	Red	tree trunk	X
Tues.	Green	hose	X
Wed.	Yellow	slide	X
Thur.	Purple	wall	

12 **MAKE PREDICTIONS** Look back through the story, and try to guess which mouse will go next. Use your crayons and draw a picture to show your prediction.
NONVERBAL RESPONSE

"It's a great cliff," he said.

230

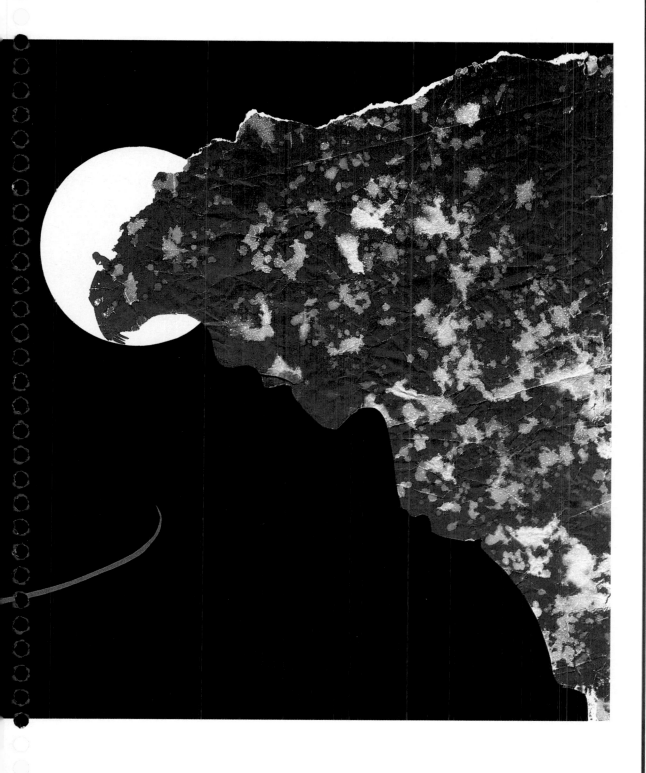

231

Skills in Context

Visualize

Model for children how visualizing can help them better understand the story. Reread **page 230**.

***THINK ALOUD** As I read, I try to make a picture in my mind to help me understand why Purple Mouse is saying what he says.*

- *I imagine Purple Mouse high on top of the strange Something.*

- *I can picture him standing at the edge of the elephant's head. This helps me understand why Purple Mouse thought the strange Something was a cliff.*

Encourage children to look back at **pages 216–217**. Have them close their eyes and pretend to be Red Mouse when he climbed up the elephant's leg. Let them explain why he might have thought the leg was a pillar.

Comprehension

STRATEGIC READING

13 **MAKE PREDICTIONS** Can you guess what Orange Mouse will tell the others? I think he's going to say it's a sail. What do you think?

INFORMAL ASSESSMENT

See if children can use the illustrations to make predictions by discussing what the parts shown in the pictures may be.

To help children with Making, Confirming, or Revising Predictions, see Reteaching lesson on page 221.

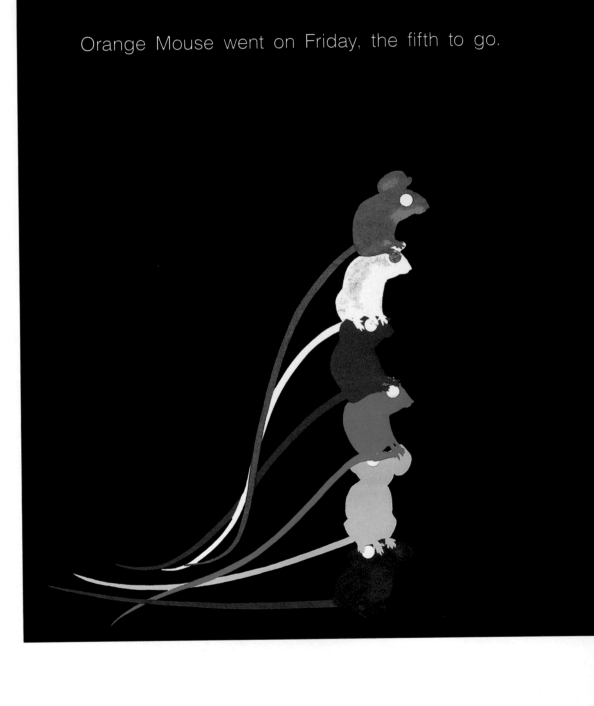

Orange Mouse went on Friday, the fifth to go.

232

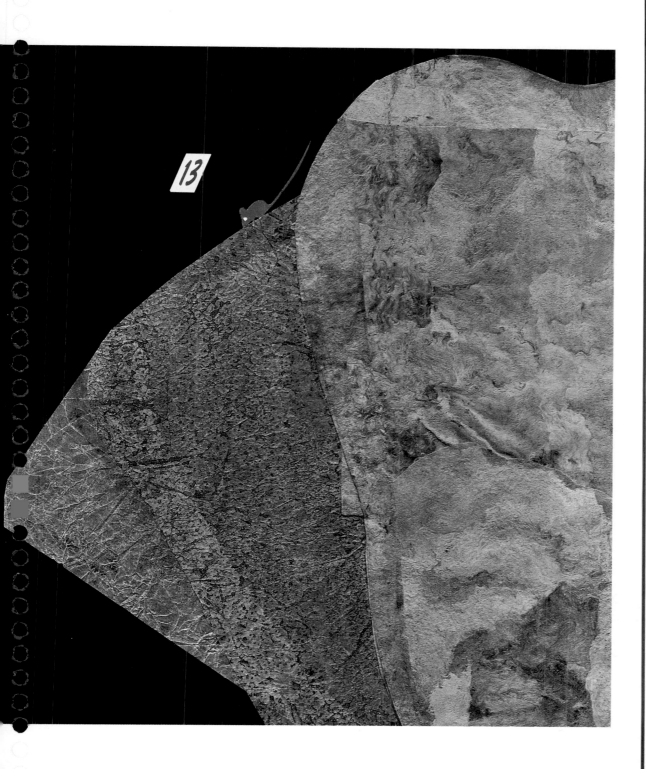

233

Skills in Context

Elephants

Share these surprising facts about elephants:

- Although an elephant's gray, wrinkled skin is up to 1–1/2 inches thick, it is surprisingly tender. Small insects like flies and mosquitoes can bite into it.

- The trunk of the African elephant has two finger-like knobs at the tip, and the Asiatic elephant has one. The trunk is used to smell, breathe, eat, and drink. It also acts like a hand to pick up very small objects.

- You may think elephants are cool, but actually, they can't sweat. To get cool, they flap their huge ears or use their trunk to give themselves a shower.

- No wonder elephants never forget! They have one of the largest brains and are highly intelligent.

Invite children to find out other surprising facts about elephants. Have them write each fact on a small cutout of an elephant. Create a "Surprising Elephants" bulletin board display.

Comprehension

14 Who would like to pretend to be the orange mouse? You just checked out the strange Something. How do you feel? What do you think you saw? Why? Who would like to volunteer to be the other mice? Do you believe Orange Mouse? **ROLE-PLAY**

"It's a fan!" he cried. "I felt it move."

234

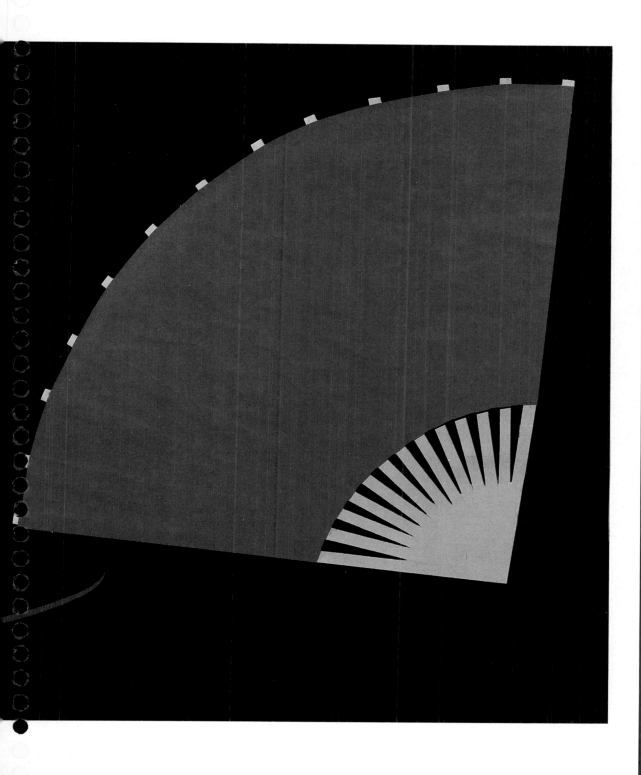

Skills in Context

COMPREHENSION

Draw Conclusions

Remind children that when we try to figure something out based on our experience and the information we have, we are drawing conclusions. Explain that each mouse has drawn a conclusion about what the strange Something is.

- Have children think about the conclusion Orange Mouse drew. Ask them to reread **pages 232–234** to determine the facts that led Orange Mouse to draw this conclusion.

Children may draw their own conclusion about what the strange Something is. Invite them to write a conclusion and the experiences or information that helped them draw it in their journals. They may illustrate it if they wish.

235

Comprehension

STRATEGIC READING

15 **MAKE PREDICTIONS** What could the strange Something be? Each mouse has said it is something different. I see something stringy that looks like it might be an old mop. I think Blue Mouse will feel it and say it's a mop. What do you think?

The sixth to go was Blue Mouse.

236

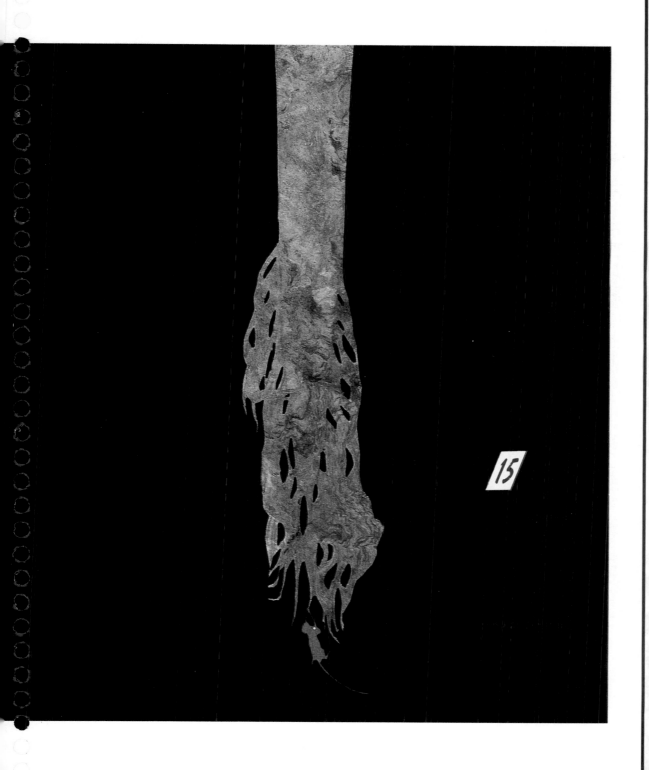

15

237

Skills in Context

SELF-MONITORING

Relate to Personal Experience

Help children see that relating what they read to their own experiences is a strategy that can help them understand the surprise in this story.

Ask children to look at the picture on **page 237**. Have children ever seen anything like it before? Since the mice are blind they must feel in order to determine what the Something is. Have children talk about what a similar-looking object might feel like to the touch.

Based on their own experience, and what they've learned from reading the story:

• Do children think that Blue Mouse will be able to identify the Something?

Comprehension

STRATEGIC READING

16 **CONFIRM PREDICTIONS** What did Blue Mouse tell the others the strange Something was? (a rope) Why did he think this? (He was only touching the part that felt like a rope.)

SELF ASSESSMENT

Help children assess how they have been reading to help themselves enjoy and understand the story better. They may ask:

• Have I used the clues in the pictures to help me make predictions about what each mouse will say?

• How do I feel about the story so far?

To help children with Making, Confirming, or Revising Predictions, see Reteaching lesson on page 221.

He went on Saturday and said, **16** "It's nothing but a rope."

238

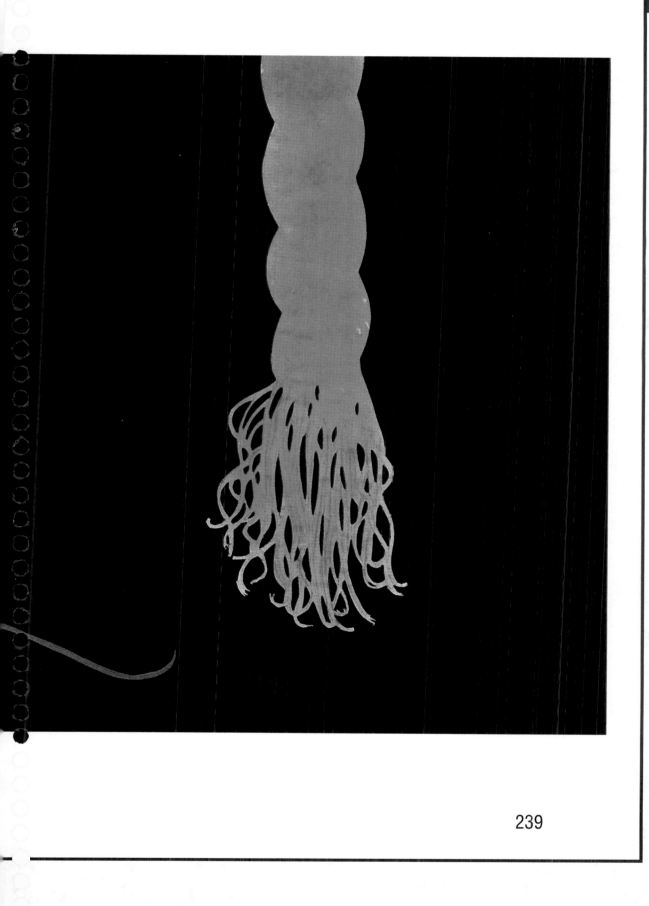

239

Skills in Context

READING FLUENCY

Choral Reading

Model fluency in reading by reading the text on **page 238** to children. As you read, pause after the introductory phrase, and read Blue Mouse's response with expression.

Encourage children to practice choral reading in small groups, monitoring each other's

• accuracy.

• expression.

• phrasing.

Comprehension

STRATEGIC READING

17 Nod your head yes or no to show whether the mice agreed that the strange Something was a rope. **NONVERBAL RESPONSE**

18 Who would like to dramatize the mice? You all disagree about what the strange Something is. What might you say to one another? **ROLE-PLAY**

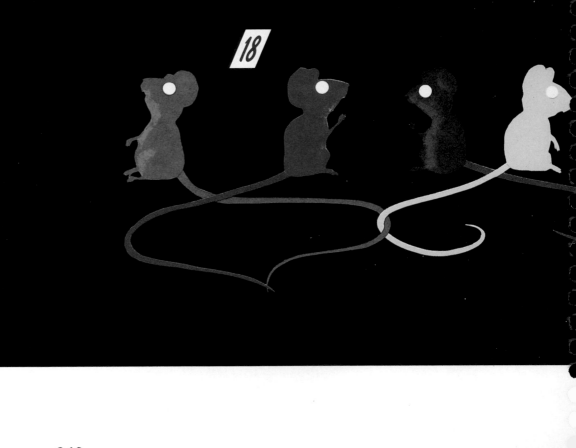

But the others didn't agree.
They began to argue.
"A snake!" "A rope!" "A fan!" "A cliff!"

240

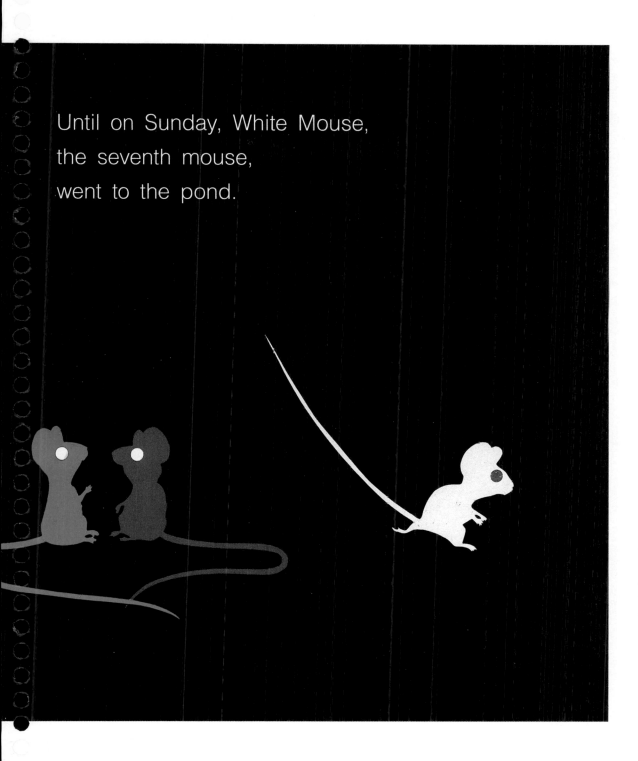

Until on Sunday, White Mouse,
the seventh mouse,
went to the pond.

241

Skills in Context

PHONICS AND DECODING

☑ Consonant Blends:
/hw/*wh*

INTRODUCE Ask children what beginning sound they hear as you say the following words: *where, when,* and *whistle.*

DEVELOP/APPLY As you write the words on the chalkboard, explain that you are using "white" chalk.

• Find the word *white* on page **241.** Point out the beginning sound /hw/.

• As you read these words, encourage children to raise their hands if they hear the *wh* blend: *hit, why, vest, while, wheel, bell.*

CLOSE Have children work in small groups to generate a list of words that begin with the /wh/ blend.

PRACTICE BOOK, page 225

See RETEACHING BLM, page 143

SKILLS TRACE

CONSONANT BLENDS /hw/, *wh-*

Tested: Progress Assessment: Level 4 Unit 2

Introduce:	Level 3: 99
Review:	Level 4: 241
Practice Book:	129, 225
Reteaching BLM:	73, 143

Comprehension

STRATEGIC READING

19 What is happening on these pages? (White Mouse is checking out the strange Something from one end to the other.) Can you guess what she might say?

PHONICS AND DECODING

/ī/-*ide* as in *side,* **page 242**
See Phonics and Decoding lesson on Long Vowels and Phonograms: /ī/-*ide* on **pages 249G–249I.**

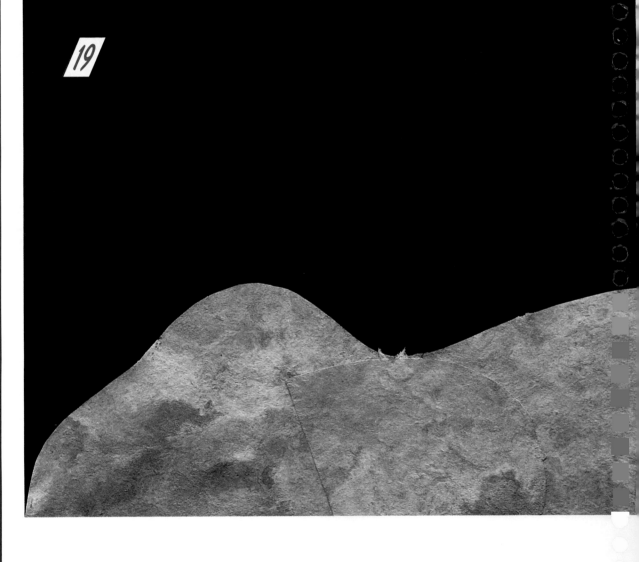

When she came upon the Something, she ran up one side, and she ran down the other. She ran across the top and from end to end.

19

242

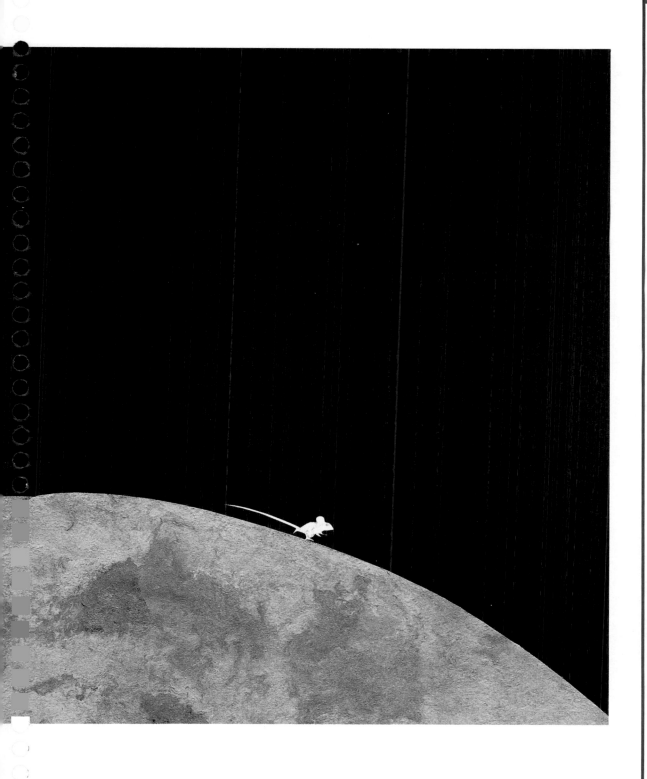

243

Skills in Context

COMPREHENSION

✓ Spatial Relationships

INTRODUCE Invite children to point up, down, and across the room. Help them understand that each word describes a direction.

DEVELOP/APPLY Explain that writers often use direction words to organize their ideas. This helps the reader picture what is happening in the story as they read.

Have children reread **page 242.** Ask:

- What words tell you where White Mouse ran? What picture do the words help you see in your mind?

CLOSE Encourage children to choose a direction word from **page 242** that they wish to illustrate. Then they can draw or trace an elephant and using their finger show the direction in which the White Mouse ran.

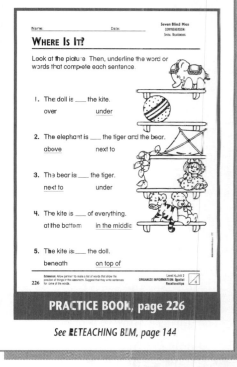

PRACTICE BOOK, page 226

See RETEACHING BLM, page 144

Comprehension

STRATEGIC READING

20 **MAKE PREDICTIONS** What do you think the White Mouse will say the strange Something is? Explain why you think as you do.

Let's add our new predictions to our chart.

Day	Mouse	I Predict Mouse Will Think It's:	Was Prediction Right?
Mon.	Red	tree trunk	X
Tues.	Green	hose	X
Wed.	Yellow	slide	X
Thur.	Purple	wall	X
Fri.	Orange	sail	X
Sat.	Blue	mop	X
Sun.	White	elephant	✓

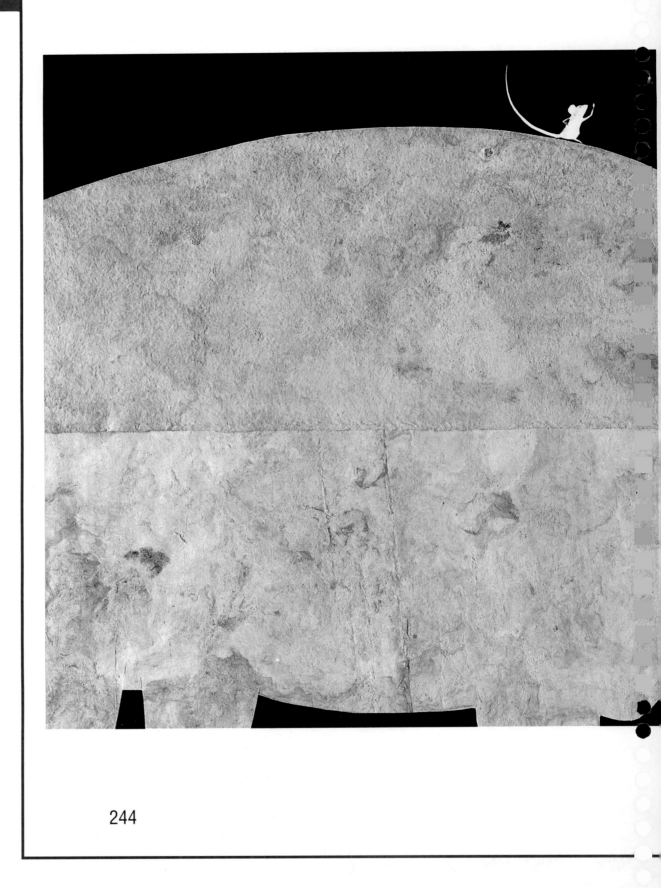

244

"Ah," said White Mouse. "Now, I see.
The Something is

       as sturdy as a pillar,

       supple as a snake,

       wide as a cliff,

       sharp as a spear,

       breezy as a fan,

       stringy as a rope,

but altogether the Something is . . .

20

245

Skills in Context

GRAMMAR REVIEW

Verbs

IS AND ARE Help children find
the verb *is* on **page 245.**

- Write *is* on the chalkboard or
  on chart paper.

- Discuss how this word shows
  what is happening now, not
  in the past.

Reread **page 245.** Lead children
to tell how the verb *is* would
change if the Something
became the Somethings.

MAKE SILLY SENTENCES Have
children create sentence subjects by brainstorming a list of
singular and plural nouns.
Record the list on the chalkboard. Children can create
sentences by adding the
descriptive phrases on **page
245** (for example, "as sturdy as
a pillar") to the nouns and con-
necting them with the appropriate form of *to be: is* or *are.*

See Take a Closer Look, **pages
105O-105P** for a lesson on *is*
and *are.*

Comprehension

STRATEGIC READING

21 **CONFIRM, REVISE PREDICTIONS**
What did White Mouse tell the others? **(The strange Something was an elephant.)** How does this compare with your prediction?

an elephant!" **21**

246

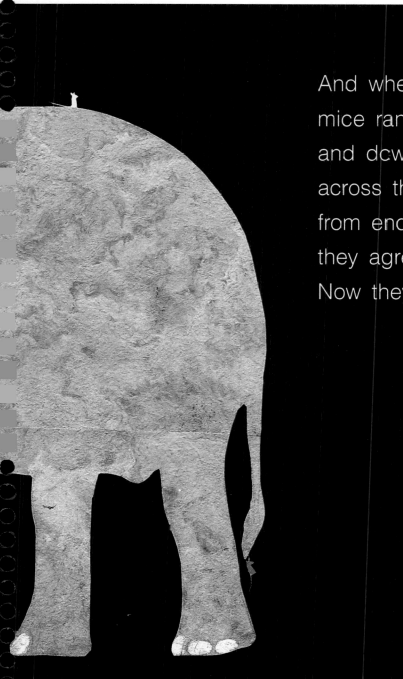

And when the other
mice ran up one side
and down the other,
across the Something
from end to end,
they agreed.
Now they saw, too.

247

Skills in Context

MULTICULTURAL
PERSPECTIVES

Elephants in India

Asiatic Elephants are found in India. The Asiatic elephant has an arched back and ears that are about half as large as those of an African elephant. They are not as large or as fierce as African elephants, and are much easier to tame.

In India, elephants are used in the logging industry. The elephant uses its trunk to lift or carry heavy logs, and also carries loads on its back.

Comprehension

STRATEGIC READING

22 What lesson did you learn from this story? (We should consider all sides of things carefully before we make decisions. If we only consider a part of something, we may make a mistake.)

ONGOING ASSESSMENT

☑ **MAKE, CONFIRM, OR REVISE PREDICTIONS**

Encourage children to personalize the strategy and its possible transfer to other situations by discussing these questions:

• In what ways might making, revising, or confirming predictions help you to understand and enjoy a story more?

• When might you use this strategy again?

FOR RESPONSE AND ASSESSMENT OPPORTUNITIES
see pages 249A–249B

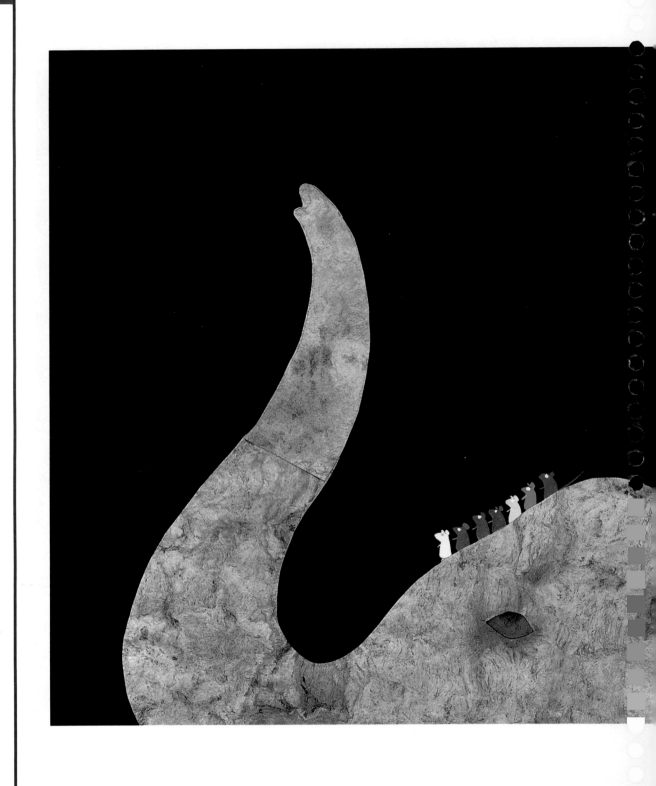

248

The Mouse Moral:
Knowing in part may make a fine tale,
but wisdom comes from seeing the whole.

22

249

Skills in Context

WRITING

Fable

Discuss the genre of "**Seven Blind Mice**" by examining these story elements:

- Did the mice in the story act like animals or people?

- Was the story true or was it make-believe?

- Did the story teach a good lesson?

Challenge children to work in small groups to plan a fable. Suggest that they begin by thinking of a lesson they would like to teach, then discuss how they could use animals to teach the lesson.

STRATEGY: CREATING CHECKLISTS Encourage each group to create a story map that outlines the setting, plot, and main characters of their fable. Ask them to make a checklist to review their story plans. They might ask themselves:

- Will our story involve animals that act like people?

- Will the story teach a lesson?

This strategy will help to prepare them for the writing process lessons on **pages 249M-N.**

Respond to the Literature

PERSONAL RESPONSE

JOURNAL WRITING

Children may use their journals to express their thoughts and questions about the selection. Their journals can be used to capture how the story made them feel. The following questions may help get them started:

- How did you feel when you found out what the strange Something was?
- What lesson was the author trying to convey?
- What surprised you as you read the selection?
- Why do you think the artist used color the way he did?

READER RESPONSE CARD 3, page T3

SMALL GROUP RESPONSE

JOURNAL ENTRIES

Children may work in small groups to discuss the selection. Encourage them to use their journals throughout the discussion.

READER RESPONSE CARD 3 is available to help guide the discussion.

To check story comprehension, you may want to assign **PRACTICE BOOK, page 227.**

WRITING ABOUT THE THEME

CRITICAL THINKING

How does **Seven Blind Mice** relate to the unit theme Surprises Along the Way? After discussions, children may understand why the mice were so surprised. Help them to realize that the animals were looking at small parts of a much bigger whole. Have children think about a time when they were surprised because they saw or heard only part of something. What lesson can children learn from reading this story?

QUICK WRITE

Invite partners to rewrite the Mouse Moral on **page 249,** using their own words.

Name: _____ Date: _____   **Seven Blind Mice** COMPREHENSION Story Comprehension

END IT

Underline the word that completes the sentence.

1. Red Mouse thought the leg was a ____.
   pillar   log
2. Green Mouse thought the trunk was a ____.
   worm   snake
3. Yellow Mouse thought the tusk was a ____.
   pin   spear
4. Purple Mouse thought the top of the head was a ____.
   cliff   mountain
5. Orange Mouse thought the ear was a ____.
   paper   fan
6. Blue Mouse thought the tail was a ____.
   string   rope
7. White Mouse thought the strange thing was an ____.
   ant   elephant
8. White Mouse was ____.
   right   wrong

Level 4/Unit 2   Extension: Challenge children to draw a picture showing something the
Story Comprehension   elephant and the seven mice might have done together.   227

PRACTICE BOOK, page 227

Comprehension Checkpoint

ACTIVITIES

INFORMAL ASSESSMENT

☑ MAKE, CONFIRM, OR REVISE PREDICTIONS

PROBLEM/SOLUTION CHART Display GRAPHIC ORGANIZER TRANSPARENCY/BLM 19 or put the following problem/solution chart on the chalkboard. Encourage children to think about the predictions they made. Guide them to see that the surprises happened because each mouse tried to solve the problem by touching just a small part of what was actually a whole elephant.

Problem What is the strange Something?	
Attempts	Outcomes
Red Mouse touches leg.	➡ Says it's a pillar
Green Mouse touches trunk.	➡ Says it's a snake
Yellow Mouse touches tusk.	➡ Says it's a spear
Purple Mouse climbs up the side to the top of the head.	➡ Says it's a cliff
Orange Mouse touches ear.	➡ Says it's a fan
Blue Mouse touches tail.	➡ Says it's a rope
White Mouse runs all over it.	➡ Says it's an elephant
Solution It's an elephant!	

Retell The Story Invite children to retell the story to a partner. Remind them to use the problem/solution chart to help them recall the events in the order in which they occurred in the story.

FORMAL ASSESSMENT

ONGOING ASSESSMENT

To test story comprehension and vocabulary, administer the multiple choice Selection Assessment for **Seven Blind Mice** in SELECTION AND UNIT ASSESSMENTS for Levels 4–5.

RETEACHING

ONGOING ASSESSMENT

For additional work with making, confirming, or revising predictions, use the Reteaching lesson on **page 221** or **RETEACHING BLM, page 141**.

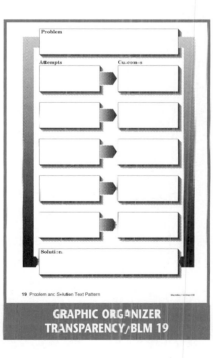

GRAPHIC ORGANIZER TRANSPARENCY/BLM 19

Extend Skills In Context

Literature-Based Instruction

To provide skills and strategies instruction to meet the needs of your children, select from these lessons.

☑ These skills are tested in the Unit Progress Assessment.

Meeting Individual Needs

*To provide additional literacy experiences tailored to specific students' needs and interests, use this literature and these resources. Activities are provided on **pages 249E–249F**.*

MULTILEVEL RESOURCES FOR FLEXIBLE GROUPING

EASY

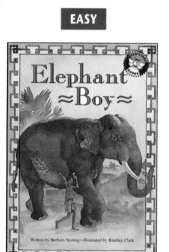

SPOTLIGHT: LITERACY SUPPORT

EARLY INTERVENTION
COMPREHENSION:
Make, Confirm, or Revise
Predictions

PHONICS AND DECODING:
Long Vowels and
Phonograms: /ī/-*ime*

EASY | AVERAGE

SPOTLIGHT: PHONICS/
DECODING

**PHONICS AND
DECODING**
☑ LONG VOWELS AND
PHONOGRAMS: /ī/-*ide*

'TRONIC PHONICS

💿 Also available on CD-ROM

EASY

SPOTLIGHT: VOCABULARY/
COMPREHENSION

VOCABULARY
• great
• strange
• agree
• elephant
• whole
• turn

COMPREHENSION
☑ MAKE, CONFIRM, OR REVISE
PREDICTIONS

EASY | AVERAGE

FISH FACES

THEME BIG BOOK

COMPREHENSION
☑ USE ILLUSTRATIONS

Meeting Individual Needs
Multilevel Resources

| **EASY** | **EARLY INTERVENTION** |

ELEPHANT BOY

REREAD A FAMILIAR BOOK
Children may read a story they have successfully read before, such as the **LITERACY SUPPORT BOOK**, *Sarah's Surprise.*

READ A NEW BOOK
Preview the **LITERACY SUPPORT BOOK** *Elephant Boy.* Use the illustrations and title to predict what the story will be about.

Read aloud the story. Point out the setting in this story. Have children chime in whenever you read *elephant.* On **page 2,** model how to make predictions. *This page tells me that Babu takes care of the elephants. I see Babu working in the picture. I predict that the next page will tell me more about Babu's work as an elephant boy.*

BUILD WORDS
Point out the word *time* in the first sentence on **page 5** of *Elephant Boy.* Children can brainstorm rhyming words for *time.* Then invite them to use the **Word Building Kit** to make other words with the *-ime* phonogram.

For a full lesson on long vowels and phonograms: /ī/-*ime* see Take a Closer Look **pages 43G–43I.**

WRITE SENTENCES
Have children compose sentences about the elephant boy's various jobs. Write the sentences on a chart or on sentence strips as children dictate. Have children copy the sentences. Invite them to reread their sentences, pointing to each word as they read. Reinforce vocabulary by having children point out specific words in their sentences. Invite children to illustrate their work.

READ INDEPENDENTLY
Have children read *Elephant Boy* independently. As they read aloud, note their achievements and praise them for their successes.

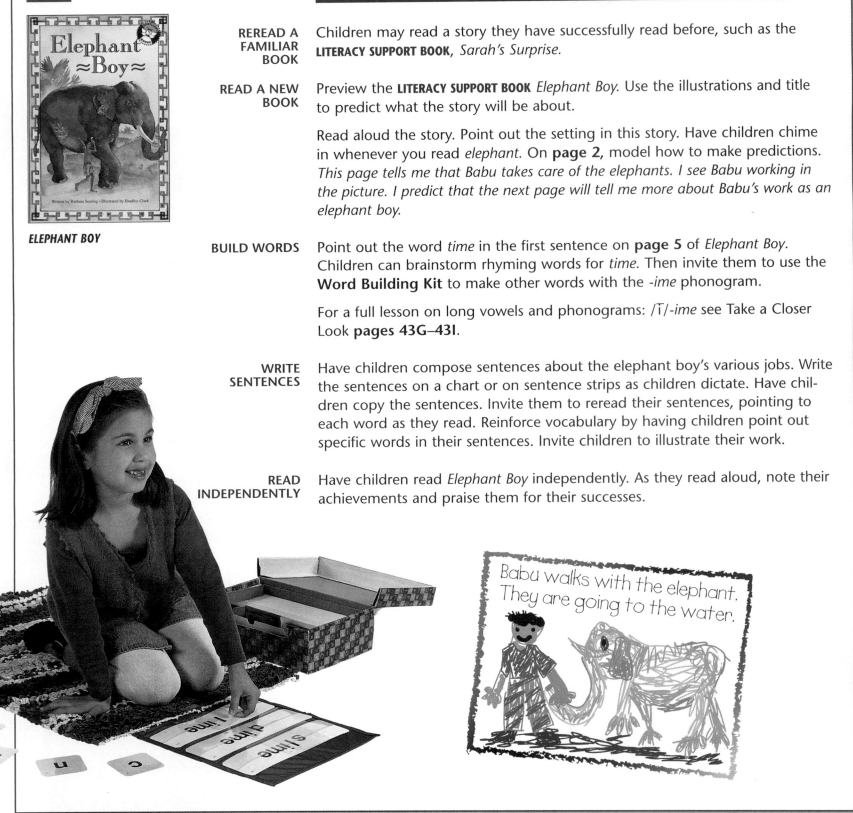

Babu walks with the elephant.
They are going to the water.

PHONICS AND DECODING

ACTIVITIES

WHAT A RIDE!

by Kathryn E. Lewis
illustrated by Esther Szededy

WHAT A RIDE!

'Tronic Phonics

☑ Long Vowels and Phonograms: /ī/-*ide*

PARTNER

PHONOGRAM SLIDE Draw an outline of a large slide on a bulletin board and label the picture *Slide*. Point out the phonogram *-ide*. As you read *What A Ride!*, have children listen for words that rhyme with *slide*. They can write the words on cards and post them on the bulletin board. **SPATIAL/LINGUISTIC**

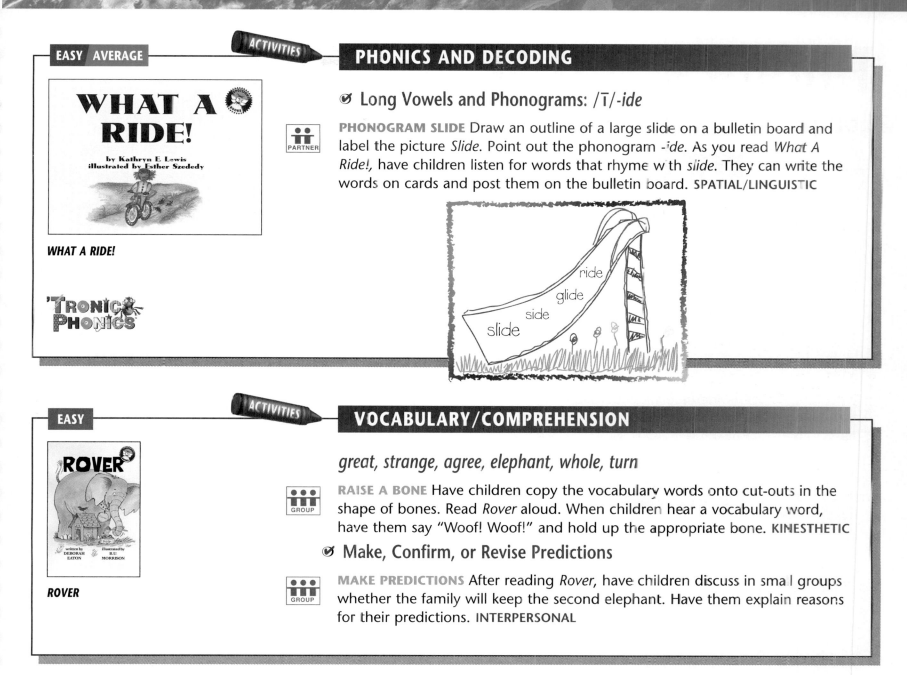

ride
glide
side
slide

VOCABULARY/COMPREHENSION

ACTIVITIES

ROVER

written by
DEBORAH
EATON

illustrated by
B.U.
MORRISON

ROVER

great, strange, agree, elephant, whole, turn

GROUP

RAISE A BONE Have children copy the vocabulary words onto cut-outs in the shape of bones. Read *Rover* aloud. When children hear a vocabulary word, have them say "Woof! Woof!" and hold up the appropriate bone. **KINESTHETIC**

☑ Make, Confirm, or Revise Predictions

GROUP

MAKE PREDICTIONS After reading *Rover*, have children discuss in small groups whether the family will keep the second elephant. Have them explain reasons for their predictions. **INTERPERSONAL**

COMPREHENSION

ACTIVITIES

FISH FACES

FISH FACES

☑ Use Illustrations

ONE

DESIGN A FISH After reading *Fish Faces*, invite children to draw their own imaginary superfish. Have children turn back and combine features from each of their favorite fish in their drawings. Encourage children to give their fish a name. **SPATIAL**

Dotted Snapper Fish

Phonics and Decoding

☑ **Long Vowels and Phonograms: /ī/-*ide***

① DEVELOP PHONEMIC AWARENESS

READ THE LITERATURE
- Reread **page 242** of "**Seven Blind Mice,**" emphasizing the word *side*. Then read the rhyme on **page 22** of the **BIG BOOK OF RHYMES AND CHIMES**, emphasizing the phonogram *-ide*.

SAY THE RHYME
- As you repeat the rhyme, encourage children to join in.
- Say the words *ride, glide,* and *side,* explaining that these words rhyme.
- As you say the following word pairs, have children hide their eyes if the words rhyme.
  wide/hide   pride/pile   tide/wide   slide/side   said/side

② DISCOVER THE SPELLING PATTERN

SHOW THE RHYME
- Display **page 22** of the **BIG BOOK OF RHYMES AND CHIMES**. As you point out the underlined letters in the word at the bottom of the page, have a volunteer read the word.
- Read the rhyme, pointing to each word. Frame the words *ride* and *glide,* and run your finger under the *-ide* phonogram in each word.
- Provide word cards with the words *side, said, tile, wide, bride, breed, hire, hide, pride.* Have children sort the cards into those that rhyme with *slide* and those that do not.

5-STEP PLAN

DECODING STRATEGIES: RHYMING, BLENDING

1 DEVELOP PHONEMIC AWARENESS

2 DISCOVER THE SPELLING PATTERN

3 USE DECODING STRATEGIES

4 WRITING

5 READING

DIGRAPHS

For additional lessons and practice with long ī, see **PHONICS SUPPORT BLM, pages 25** and **82.**

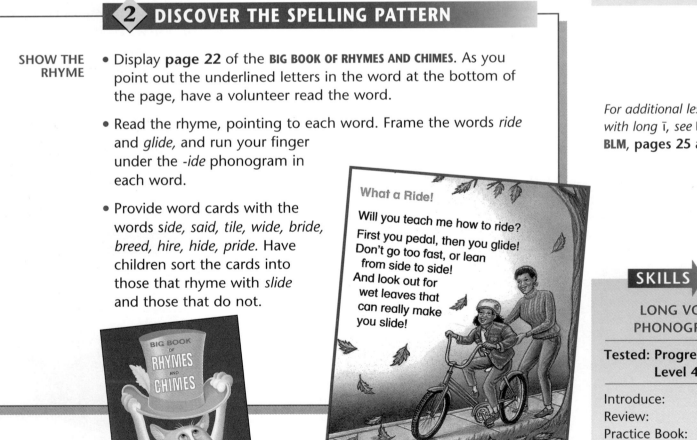

What a Ride!

Will you teach me how to ride?
First you pedal, then you glide!
Don't go too fast, or lean
from side to side!
And look out for
wet leaves that
can really make
you slide!

slide

BIG BOOK OF RHYMES AND CHIMES, page 22

SKILLS ▶ TRACE

LONG VOWELS AND PHONOGRAMS: /ī/-*ide*

Tested: Progress Assessment, Level 4, Unit 2

Introduce: Level 4: 249G
Review: Level 4: 261
Practice Book: 228, 233
Reteaching BLM: 145, 149

ACTIVITIES

③ DECODING STRATEGIES: BLENDING ACTIVITIES

MODEL THE STRATEGY
• Write the phonogram *-ide* on the chalkboard. Model the blending strategy by blending *r* and *-ide*.

THINK ALOUD *Now I'm going to build words with* -ide. *Let's add* r *to make the word* ride. *Listen as I blend the letters together:* r-ide. *Now let's build more words.*

CREATE WORDS
• Write the phonogram *-ide* on chart paper. Have children write letters on self-stick notes and hold them up in front of the phonogram.

• Help children blend the letters to see if they have made words. Record created words on the chart.

USE THE WORD BUILDING KIT
• Use the word building kit to continue modeling the blending strategy. Put cards with the phonogram *-ide* into each slot of the mini-pocket chart.

• Show how to place an acetate letter such as *r, h,* or *s,* in front of the phonogram to build a word, and model the blending strategy.

• Let children build more words, applying the blending strategy you modeled.

CONSONANT AND VOWEL PATTERNS: CVC*e*
• Write the word *ride* on chart paper. Point out the consonant/vowel/consonant/*e* pattern of the word. Write the word *hide* underneath. Point out the pattern again. Together, say the two words aloud, emphasizing the long *ī* sound. Point out that in a one-syllable word with a consonant/vowel/consonant/*e*, the vowel is usually long.

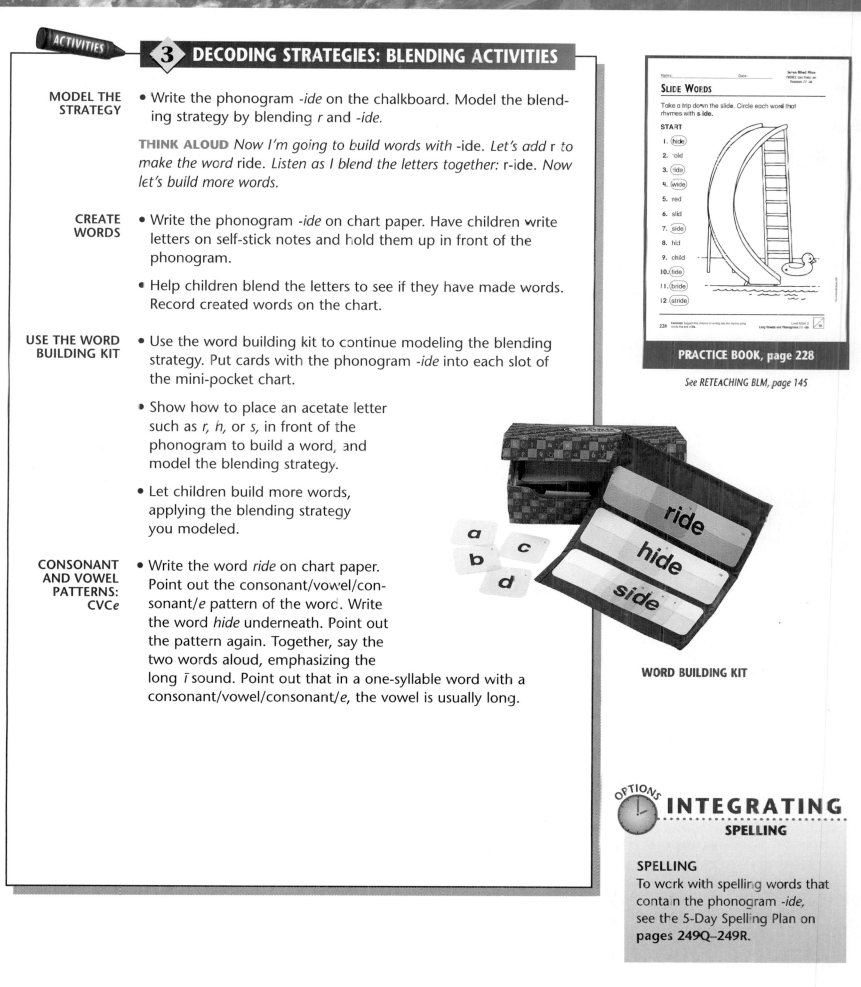

PRACTICE BOOK, page 228

See RETEACHING BLM, page 145

WORD BUILDING KIT

OPTIONS
INTEGRATING
SPELLING

SPELLING
To work with spelling words that contain the phonogram *-ide,* see the 5-Day Spelling Plan on **pages 249Q–249R.**

Phonics and Decoding

☑ **Long Vowels and Phonograms: /ī/-*ide***

ACTIVITIES

◆ 4 ◆ WRITING

USE THE PHONOGRAM

• Encourage children to work with a partner to brainstorm sentences containing two *-ide* words. Have them write and illustrate their sentences.

I can hide by the slide.

The bride took a ride.

The slide is wide.

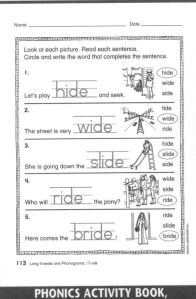

Name _____ Date _____

Look at each picture. Read each sentence.
Circle and write the word that completes the sentence.

1. Let's play ‾hide‾ and seek. hide / wide / side
2. The street is very ‾wide‾. tide / wide / ride
3. She is going down the ‾slide‾. hide / slide / side
4. Who will ‾ride‾ the pony? wide / side / ride
5. Here comes the ‾bride‾. ride / slide / bride

113 Long Vowels and Phonograms: /ī/-ide

PHONICS ACTIVITY BOOK, pages 113–114

ACTIVITIES

◆ 5 ◆ READING

READ "SEVEN BLIND MICE"

Remind children they will be encountering words with the phonogram *-ide* in books they read. As you reread **"Seven Blind Mice"** together, have volunteers point out the word *side* and suggest words that rhyme with it.

READ "WHAT A RIDE!"

Introduce small groups to "What a Ride!" Tell children to make a list of words with the phonogram *-ide* as they read the selection aloud. Children may recognize the rhyme from the **BIG BOOK OF RHYMES AND CHIMES**.

'TRONIC PHONICS

"What a Ride!" is also available in **'TRONIC PHONICS™** on CD-ROM. Children can work independently or in pairs to read the story, engage in blending activities, and write their own story.

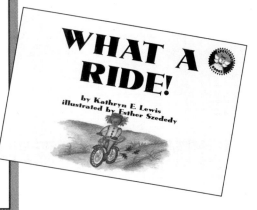

WHAT A RIDE!
by Kathryn E. Lewis
illustrated by Esther Szededy

SPOTLIGHT: PHONICS AND DECODING
What a Ride!

✔ Consonant Digraphs: /th/ *th*

DEVELOP PHONEMIC AWARENESS FOR /th/ *th*

READ ALOUD
- Ask children to listen as you read **page 226** of "Seven Blind Mice." Emphasize the digraph in the word *third*.
- Have children hold their thumbs up if the word you say has the same sound as *thumb*.

DEVELOP PRINT AWARENESS FOR /th/ *th*

FIND THE DIGRAPH
- Write the words *third* and *thumb* on the chalkboard and have volunteers underline the digraph in each word.
- Have children find the digraph *th* in the word *something* on **page 215** and on other pages of **"Seven Blind Mice."**
- Help children generate more words that begin with the digraph *th* and list them on the chalkboard.

ACTIVITIES

READ AND WRITE

HIDE AND FIND OTHER WORDS
- Invite children to look through their books for words that begin with the digraph *th*. Have them write words they find on cards and hide them around the classroom.

CREATE CLUE CARDS
- Have children brainstorm words that begin with the same sound as *third,* and write their suggestions on the chalkboard.
- Children can choose a word, and write clues telling what their word means.
- Children can exchange cards and guess the word.

PRACTICE BOOK, page 229

See RETEACHING BLM, page 146
See PHONICS ACTIVITY BOOK, pages 115–116

I think you sew with it.

SKILLS ✕ TRACE

CONSONANT DIGRAPHS: /th/ *th*

Tested: Progress Assessment, Level 4, Unit 2

Introduce:	Level 4: 249J
Review:	Level 5: 175
Practice Book:	229, 304
Reteaching BLM:	146, 206

Vocabulary

VOCABULARY REVIEW

great	strange	agree
elephant	whole	turn

WORD SEARCH Children can work in groups of three or four to search through old children's magazines or newspapers to find the vocabulary words. Have them cut out the paragraph containing the word and cross out the word with a marker. Children may then paste the paragraph to an index card and write the missing vocabulary word on the back of the card. The cards may be used to play a game: children earn points for their team by drawing a card and providing the correct vocabulary word.

great

strange

agree

elephant

whole

turn

VOCABULARY STRATEGY: Irregular Plurals

LINK TO LITERATURE Help children use context on page 215 of "**Seven Blind Mice**" to understand that *mice* is the irregular plural form of *mouse.*

"One day seven blind mice were surprised to find a strange Something by their pond."

Write *mouse* and *mice,* and have children identify which one means one and which means more than one. Elicit that *mice* is irregular because an "s" is usually added to a word to form the plural.

EXPLORE Children can sit in a circle and brainstorm examples of words that name more than one. Have them write the plural words on cards.

DISCUSS Talk about how the plural words on their cards differ from the singular form. Emphasize irregular plurals like *feet* and *hair.*

USE DIFFERENT MODALITIES Invite children to draw and label pictures illustrating the singular and plural form of an irregular plural noun.

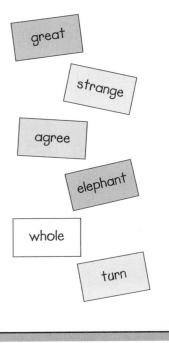

Listening, Speaking, Viewing

ROLE-PLAY

 Invite children to choose their favorite mouse from the story to role-play. Encourage them to verbalize the thoughts of the mouse as it encountered the elephant and came to a conclusion.

VIEWING AND LISTENING TIPS Encourage children to recall the story as they watch the role-plays and then compare the dramatization with the text. Remind them to listen carefully to see if role-plays accurately portray the mice and their conclusions.

ORAL LANGUAGE DEVELOPMENT

VIEW AND EVALUATE ILLUSTRATIONS Have children study the illustration that shows their favorite mouse examining the elephant in **"Seven Blind Mice."** Invite them to select the illustration they like best and explain to their partner why they like it. Children can also discuss what else each mouse may have thought the strange Something was. Encourage partners to ask each other questions, such as 'How did the strange Something feel?" and "Were you scared to touch it?"

CHORAL READING

Invite children to participate in the choral reading "Yellow Butter" from the book of **Read Alouds, Plays, and Choral Readings.** Children may also want to perform the play "A Pinch of Pepper" in a Reader's Theater.

SPEAKING TIPS Encourage children to adjust their volume and tone to add life to the words as they perform their roles.

ADDITIONAL RESOURCES

STORYTELLING Read aloud the folk tale "Test of a Friendship" from the book of **Read Alouds, Plays, and Choral Readings.**

LISTEN TO THE STORY If children haven't already done so, they can listen to the **LISTENING LIBRARY AUDIOCASSETTE** for a dramatic reading of "Seven Blind Mice."

LISTEN TO THE SONG Invite children to listen to the song "Surprise! Surprise!"on the **SONGS AND STORIES AUDIOCASSETTES.**

PORTFOLIO

Tape record children's choral readings. You may also want to videotape their role-plays and performances to include in their portfolios.

OPPORTUNITIES

Writing

Writing Process: Explanatory Writing

Remind children that the mice in **"Seven Blind Mice"** liked to go to the pond. Invite children to talk about favorite places they like to go. Perhaps they have a favorite pet or toy. Encourage them to write a paragraph, explaining why the place or thing is their favorite.

PREWRITING

Help children brainstorm a list of details that describe their topic. Tell them to imagine they are telling their best friend about it. Children might think, "What do I like about it?" or "What makes it special?"

DRAFTING

Children can use their lists to help them write their explanations. Remind them that now is the time to link ideas. They can check their grammar, spelling, and punctuation at a later point.

REVISING

Help children go over their drafts to see if their paragraph needs improvement. Is it interesting to read? Does it explain why something is their favorite? They may want to have a partner read it and suggest corrections.

REVISING STRATEGY: CREATING CHECKLISTS

Sometimes writers make a list of things they will look for as they read their draft. Creating checklists is a useful tool for improving writing. Have children create checklists to help them revise their writing. They might check for things such as:

• Do I have an interesting opening sentence?

• Have I included the most important ideas about my favorite thing?

• Did I repeat any information?

PROOFREADING

After children have finished rewriting their story, help them create and use another checklist for spelling, grammar, and punctuation. If you have presented the grammar lesson on **pages 249O–249P**, encourage them to check for the correct use of the verbs *go* and *went*.

PUBLISHING

Children may draw a picture of their favorite thing to accompany their paragraphs. Display their work in a classroom exhibit for everyone to enjoy.

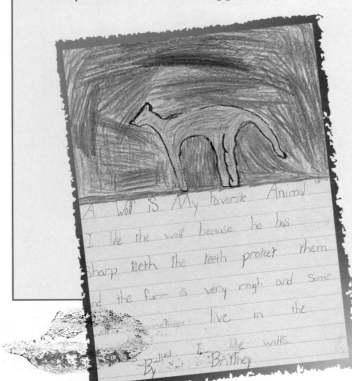

RUBRIC FOR EXPLANATORY WRITING	
4	**EXCELLENT** This paper clearly sets forth a variety of reasons for the writer's choice. The ideas are developed well and organized thoughtfully.
3	**GOOD** This explanation sets forth a variety of reasons for the writer's choice.
2	**FAIR** The details in this explanation may be too few and not adequately developed.
1	**POOR** This paper does not fulfill the assignment. It may neglect to offer reasons for the writer's opinion.

Writing Projects

 Tronic Phonics *The* **Make a Book** *section allows children to write and illustrate their own stories.*

PROJECT 1

WEEKLY CALENDAR In the story, a different mouse went to inspect the strange Something each day. Make a calendar that shows the days of the week. Draw and label something you might see on each day. Be sure to show seven different things. **EASY**

PROJECT 2

ANIMAL SURPRISES Animals are full of surprises! Draw a picture of an unusual animal. Then list two or three surprising facts about it. You may wish to use an encyclopedia or other reference book to help you.

AVERAGE

PROJECT 3

WHO AM I? PARAGRAPH Each part of the elephant was mistaken for a similar object in the story **"Seven Blind Mice."** Choose another animal. What parts of the animal remind you of other familiar items? Write a short paragraph that describes how the animal is like some of the objects you see around you. **CHALLENGE**

GRAMMAR, MECHANICS, AND USAGE If you have already presented the grammar lesson on **pages 249O–249P** or in the **GRAMMAR MINILESSONS, page 22,** remind children to check their use of the verbs *go* or *went* in their writing.

SPELLING Children may pick words from their writing to add to their personal spelling list. See also the spelling lesson on **pages 249Q–249R.**

PORTFOLIO

OPPORTUNITIES

Invite children to choose examples from their writing to include in their portfolios.

5-Day Plan
Grammar

GO AND *WENT*

MEETING INDIVIDUAL NEEDS

Second-Language Support
To emphasize verb tense, children may pantomime sentences such as "Three children go to the front." Then have them discuss what they just did.

DAY 1

Daily Language Activity

Write the sentences on the chalkboard each day or use Transparency 7. Have children orally make each sentence tell about the past.

1. One day the mice go to the pond. went
2. They go last week. went
3. Then they all go home. went

DAY 2

Daily Language Activity

Present these sentences and have children orally make each sentence tell about now.

1. Now the mice went one at a time. go
2. Red Mouse went to look first. goes
3. Green Mouse went next. goes

TEACH GO AND *WENT*

FROM THE LITERATURE

INTRODUCE Read the second sentence on **page 228** of "**Seven Blind Mice**": "He went on Thursday." Ask children to identify the verb and tell when the action is happening. (*went;* in the past)

IDENTIFY PRESENT AND PAST TENSE

DEVELOP/APPLY Present the sentences shown below. Ask children to explain how the verbs are different.

Harold goes home in the car today.
The children go home on the bus today.
They went home on the bus yesterday.

The verb *went* shows action that happened in the past. The verbs *go* and *goes* show the same action happening now. Point out the special spelling of *goes,* which tells what one person does now.

SUMMARIZE

CLOSE Help children list rules for *go* and *went*.

GO AND *WENT*

• The words *go* and *goes* tell about something that is happening now.
• The word *went* tells about something that happened in the past.

USING GO AND WENT

Remember
Some verbs have special forms for the past. The past tense of **go** is **went**.

Read each sentence.
Draw a line under the past tense verb.

1. The children went to the fair.
2. Jojo went to the ring.
3. The boys and girls go to school.
4. They went around the ring.
5. Circle the numbers of the sentences that have the past tense verb **went**.

   1   2   3   4

DAY 1, GRAMMAR PRACTICE BOOK, page 101

USING GO FOR PRESENT TENSE

Remember
The verb **go** tells about actions that happen now.
Use **goes** when you tell about one person.
Use **go** when you tell about more than one person.

Look at the pictures.
Write **go** or **goes** in each sentence.

1. Pat _____ for her _____ lesson.
2. Pete also _____ today to play the _____ .
3. Lee and Ann _____ next for _____ lessons.
4. Who _____ last to play the _____ ?

DAY 2, GRAMMAR PRACTICE BOOK, page 102

DAY 3

Daily Language Activity

Present these sentences and have children orally make each sentence tell about the past.

1. Yellow Mouse goes to the pond on Wednesday. **went**
2. Purple Mouse goes on Thursday. **went**
3. Orange Mouse goes on Friday. **went**

WRITING APPLICATION

DESCRIBING A PLACE

PARTNER

Children can work in pairs to write a description of a place they have visited. Encourage them to tell how often they go there and what they did when they went there. Have children identify the verbs *go* and *went* in their paragraphs.

GRAMMAR/MECHANICS CHECKLIST

Children may check that

- they have used *goes* to tell what one person or thing does now.
- they have used *go to* tell what more than one person or thing does now.
- they have used *went* to tell about things that happened in the past.

DAY 4

Daily Language Activity

Present these sentences and have children orally make each sentence tell about now.

1. All the mice went to see the strange Something. **go**
2. Each mouse went right up to it. **goes**
3. Purple Mouse went up a cliff. **goes**

QUICK WRITE

TELL WHAT HAPPENED

Ask children to write a sentence telling what any one of the mice did to find out what the strange Something was. Have children check verb tenses when finished.

DAY 5

Daily Language Activity

Present these sentences and have children orally make each sentence tell about the past.

1. Finally White Mouse goes to the pond. **went**
2. The mice go up and down the elephant. **went**
3. They go from end to end. **went**

See pages 22 of the GRAMMAR MINILESSONS *for more information on go and went.*

USE WENT FOR PAST TENSE

Remember
Some verbs have special forms for the past tense. Use **went** for the past tense of **go**.

Fill in the missing verb. Write the past tense form **went**.

1. Jason _____ to see the fan.
2. Pam _____ the next day.
3. Soon the whole class _____ .
4. Our teachers _____ with us.
5. Color the bands on the fan. Use red for present tense. Use blue for past tense.

DAY 3, GRAMMAR PRACTICE BOOK, page 103

USING GO OR WENT

Remember
Use **go** to tell about actions that happen now. Use **went** to tell about past actions.

Write **go** or **went** in each sentence. Write **went** to tell about past actions.

1. Now, the children _____ out.
2. Yesterday, Lily _____ to see her friend.
3. The day before, Manny _____ , too.
4. Now, Janet and Lee _____ for a walk.
5. Yesterday, Jasper _____ to the pond.

DAY 4, GRAMMAR PRACTICE BOOK, page 104

WRITING WITH GO AND WENT

Remember
Use past tense verbs when you tell about something that already happened. The children **went** out in the snow.

The sentences tell about an event. Write **went** to tell about past actions.

1. Boys and girls _____ to the top of the hill.
2. Each child _____ down the hill on a sled.
3. Everyone _____ down more than once.
4. Lee _____ down on her sled five times.

DAY 5, GRAMMAR PRACTICE BOOK, page 105

5-Day Plan
Spelling

DAY 1

BEGIN WITH A PRETEST

ASSESS PRIOR KNOWLEDGE: WORDS WITH /ī/-*ide*

Use the dictation sentences below and **page 101** of the **SPELLING ACTIVITY BOOK** for the pretest. A Student Record form is provided.

Allow children to correct their own papers. Ask them to pay special attention to the words they misspelled.

SPELLING WORDS /ī/-*ide*			CHALLENGE WORDS	
side	slide	hide	first	find
wide	ride			

*Note: Words in **dark type** are from the story.*

DICTATION SENTENCES

SPELLING WORDS

1. The mouse ran up the elephant's <u>side</u>.
2. She thought the Something was very <u>wide</u>.
3. One mouse thought a tusk was a <u>slide</u>.
4. Did any of the mice get a <u>ride</u>?
5. Where can an elphant <u>hide</u>?

CHALLENGE WORDS

6. Who will be the <u>first</u> to go?
7. We will <u>find</u> out what it is.

DAY 2

EXPLORE THE SPELLING PATTERN

IDENTIFY THE PHONOGRAM -*ide*

Write the following consonants or blends on the chalkboard or chart paper: *s, w, h, r, sl*. Provide children with 6" x 6" cards and have them write the letters *ide* on them. Invite volunteers to come to the board and place their cards next to one of the consonants or blends. Together read the word that is formed. When all five spelling words have been formed, have children copy them onto a piece of paper, circling the *ide* in each word.

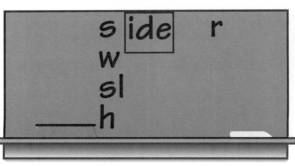

DAY 1, SPELLING ACTIVITY BOOK, page 101

DAY 2, SPELLING ACTIVITY BOOK, page 102

DAY 3

CONSTRUCTING WORDS

CREATING COLORFUL WORDS

Give each child five yellow strips of paper (2" x 2") and five orange strips of paper (3" x 2"). On each of the yellow strips, have children write one of the following consonants or blends: s, w, sl, r, h. On each of the orange strips, have children write the phonogram *ide*. Have children place all the strips face down on their desk. Then invite them to turn over one yellow strip and one orange strip and place them together. Have them read the word they have created and write it on another sheet of paper.

WORK WITH MEANING

MAKE A PICTURE DICTIONARY

Remind children that many dictionaries include illustrations of some of the words. Talk about the spelling words, and discuss the kind of pictures that might help a person understand their meanings. Invite pairs of children to select a Spelling Word and draw a picture that illustrates its meaning.

The optional extension activity for the Challenge Word on **page 103** of the **SPELLING ACTIVITY BOOK** may be assigned on Day 3.

DAY 4

SPELLING AND WRITING

SILLY PHRASES

Invite partners to create silly phrases using two or more Spelling Words. Encourage them to illustrate their phrases.

a wide slide

Hide on the side of the slide.

DAY 5

END WITH A POSTTEST

REASSESS CHILDREN'S KNOWLEDGE

Use **page 105** of the **SPELLING ACTIVITY BOOK** or the dictation sentences on **page 249Q** for the posttest. Children can record their scores on the Student Record form provided.

DAY 3, SPELLING ACTIVITY BOOK, page 103

DAY 4, SPELLING ACTIVITY BOOK, page 104

DAY 5, SPELLING ACTIVITY BOOK, page 105

Reading Resources
Study Skills

BOOK PARTS

For PUPIL EDITION, see page 288

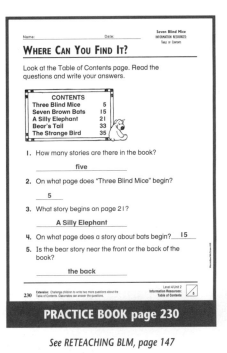

PRACTICE BOOK page 230

See RETEACHING BLM, page 147

☑ Use Parts of a Book

INTRODUCE Discuss with children how the mice in **"Seven Blind Mice"** learned about the elephant. Invite ideas about how children might find information about elephants. Point out that books have special parts to help readers locate certain types of information.

DEVELOP/APPLY Have children turn to **page 290** in their anthologies and describe what they see. Point out that both of these pages would be found at the front of a book.

Direct attention to the **title page.** Have children identify the kind of information provided, including the book title, subtitle, author, photographer, publisher, and place of publication. Mention other items that may also be found, including the illustrator, translator, and publication date. Have children find the book title, author, photographer, and publisher on **page 290.**

Ask children to identify the information on the **table of contents** page. Discuss that this is a list of the stories,

chapters, units, or other parts of a book. Then have them refer to the table of contents to answer these questions:

- On what page does information about elephant families begin?
- Would you look in the beginning, middle, or back part of the book for "Elephants in Danger"?
- Where would you find information about the elephant's trunk?

CLOSE Invite each child to choose a book from the classroom or library and identify the author, title, illustrator (if there is one), publisher and place of publication.

Instruct children to find the table of contents in this book. Assign a unit or selection to children and have them find the page on which it begins.

Multicultural Perspectives

FABLES

◆◆

Seven Blind Mice" is based on an ancient form of storytelling called the fable—a part of many cultures for over a thousand years. Fables are short narratives meant to teach a moral lesson. Generally, the characters in fables are animals who engage in an act that is meant to convey wisdom about proper behavior.

Perhaps the best known fables are those attributed to the ancient Greek, Aesop. It is believed that he lived in Greece between 620 and 560 B.C. Aesop used his fables to express his political beliefs at a time when free speech was prohibited.

The Panchatantra was written in Kashmir in about 200 B.C. Unlike the pithy tales of Aesop, these stories were long and involved, and even included lengthy poems.

> *Fables have been an important cultural tradition the world over for more than one thousand years.*

Jean de la Fontaine became one of the most famous writers of fables. He wrote in France in the seventeenth century, and was called the fable-teller. La Fontaine wrote in verse, and followed Aesop's technique of using animal characters to convey a moral message.

In African fables, often the "star" of such tales is Anansi, a spider who outwits every creature in the jungle through his craftiness.

In the Americas, the Yurok of the Southwest weave stories around Coyote, a foolish fellow whose greed and stupidity lead him into misadventure. In the Southeast, the Muskogee use the heron and hummingbirds in fables. One tale features these creatures in a race similar to Aesop's "Hare and the Tortoise."

Fable Fest

Invite children to visit the library and ask the librarian to show them collections of fables. Have each child choose a favorite fable and present it orally to the class. Children may wish to use puppets in their retellings.

Across the Curriculum

MATH

GROUP

MICE IN A ROW
30 minutes

Materials: chalk; chalkboard; colored paper; stapler; scissors; marker; labels

LEARNING ABOUT NUMBERS

Children can learn about ordinal numbers.

- Invite volunteers to be the seven blind mice. Identify each mouse by having the child wear a headband of colored construction paper.

- Volunteers should arrange themselves in the order in which the mice appear in the story.

- Label each mouse with the numerals 1 through 7. Then discuss who went first, second, third, and so on, writing the ordinal number names on the chalkboard.

KINESTHETIC/LOGICAL/MATHEMATICAL

MUSIC

PARTNER

SEVEN BLIND MICE
2 hours

Materials: paper; pencil

CREATING SONGS

Children can substitute story-related lyrics for the lyrics of the song "Three Blind Mice."

- Hum the melody to the song "Three Blind Mice." Invite partners to create a similar song called "Seven Blind Mice."

- Encourage them to use story events in the correct order for the lyrics of their song.

- Allow children time to revise their songs if necessary.

- Invite children to sing their song to others.

LINGUISTIC/MUSICAL

SCIENCE

A JUNGLE ANIMAL
45 minutes

Materials: reference books on jungle animals; art supplies

MAKING WORD WEBS
Children can make animal word webs.

- Talk about where the elephant in this story might live. Use this opportunity to invite children to learn about jungles and other animals that might live there with the elephant.

- Children may choose a jungle animal. Have them find out what it looks like, where it lives, and what it eats.

- Help children make a word web for their animal. Have them draw and label a picture of the animal. They can add facts in boxes around the drawing with lines leading to the animal.

SPATIAL/LOGICAL

ART

STRANGE SOMETHINGS
40 minutes

Materials: art supplies; wallpaper; wrapping paper; fabric scraps

MAKING AN ANIMAL COLLAGE
Children can make textured collage pictures.

- Refer to the collage picture of the elephant in **"Seven Blind Mice."** Invite children to make a picture of an animal of their choice using a variety of differently textured materials.

- When they have dried, display them on a table and invite children to close their eyes and gently feel one of the collages. Can they guess which animal it is by feeling the shape?

SPATIAL/KINESTHETIC

Spotlight on Inquiry

EXPLORE MULTIPLE SOURCES

Encourage children to use various resources, including this selection, to pursue ideas related to "**Seven Blind Mice.**" Use the questions below as well as children's questions to generate interest and inquiry.

- How else can we learn about elephants?

- What other things can be confusing if looked at only in parts?

THE ELEPHANT'S TRUNK

PREVIEW/QUESTIONS Introduce the selection to answer the first inquiry above. Then ask:

- As you scan the pictures, do you think this reading will be a story or will give facts about elephants?

- What kind of information about elephants will this reading provide?

THE ELEPHANT'S TRUNK

The elephant's trunk is wonderful. It can do many things.

A mother elephant gently pushes her calf with her trunk. She lets her calf know she is close behind.

250

- *Look Again!* Tana Hoban, New York: Macmillan Publishing Co., Inc., 1971. A book of photographs shown first in part, then in their entirety. No text.
- *Mouse Views: What the Class Pet Saw.* Bruce MacMillan, New York: Holiday House, 1993. Close-up photos are revealed to be everyday things by turning the page.

An elephant gets food with its trunk. It uses the trunk to pull up grass and lift it to the mouth.

When an elephant sleeps, it rests its trunk. It can fold the trunk on its tusks.

251

STRATEGIC READING

Read each portion of the text aloud with the class. Encourage children to analyze the text and photographs to find out general facts about elephants. Invite children to help you chart their observations and see how they add to understanding elephant behavior. **(GRAPHIC ORGANIZER TRANSPARENCY/BLM 31) ANALYZE INFORMATION**

OBSERVATIONS	INFORMATION
Mother elephant pushes calf along.	Baby elephants are cared for by adults.
Elephant pulls up grass.	Elephants eat plants.
Elephant sleeps and rests trunk	Elephants need rest just like we do.
Elephants play and hold each other.	Elephants enjoy being together.

31 Chart

GRAPHIC ORGANIZER TRANSPARENCY/BLM 31

Spotlight on Inquiry

LINKS ACROSS THE LITERATURE
Invite children to discuss thoughts about why and how **"The Elephant's Trunk"** and **"Seven Blind Mice"** go together. Have them compare ways in which each selection looks at elephants. How do we learn about elephants from each selection? What type of pictures does each include? Which reading is more enjoyable? Enter responses in a chart such as the one below.
(GRAPHIC ORGANIZER TRANSPARENCY/ BLM 31) ORGANIZE INFORMATION

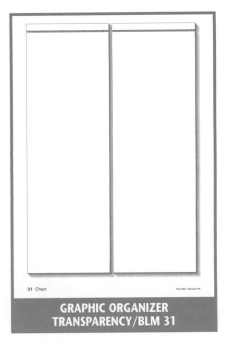

31 Chart   Macmillan / McGraw-Hill

**GRAPHIC ORGANIZER
TRANSPARENCY/BLM 31**

252

SEVEN BLIND MICE	THE ELEPHANT'S TRUNK
• Story	• Magazine Article
• We learn about elephants through experiences of blind mice.	• We learn about elephants through information presented in text and photographs.
• Creative Illustrations	• Nature Photographs

MAKE IT REAL!

PARTNER Have children work in pairs to create two drawings of an animal. Partners should choose an animal and discuss the ways one of the seven blind mice might "see" a part of the animal. Let partners decide who will draw the animal in the way discussed and who will draw the entire animal as it might really look. Encourage children to create captions for each drawing before displaying them in a central area. Provide time for children to visit the class "gallery" and view one another's work.

Elephants use their trunks to play.
They tug and push.
They hold on to each other.

253

Poetry

READING THE POEM

TEACHER READ ALOUD Before children look at the illustration, have them listen carefully as you read the poem aloud. Then have them sketch their favorite thing described in the poem. Children can discuss how their images are different or similar to those the artist imagined. Use **LISTENING LIBRARY AUDIOCASSETTE** for a reading of "**Things That Happen.**"

CRAWLING CRITTERS This poem lends itself especially well to dramatic interpretation. Divide the class into groups, assigning each a creature from the poem. Have each group pantomime the particular action described as you read the poem aloud. All groups can pantomime the rising sun at the end of the poem. Invite the children to chime in the final four lines.

LITERARY DEVICES AND TECHNIQUES

IMAGERY Point out to children that poets use words to paint pictures in the minds of readers. The pictures can make us feel happy, sad, angry, or excited. Read the poem again, inviting children to identify the pictures the poet has painted in their minds. Have children share how the images made them feel.

THINGS THAT HAPPEN

Only a while ago,
I saw a snail
running
down the road,
a worm
hopping,
and heard
a toad
singing
like a bird.

The sun rises!
The sun rises!
Can there be
Still more surprises?

Felice Holman

254

POETRY TALK

GROUP Children can discuss their personal responses to the poem and talk about these and other questions in small groups.

- The poet talks about many surprises. Which one would surprise you the most?

- How would you feel if you saw animals doing the things the poet talks about?

- How do you think the poet feels about the sun rising? How would a sunrise make you feel?

- Which would make you more excited—a sunrise or a singing toad? Why?

- Why did the poet say "Can there be still more surprises?"

MEET THE POET

ABOUT FELICE HOLMAN Felice Holman says that, since the time she was a child, she has always been writing something. She especially likes writing for children. She explains, "Since young people are going to be grown up people very soon, I think they are probably the most important people around. It gives me a lot of satisfaction to be talking to the most important people around."

The Surprise Family

Selection Summary

A boy becomes a chick's unlikely mother. The beloved bird soon grows up and decides she wants to become a mother, too. The two of them come across a nest of eggs only to find out later that the hen's adopted brood is not quite what a hen would expect. The babies turn out to be ducks. But the chicken loves them anyway.

Linking Skills to Literature

Key Comprehension Strategies/Skills

☑ **ANALYZE CHARACTER, PLOT, SETTING**

ANALYZING CHARACTER, PLOT, SETTING The offbeat nature of this story—a hen mothering a group of ducklings—is perfect for children to explore character types. What the characters do is directly related to their setting and relationship to one another.

INTERACTING WITH THE TEXT

ENGAGE THE READER Children will have an opportunity to intereact with the text through analyzing the characters, plot and setting. Charting characters' actions and acting out the story are enjoyable ways to build comprehension.

See **pages 256H** and **256,** where the story pages begin.

WRITER   ILLUSTRATOR

LYNN REISER

Lynn Reiser wrote "**The Surprise Family**" to show that families are full of surprises. "All families are surprise families. Parents and children meet as strangers and grow up together, surprising one another with interests and talents that are not exactly what had been expected. And they continue to love each other anyway."

Lynn would like to write and illustrate more children's books. She says, "One of the most rewarding things about writing is that it can be shared with other people. I want children to enjoy reading as much as I do."

Other Books by Lynn Reiser
• *Two Mice in Three Fables* (Greenwillow, 1995)
• *Bedtime Cat* (Greenwillow, 1991)

Suggested Lesson Planner
With Flexible Grouping Options

WEEK AT A GLANCE	PART 1 — DAY 1 — FOCUS ON READING	PART 2 — DAY 2 — READ THE LITERATURE
THE SURPRISE FAMILY by LYNN REISER ◆ **Reading** ◆ **Writing** ◆ **Listening, Speaking, Viewing**	Preview the Selection, 256E ● Build Background, 256E Graphic Organizer Transparency/BLM 14 ● Oral Language Activities, 256F See also ESL/Second-Language Teacher's Guide, 215–223 Vocabulary, 256G Instructional Vocabulary *everywhere* *drink* *afternoon* *swim* *farther* *nest* Vocabulary Transparency/BLM 8 Practice Book, 231 If you wish to have children begin reading the selection at this point, see page 256H.	Set Purposes, 256H Journal Writing Suggestions for Reading, 256H ● Read Independently ●● Read Aloud ● Read Together Read and Teach Teach Strategic Reading, 256H-285 ☑ Analyze Character, Plot, Setting
◆ **Phonics and Decoding**	☑ Develop Phonemic Awareness for *-ay*, 285G Long *a*: Lessons and Practice ● Phonics Support BLM 24,80	☑ Discover the Spelling Pattern *-ay*, 285G
◆ **Spelling**	For a detailed 5-day lesson plan for spelling, see pages 285Q–285R. Pretest (long *a*), 285Q Words in dark type appear in the story. *away* *anyway* bay *day* say Spelling Activity Book, 106	● Challenge Words *every* *only* Explore the Pattern, 285Q–285R Spelling Activity Book, 107
◆ **Grammar, Mechanics, and Usage**	Daily Language Activity: *Was* and *Were* 1. The egg were ready to hatch. (was) 2. The chick's mother were a boy. (was) 3. The boy and the chick was happy together. (were) Grammar Practice Book: *Was* and *Were*, 106 ● Grammar Minilessons, 22 See pages 285O–285P	Daily Language Activity: *Was* and *Were* 1. The boy were kind to the chick. (was) 2. She were safe in his pocket. (was) 3. Both of them was warm under the quilt. (were) 5-Day Grammar Plan: *Was* and *Were*, 285O–285P Grammar Practice Book: *Was* and *Were*, 107

Flexible Grouping Options
● Extra Support
● Challenge
● Second-Language Support
☑ These core skills are tested in the Unit Progress Assessment.

DAY 3 *READ THE LITERATURE*	PART **3** **DAY 4** *EXTEND SKILLS IN CONTEXT*	**DAY 5** *EXTEND SKILLS IN CONTEXT*
Respond to the Literature Journal Writing, 285A ● Writing About the Theme, 285A Practice Book, 239 Comprehension Checkpoint, 285B ☑ Analyze Character, Plot, Setting Practice Book, 235 Graphic Organizer Transparency/BLM 30 ● Reteaching ☑ Analyze Character, Plot, Setting, 271 Practice Book, 235 Vocabulary Selection Assessment Selection Assessment/Unit Progress Assessment, Levels 4/5	Skills in Context ☑ Problem and Solution, 259 Practice Book, 232 ●☑ Long Vowels and Phonograms: /ī/ -*ide*, 261 Practice Book, 233 Foreshadow, 263 Directionality, 265 Unfamiliar Words, 267 ●☑ Short Vowels and Phonograms: /a/ -*at*, 269 Practice Book, 234 ●☑ Character, Plot, Setting, 271 Practice Book, 235 ●●● Multilevel Resources, 285B–285D ●● Vocabulary, 285K Listening, Speaking, Viewing, 285L Across the Curriculum, 285U	Skills in Context Humor, 273 ●☑ Consonant Blends: /sw/*sw*, 275 Practice Book, 236 Reread, 277 ☑ Summarize, 279 Practice Book, 237 ☑ Compare and Contrast, 281 Practice Book, 238 Ducks, 283 Story: Beginning, Middle, End, 285 Writing Process: Descriptive Paragraph, 285M ●● Writing Projects, 285N Study Skills/Reading Resources: Follow Directions, 285S Practice Book, 242 Multicultural Perspectives What Makes a Family?, 285T Across the Curriculum, 285V
☑ Decoding Strategies: Blending Activities, 285H Practice Book, 240 b|ay d|ay s|ay	☑ Writing with the Phonogram, 285H ● Phonics Activity Book, 117–118	☑ Reading with the Phonogram, 285I ☑ Consonant Blends: /skw/*squ*, 285J Practice Book, 241 ● Phonics Activity Book, 119–120 ● 'Tronic Phonics™
Constructing Words, 285R Work with Meaning, 285R Spelling Activity Book, 108	Spelling and Writing, 285R Spelling Activity Book, 109	Posttest, 285R Spelling Activity Book, 110
Daily Language Activity: *Was* and *were* 1. Soon the chick were a hen. (was) 2. The hen were afraid to swim. (was) 3. Her babies was all good swimmers. (were) Writing Application: A News Story, 285P Grammar Practice Book: *Was* and *Were*, 108	Daily Language Activity: *Was* and *Were* 1. The hen's babies was ducklings. (were) 2. Their beaks was not pointed. (were) 3. Their feet was webbed. (were) Quick Write: Personal Narrative, 285P Grammar Practice Book: *Was* and *Were*, 109	Daily Language Activity: *Was* and *Were* 1. The babies was not chicks. (were) 2. The hen were surprised. (was) 3. The hen and the ducks was a family. (were) Grammar Practice Book: *Was* and *Were*, 110; Answer Key and Grammar Assessment, 25

Prepare to Read

PREVIEW THE SELECTION

AUTHOR, ILLUSTRATOR Read about author/illustrator Lynn Reiser on **page 285**, and skim the pictures in the story. Ask children where they have seen Reiser's work before. (She wrote and illustrated **"Any Kind of Dog,"** pages **46–69**.)

GENRE: REALISTIC FICTION Have children use the title and illustrations to predict what this story will be about. Who are the characters? Where does the story take place? Could this story be true? Why or why not?

EVALUATE PRIOR KNOWLEDGE

FARMYARD BIRDS Ask children to brainstorm characteristics of chickens and ducks. Create a Venn Diagram like the one below or use **GRAPHIC ORGANIZER TRANSPARENCY/BLM 14**.

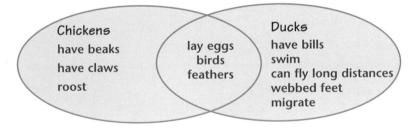

Chickens
have beaks
have claws
roost

lay eggs
birds
feathers

Ducks
have bills
swim
can fly long distances
webbed feet
migrate

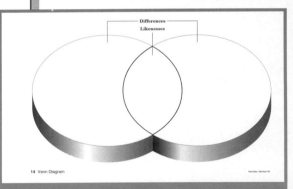

GRAPHIC ORGANIZER TRANSPARENCY/BLM 14

 ## ACTIVITIES FOR BUILDING BACKGROUND

MAKE IT REAL: BIRD DIAGRAMS Find photographs of chickens and ducks, or use a copy machine to enlarge the picture of the chicken on **page 265** and the duck on **page 283**. Have children paste the pictures to a large sheet of paper and color them in. Then invite them to create labels for the different characteristics of the birds and paste them onto the pictures.

INTEGRATING
SPELLING AND GRAMMAR

SPELLING
You may want to present the spelling pretest of words with /ā/-*ay*. See **pages 285Q–285R** for the 5-Day Spelling Plan.

PHONICS AND DECODING CONNECTION
See lesson on Long Vowels and Phonograms: /ā/-*ay* on **pages 285G–285I**.

GRAMMAR
See **pages 285O–285P** for Daily Language Activities. A 5-Day Grammar Plan is also presented.

ORAL LANGUAGE ACTIVITIES

MAKING VISUAL CONNECTIONS

In keeping with the selection theme of Surprises, bring the class a "surprise" feather or feathers. Pass the feather(s) around, and encourage children to make observations. Invite pairs to draw the animal they think the feather comes from.

Pair children who are acquiring English as a second language with bilingual children who speak their language. Have these partners label their drawings in both languages.

BUILD VOCABULARY

After children draw their bird, encourage them to brainstorm words or phrases to tell about it. Where does their bird live? What does their bird eat? Can it fly very high like an eagle, or is it more like an ostrich that runs along the ground?

Invite partners to share information about their bird with the rest of the class. Encourage children to ask questions about their classmates' bird. Partners can then add more phrases to their pictures.

NONVERBAL RESPONSES

How did the bird lose its feather? Pairs or small groups of children can work together to act out a scene showing how the bird may have lost the feather.

TEACHING
TIPS

English-speaking children can model for children learning English. Have them start with a single word and add words to make a meaningful phrase.

LANGUAGE DEVELOPMENT

You may want to present the following words, idioms, and phrases to children who need language support:

cracked open, p. 257
expected, p. 259
too close, p. 260
went for a walk, p. 261
not enough, p. 262
farther away, p. 275
out of sight, p. 277
was left, p. 277

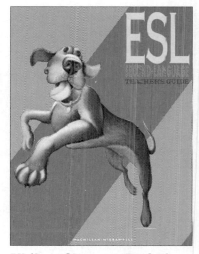

ESL/Second-Language Teacher's Guide
A full teaching lesson for students acquiring English is available in the ESL/SECOND-LANGUAGE TEACHER'S GUIDE.

Vocabulary

INSTRUCTIONAL VOCABULARY

everywhere	in all places
drink	a liquid you put in your mouth and swallow
afternoon	the part of the day between noon and evening
swim	to move in the water
farther	comes from the word far; more far
nest	a bird's house, built by birds with leaves, sticks, and mud

VOCABULARY ACTIVITIES

ILLUSTRATING A SCENE

Present the vocabulary as a series of sentences. Invite children to listen and draw the scene as they imagine it to appear. Ask them to compare their drawings and describe the places they imagined.

PERSONAL EXPERIENCE

After you present the vocabulary, have partners talk about a time they went for a *swim* or about what they like to do in the *afternoon* before dinner. Then have each child share with the class what their partner told them.

WORDS IN CONTEXT

For more vocabulary practice, assign **PRACTICE BOOK**, page 231.

VOCABULARY STRATEGY TRANSPARENCY /BLM 8

PRACTICE BOOK, page 231

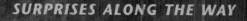
Strategic Reading

SET PURPOSES

JOURNAL WRITING   With partners, children can discuss and record their reasons for reading the selection. Children may read to learn more about

- the boy.

- the chicken and the ducks.

- why the family is called "The Surprise Family."

ENGAGE THE READER Opportunities to **role-play** story characters are provided in the Strategic Reading suggestions. As children read, you may also encourage them to **list** characters' actions and feelings in this story.

Hen	Boy

As they read, children can note in their journals any comments or questions they may want to explore. Invite children to refer to their journals and their character charts in the after-selection discussion **(pages 285A–285B)**.

<table><tr><td>OPTIONS</td></tr></table> **MANAGEMENT**
TIPS

Books for Meeting Individual Needs, **pages 285D–285F**, offer teaching suggestions for working with groups of children who have specific needs.

SUGGESTIONS FOR READING

READ INDEPENDENTLY

Independent readers can read the selection silently, noticing where the story takes place and how the characters' feelings affect what happens in the story.

READ ALOUD

Read the story aloud or play the **LISTENING LIBRARY AUDIOCASSETTE.** Encourage children to notice ways in which the characters react to each other.

READ TOGETHER

Ask children to work in pairs and alternate reading the text after each page.

READ AND TEACH

☑ **Analyze Character/ Plot/Setting**

Use comprehension strategies beginning on **page 256** as you and your children read the literature, or use the strategies after any other **SUGGESTION FOR READING** option.

Comprehension

STRATEGIC READING

☑ **ANALYZE CHARACTERS, PLOT, SETTING**

Share the comprehension strategies that will be focused on.

The author doesn't always tell you how characters are feeling or what they are thinking. You must pay close attention to the things that characters say and do. Their actions and feelings affect the plot, or what happens in the story.

Where the story takes place, or the setting, also affects the plot. When you pay attention to characters' actions and feelings, and to the story clues in the setting, you will understand and enjoy the story more.

TEACHING
TIPS

Tell children that, as they read, you will model how readers use these strategies, and that they will have a chance to use these strategies, too.

First there was an egg.

One day it cracked open.

257

Skills in Context

*To provide **Skills** and **Strategies** instruction, select from these lessons.*

☑ These core skills are tested in the Unit Progress Assessment.

Comprehension

STRATEGIC READING

1 **CHARACTER** Who is the first character we meet in this story? **(a baby chick)**

2 **CHARACTER** Why do you suppose the chick thinks the boy is her mother?

3 **CHARACTER** Who will volunteer to play the role of the boy? As the boy, what do you think of the little chick? How can you let her know how you feel about being her "mother"? **ROLE-PLAY**

PHONICS AND DECODING

/ā/-*ay* as in *anyway*, **page 259** See Phonics and Decoding lesson on Long Vowels and Phonograms: /ā/-*ay* on **pages 285G–285I**.

 A baby chick looked out.
Nobody was there.

Where was her mother?

258

The baby chick looked up and saw—

a boy.

Her mother was a boy!
The boy was not the kind of mother
the chick had expected,
but she loved him anyway.

259

Skills in Context

COMPREHENSION

✒ Problem and Solution

INTRODUCE Remind children that people solve problems in different ways. By watching a character solve a problem, they can learn about what the character is like.

DEVELOP/APPLY Have children reread **pages 257–259**, and ask them what problem the chick faces. Encourage them to use their own words to tell how the chick solves her problem and what this solution tells about her.

CLOSE Invite children to talk about how they have solved problems of their own.

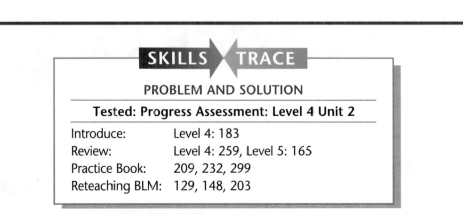

PRACTICE BOOK, page 232

See also RETEACHING BLM, page 148.

SKILLS TRACE

PROBLEM AND SOLUTION

Tested: Progress Assessment: Level 4 Unit 2

Introduce:	Level 4: 183
Review:	Level 4: 259, Level 5: 165
Practice Book:	209, 232, 299
Reteaching BLM:	129, 148, 203

Comprehension

STRATEGIC READING

4 **CHARACTER, SETTING** Where is this story taking place? **(in boy's house)** What might you learn about chicks by reading about what this one needs? **(Chicks eat and drink and need grit; they fear hawks and loud noises; they need fresh air and exercise; and they like to be warm while they sleep at night.)**

5 **CHARACTER** I can tell a lot about the boy from the information on these pages. He shows the chick how to find water and food, and he even keeps her warm at night. I think he must be a very caring little boy, and he probably loves animals very much. How would you describe him?

She followed him everywhere. The boy showed his baby chick how to find water and food and grit for her gizzard.

He taught her how to hide safe inside his jacket when a hawk flew by or when the vacuum cleaner came too close.

260

Every afternoon
the boy
and his baby chick
went for a walk
around the garden.

At night
she slept warm
under the edge
of his quilt.

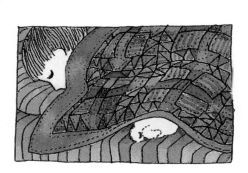

5

261

Skills in Context

☑ Long Vowels and Phonograms: /ī/-*ide*

INTRODUCE Reread the last paragraph on **page 260**. Write on the chalkboard, *He taught her how to hide safe inside his jacket.* Underline *hide* and *inside*, asking children to identify what sound these words have in common.

DEVELOP/APPLY Circle the *-ide* in each word. Read and say the sound with children. Elicit from them that the *i* is long because of the phonogram pattern. Encourage them to think of other words that contain this phonogram.

CLOSE Invite partners to draw a playground scene that includes a girl on a slide, a baby going for a wagon ride, and a boy playing hide and seek. Help them write sentences about the picture.

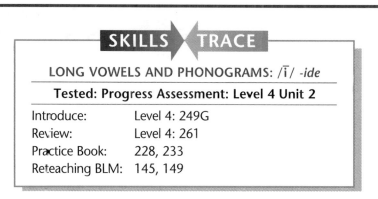

PRACTICE BOOK, page 233

See also RETEACHING BLM, page 149.

SKILLS TRACE

LONG VOWELS AND PHONOGRAMS: /ī/ -*ide*

Tested: Progress Assessment: Level 4 Unit 2

Introduce:	Level 4: 249G
Review:	Level 4: 261
Practice Book:	228, 233
Reteaching BLM:	145, 149

Comprehension

6 **PLOT** What has happened to the chick to make her want a family? **(She has grown up and become a hen.)**

7 **PLOT** What did the boy find for the hen? **(some eggs)** Why do you think he did this? **(He cares about her and wants her to be happy and have a family.)**

Let's begin our Character Chart by writing what we know about the hen and the boy so far.

Hen	Boy
Thinks the boy is her mother.	Takes care of the hen when she's a chick.
Feels happy and safe.	Boy is helpful and loves chick.
Grows up and wants a baby of her own.	Finds her eggs to take care of when she grows up.

The baby chick grew and grew and became a little hen.

She still followed the boy everywhere, but now following the boy was not enough. She wanted a family to follow her. /6/

She built a nest.

262

The boy found a clutch of eggs.

He gave them to the little hen.

263

Skills in Context

LITERARY ELEMENT

Foreshadowing

Tell children that writers and illustrators often give clues about what's going to happen next in a story.

Ask children to look on **pages 262–263** for clues about what is going to happen. Lead them to see that a fox is dragging a duck away from her nest. Model how to use this picture clue to predict what might happen.

THINK ALOUD *When I see the fox dragging the duck away, I remember something about ducks. They lay eggs, too! Now the boy is giving the duck's eggs to the chicken. The chicken is going to hatch the baby ducks.*

Challenge children to use foreshadowing to make predictions in other parts of the story.

Comprehension

8 Why does the hen have to sit on the eggs so much? (She has to keep them warm until the chicks are ready to hatch.)

9 How do you think the hen feels when she sees the babies hatch from the eggs? Who would like to volunteer to be the hen? Show us what she might say and do at this point. **ROLE-PLAY**

She sat
and warmed the eggs,
and every day she turned the eggs,

8

and she sat

and she sat

and she sat

and she sat

and she sat—

CRACK!

264

The eggs cracked open.

The babies looked out
and saw the little hen.

Skills in Context

CONCEPTS OF PRINT

Directionality

Refer children to **pages 258–259,** and ask them to help you figure out how to read these pages.

- Have them identify the order in which they should read the text on **page 264.** Then ask them to use a finger to track print in the correct order.

- Be sure children understand that they must read all of **page 264** before they can read **page 265.**

- Ask them to identify which egg "speaks" first, then point to each one in the order in which each cracks.

After discussing this page, help children by explaining that when reading they should follow the text from left-to-right and top-to-bottom.

Comprehension

STRATEGIC READING

10 **CHARACTER** The hen is showing her babies how to find water and food and she is teaching them to run from danger. I think she takes good care of these babies, just like the boy took care of her. Let's add this information to our Character Chart.

Hen	Boy
Thinks the boy is her mother.	Takes care of the hen when she's a chick.
Feels happy and safe.	Boy is helpful and loves chick.
Grows up and wants a baby of her own.	Finds her eggs to take care of when she grows up.
Takes good care of the babies. Is a good mother.	

11 Make the noise the hen makes when she thinks something dangerous is near.
ROLE-PLAY

INFORMAL ASSESSMENT

Ask children to retell the story up to this point. Check to see if they have an understanding of the main characters and can recall the story events in sequence.

To help children with Character, Plot, and Setting, see Reteaching lesson on **page 271**.

They followed her everywhere. She showed them how to find water and food

and grit
for their gizzards.

266

She taught them to run to her
when she sang a danger song
and danced a danger dance

and to hide
safe under her feathers.

267

Skills in Context

Unfamiliar Words

Most children won't understand the meaning of the phrase "grit for their gizzards." Encourage them to use context clues and illustrations to speculate on the meaning of this phrase.

Model for them the following think aloud.

THINK ALOUD *When I read the phrase grit for their gizzards I look for clues in the words around it that will help me with its meaning. First, I know that gizzards must be something the chicks have because of the word* their. *Then I read that the mother chicken showed the babies how to find this. Grit must be a thing. I look at the illustration and see the baby chicks and the chicken eating. Grit is a thing the chicks eat which is good for their gizzards.*

Invite children to use this skill to figure out the meaning of other words throughout the story.

Comprehension

STRATEGIC READING

12 **SETTING** Where is this story taking place now? **(a garden)** How would it be different if it were taking place on a farm?

🔬 SCIENCE CONNECTION

Chickens not only cannot swim, but, because their wings are short and weak, they're not very good fliers, either. Chickens usually have four toes on each foot. There are many kinds of chickens, often named after the area where they originated. The Yokohama chicken, a Japanese fancy breed, has tail feathers that are 12 to 15 feet long!

Every afternoon the boy and the little hen and the babies went for a walk around the garden.

268

At night the babies slept

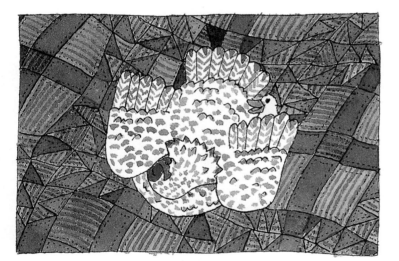

warm under the little hen's wings.

269

Skills in Context

PHONICS AND DECODING

✓Short Vowels and Phonograms: /a/-at

INTRODUCE Read aloud the first sentence on **page 269.** Write the word *at* on the chalkboard, pronouncing it with children. Write *c* in front of the word and ask what the new word is.

DEVELOP/APPLY Write the following sentences on the chalkboard, and have children join you in reading them: *The hen sat on the hat. Look at that. The boy's hat is flat.*

Ask children to identify words in the sentences that contain the *-at* phonogram.

CLOSE Invite children to work in pairs to list as many /a/-*at* words as they can. Then have them write a sentence using two words from their list.

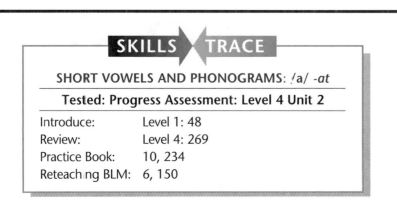

PRACTICE BOOK, page 234

See also RETEACHING BLM, page 150.

SKILLS ▶ TRACE

SHORT VOWELS AND PHONOGRAMS: /a/ -at

Tested: Progress Assessment: Level 4 Unit 2

Introduce:	Level 1: 48
Review:	Level 4: 269
Practice Book:	10, 234
Reteaching BLM:	6, 150

Comprehension

STRATEGIC READING

13 **CHARACTERS** The babies are growing. What do you notice about the babies? **(They don't look like their mother, the hen. They look like ducks.)** Where do the babies want to go? **(to the pond)** What do the boy and the hen do now? Let's add what they do to our Character Chart.

Hen	Boy
Thinks the boy is her mother.	Takes care of the hen when she's a chick.
Feels happy and safe.	Boy is helpful and loves chick.
Grows up and wants a baby of her own.	Finds her eggs to take care of when she grows up.
Takes good care of the babies. Is a good mother.	
The hen takes them for a walk by the pond.	Goes with the hen and the babies by the pond.

14 Show how you think the babies feel about being at the pond. **ROLE-PLAY**

15 **CHARACTER** What do you think the babies will do next? Why do you think as you do?

The little hen's family grew.
They still followed her everywhere,
but now walking around the garden
was not enough.
They wanted to walk by the pond.

So the boy
and the hen
took them to walk
by the pond.

270

They stood at the edge of the water.

They looked at the water.

They took a drink of the water. 15

271

Skills in Context

☑ Comprehension
Character, Plot, Setting

INTRODUCE Remind children that different elements work together to make a story: characters are the *who* of the story; setting is *where* the story takes place; plot is the *what, how* and *why* of the story.

DEVELOP/APPLY Ask children to look at words and pictures in **"The Surprise Family"** to answer these questions:

* Who are the characters in this story?

* What is the setting?

* What is the plot?

CLOSE Change one element of the story and discuss how the story would change.

* Character change: The ducklings have an eagle for a mother instead of a hen.

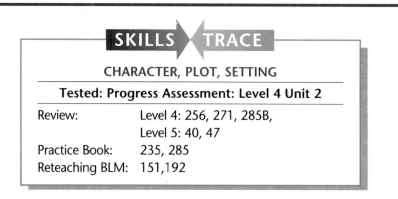

PRACTICE BOOK, page 235

See also RETEACHING BLM, page 151.

SKILLS TRACE

CHARACTER, PLOT, SETTING

Tested: Progress Assessment: Level 4 Unit 2

Review:	Level 4: 256, 271, 285B,
	Level 5: 40, 47
Practice Book:	235, 285
Reteaching BLM:	151,192

Comprehension

STRATEGIC READING

16 **CHARACTER** Why is the hen so upset? (She is afraid the babies will drown because chickens don't know how to swim.) Do you think the babies will be able to swim? Raise one hand if you think they will and two hands if you think they won't. **NONVERBAL RESPONSE**

SELF ASSESSMENT

As children discuss the characters in this story, encourage them to ask themselves:

• Why does the hen do this?

• Would any of the other characters do this?

• What makes this character different?

To help children with Character, Plot, and Setting, see Reteaching lesson on page 271.

They jumped into the water!

272

The little hen cried her DANGER cry—
her babies splashed.

273

Skills in Context

Humor

Discuss with children that sometimes illustrators create funny pictures when something awful is happening. This lets readers know that the event will end happily. Have children look at the illustrations on these pages.

Ask children to guess what is going on without reading the text. Discuss children's responses to the action on these pages.

Ask children:

- What is happening in the picture?

- What makes the illustration seem funny?

- How does this picture make you feel?

Comprehension

STRATEGIC READING

17 **PLOT** Describe what's happening in this picture. **(The hen is doing her danger dance.)** Why does the author/illustrator use two pages to show this? **(to emphasize what a scary thing it is for the hen to have her babies go swimming)** Explain to children that this event is a *turning point* in the story's plot because suddenly things change: the ducklings swim away, leaving the hen alone.

Let's add what the hen does and how she feels to our chart.

Hen	Boy
Thinks the boy is her mother.	Takes care of the hen when she's a chick.
Feels happy and safe.	Boy is helpful and loves chick.
Grows up and wants a baby of her own.	Finds her eggs to take care of when she grows up.
Takes good care of the babies. Is a good mother.	
The hen takes them for a walk by the pond.	Goes with the hen and the babies by the pond.
Gets very worried and does danger dance when babies go into pond.	

TEACHING
TIPS

Focus on the reasons for the hen's distress by asking children, "Can you think of anything that might cause someone to get very worried about you? How do they act when they are very worried about you?"

The little hen danced her DANGER dance—
her babies swam.
The little hen held out her wings
for her babies to run under—

274

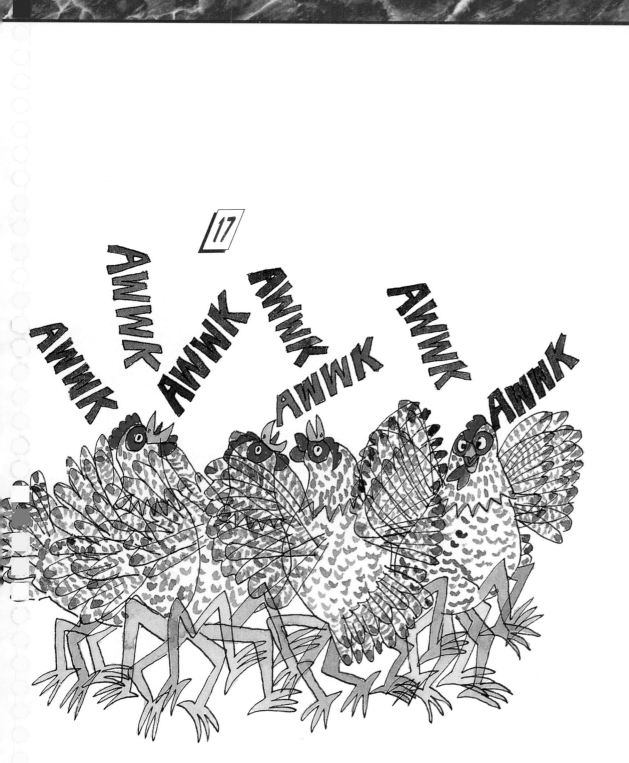

17

but they kept on swimming farther and farther away.

275

PHONICS AND DECODING

☑ Consonant Blends: /sw/ *sw*

INTRODUCE Remind children that a consonant blend is a combination of two consonant sounds. Each consonant keeps its own sound.

DEVELOP/APPLY Direct children's attention to the word *swam* on **page 274**.

- Ask what two consonants form a blend at the beginning of *swam*.

- Have children find a word on **page 275** that begins with the same blend as *swam*.

- Invite children to think of other words that begin like *swam* and *swimming*.

CLOSE As you say the following words, ask children to pretend to swim when they hear the /sw/ sound: *swell, sail, switch, swan, wish, swallow, sand.*

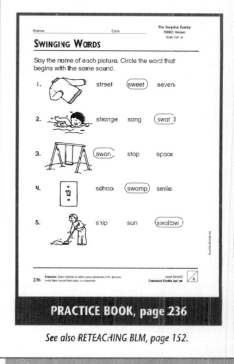

PRACTICE BOOK, page 236

See also RETEACHING BLM, page 152.

SKILLS ✕ TRACE

CONSONANT BLEND: /sw/ *sw*

Tested: Progress Assessment: Level 4 Unit 2

Introduce:	Level 4 : 207J
Review:	Level 4: 275
Practice Book:	219, 236
Reteaching BLM:	138, 152

Comprehension

STRATEGIC READING

18 Why were the babies able to swim when the chicken could not? (because they weren't baby chickens; they were ducklings)

19 CHARACTER How do you think the hen feels now? (confused, lonely, sad) Pretend that you are the hen. Tell us how you are feeling and what you are thinking. **ROLE-PLAY**

20 CHARACTER What is the boy doing that shows he cares about the hen's feelings? (He's patting her.)

INFORMAL ASSESSMENT

Draw a story map on the chalk-board or on a transparency. Observe if children can identify the main characters, setting, and plot up to this point in the story.

To help children with Character, Plot, and Setting, see Reteaching lesson on page 271.

The little hen ran after them,
but when her feet got wet,
she stopped.
She was a chicken.
Chickens cannot swim.

276

The little hen's babies swam out of sight.

Only her boy was left.

277

SELF-MONITORING

Reread

Model for children how rereading can sometimes help make sense of a confusing part in a story.

THINK ALOUD On this page, I started looking at the pictures, and I wasn't sure where the babies had gone. I'm going to read this again to make sure I understand what is happening.

Reread the page with children. Then say: *Now I understand. The babies are in the water, and the hen is really afraid they are going to get hurt. That's why she's holding out her wings and making all these loud noises.*

Work with children to create a list of things they can do if they get confused when reading:

- I can go back to the last part I understood and reread the words slowly.

- I can study the pictures and then reread the words to find out what is happening.

- I can reread the text aloud.

Comprehension

STRATEGIC READING

21 **CHARACTER** How do you think the hen will feel about swimming now? (She may still think it's dangerous for herself but may realize it's safe for her babies.) How do you think she feels? (Very happy and excited to see her babies) How do you think the babies feel? (Happy and excited to see their mother.)

Then the little hen's babies
turned around,

swam back,
hopped out of the water,

flapped their wings,
shook their tails,

and ran to their mother hen.

278

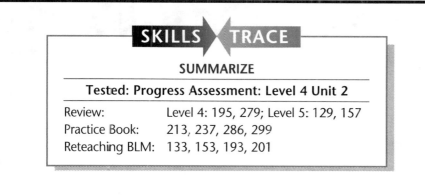

She gathered her babies in,
warm under her wings.
She looked at them.
They were safe.

 She looked at them
again.
Carefully.

279

Skills in Context

COMPREHENSION

✓Summarize

INTRODUCE Remind children that a summary is a retelling of a story in their own words. It includes only the most important details.

DEVELOP/APPLY Ask children to recall what has happened in the story so far. Record their ideas on the chalkboard. Ask them to look at the ideas they have written and circle the ones that are the most important. Help children put the circled ideas in order to write a class summary.

CLOSE Have children draw pictures about the story to go with the summary. Guide children to understand that their pictures can also give a summary of the story.

Name: _____ Date: _____   The Surprise Family
COMPREHENSION
Summarize

KEEP IT SHORT

Read each story. Then write one sentence that tells what the story is about.

1. A frog lived in the pond. He did not like it when the ducklings went swimming. They would splash him and make noise. He would croak at them. One duckling told him to hop on her back. The duckling gave the frog a ride. The frog had fun. After that, he played with the ducklings when they came to the pond.

The frog learned to get along with the

ducklings.

2. All of Fuzzy Duckling's brothers and sisters could quack. Fuzzy Duckling could not. She tried and tried. One day her brother said, "Boo!" Fuzzy Duckling jumped and said, "Quack." Then everyone laughed. Fuzzy Duckling was happy.

Fuzzy Duckling learned to quack.

Level 4/Unit 2
Summarize   237

PRACTICE BOOK, page 237

See also RETEACHING BLM, page 153.

Comprehension

STRATEGIC READING

22 **PLOT** What is happening on these pages? (The hen is finally noticing that her babies look different from her, and from the boy.)

23 **CHARACTER** Now that the hen realizes the babies are ducklings, how do you think she will feel about them? (She will still love them.)

Their beaks were not pointed
like her beak,
or soft
like her boy's mouth—
they were flat.

Their feet were not sharp
like her feet,
or hard
like her boy's shoes—
they were webbed.

Their feathers were not fluffy
like her feathers,
or fuzzy
like her boy's jacket—
they were waterproof.

22

280

Her babies did not look like chicks
or like boys.
They looked like ducklings.

Ducklings were not the kind of family
she had expected,

281

Skills in Context

☑ Compare and Contrast

INTRODUCE Remind children that comparing and contrasting characters in a story can help them understand more about the characters.

DEVELOP/APPLY Invite children to find out how chickens and ducks are alike by comparing and contrasting the chicken and the ducklings in the story. Let them know that they can use the words and the illustrations for clues about the characters.

CLOSE Ask children to draw a picture of a hen and a duck that shows a way the two birds are alike or a way they are different. Have them write a sentence to describe the similarity or difference.

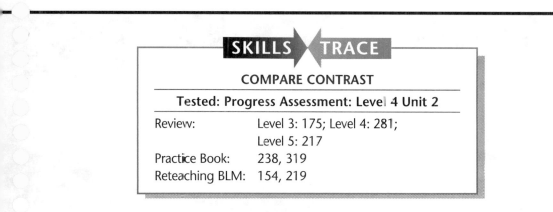

PRACTICE BOOK, page 238

See also RETEACHING BLM page 154.

SKILLS TRACE

COMPARE CONTRAST

Tested: Progress Assessment: Level 4 Unit 2

Review:	Level 3: 175; Level 4: 281; Level 5: 217
Practice Book:	238, 319
Reteaching BLM:	154, 219

Comprehension

STRATEGIC READING

24 Look at this page! Why are these words all alone on the page this way? (probably to show that this is a very important idea, the most important idea in the story—that people love each other despite their differences.)

25 CHARACTER, PLOT, AND SETTING
Things seem pretty calm now. How have all the characters worked things out so that everyone is happy and has what they need? (The ducks get to go swimming in the pond, and the boy keeps the hen company.)

Let's add this information to our Character Chart.

Hen	Boy
Thinks the boy is her mother.	Takes care of the hen when she's a chick.
Feels happy and safe.	Boy is helpful and loves chick.
Grows up and wants a baby of her own.	Finds her eggs to take care of when she grows up.
Takes good care of the babies. Is a good mother.	
The hen takes them for a walk by the pond.	Goes with the hen and the babies by the pond.
Gets very worried and does danger dance when babies go into pond.	Comforts her when ducklings go swimming in the pond.
Realizes the babies are ducklings, but loves them anyway.	Boy loves hen and wants to help her.

but she loved them anyway.

282

The ducklings grew
and grew and became
big ducks.
Some afternoons
while the ducks
swam in the pond,
the boy
walked around the garden,
and the hen followed him.
Some afternoons
while the ducks
swam in the pond,
the hen
walked around the garden,
and the boy followed her.
Other afternoons
while the ducks
swam in the pond,
and the boy waded after
them, the hen watched.

Skills in Context

AMAZE YOUR STUDENTS

Ducks

Share these facts about ducks:

- Ducks are "waterproof" because of oil secreted by a gland near their tails. They spread this oil all over their feathers, so the water rolls right off of them.

- Ducks don't mind cold weather because their outer feathers are packed tightly together over a layer of thick, soft light feathers called "down." The down keeps them warm.

- Ducks' legs are set far back on their bodies. This is why they are good swimmers; it's also why they waddle when they walk.

Comprehension

STRATEGIC READING

26 **CHARACTER** How has each character changed since the beginning of this story? (They have all grown up and become good at taking care of one another.)

ONGOING ASSESSMENT

☑ **CHARACTER, PLOT, AND SETTING**

Encourage children to think about the strategies and their possible transfer to other situations by asking these questions:

• How did thinking about where the story took place, what the characters did, and how the characters felt help me to understand this story better?

• When might I use this strategy again?

FOR RESPONSE AND ASSESSMENT OPPORTUNITIES
see pages 285A–285B

▼

But every afternoon
in the garden
beside the pond, *26*
after walking and swimming and wading,
there they all were,
together,
under the little hen's wings.

QUACK

MEET LYNN REISER

Lynn Reiser has written seven books for children. She has also made the drawings for these books. Ms. Reiser likes nature and animals very much. She has a special way of drawing. Her pictures are full of people and animals. Sometimes they are doing funny things. She wrote *The Surprise Family* to show that families are full of surprises. The surprises make families fun. Families can love each other no matter what happens.

285

Respond to the Literature

PERSONAL RESPONSE

JOURNAL WRITING

Children may use their journals to express their feelings, ideas and questions about the selection. The following questions may help them get started:

- What did you think about the boy in this story? the hen? the ducklings?

- Have you ever had a pet that thought of you as its mother? Tell about it.

- Which part of the story did you like the best?

- Which picture was your favorite? Why?

READER RESPONSE CARD 4, page T3

SMALL GROUP RESPONSE

JOURNAL ENTRIES

Children may work in small groups to discuss the selection. Encourage them to use their journals throughout the discussion.

READER RESPONSE CARD 4 is available to guide the discussions.

To check story comprehension, you may want to assign **PRACTICE BOOK, page 239.**

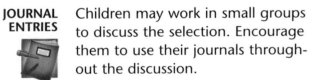

WRITING ABOUT THE THEME

CRITICAL THINKING

How does **"The Surprise Family"** relate to the unit theme of Surprises Along the Way? After their discussions, children may see that the hen was surprised by the needs of her babies, but she chose to accept and love them anyway. They may realize that even when things turn out differently than we expect, we can still find happiness and pleasure, just like the hen did.

QUICK WRITE

What might the hen have said to the ducklings after their first swim? How might the ducklings have answered? Have partners act out, then write, a dialog that might have taken place.

Name: _____ Date: _____ The Surprise Family
COMPREHENSION
Story Comprehension

REMEMBERING THE STORY

Underline the words that finish the sentence.

1. The boy showed the chick _____.
   how to find water and food
   how to fly and scratch

2. The boy gave the little hen _____.
   a soft nest
   a clutch of eggs

3. The boy and the little hen took the babies for a walk _____.
   in the yard
   around the garden

4. When the babies jumped into the water, the little hen _____.
   jumped into the water, too
   cried her danger cry

5. When the babies came back from their swim, the little hen _____.
   looked at them carefully
   danced her danger dance

Level 4/Unit 2   Extension: Challenge children to write other sentences about the story   239
Story Comprehension   and to leave blanks for classmates to fill in.

PRACTICE BOOK, page 239

Comprehension Checkpoint

INFORMAL ASSESSMENT

☑ ANALYZE CHARACTER, SETTING, PLOT

CHARACTER CHART Display **GRAPHIC ORGANIZER TRANSPARENCY/BLM 30,** or put the following chart on the chalkboard. Ask children to contribute ideas from the story to fill in the chart. If children began this chart during Strategic Reading, invite them to add the third column at this time.

Hen	Boy	Ducklings

Children can use their charts to analyze the characters, setting, and plot in this story. Encourage them to **retell** the story to a partner.

ONGOING ASSESSMENT

COMPREHENSION

Assessment Checklist

- When you assess children's charts, look for **Concepts** and **Comprehension.** Have children understood how setting, characters, actions, and feelings affected what happens in the story?

- In their retellings, look for **Sequence of Events.** Do children understand the order in which the plot was developed in this story?

30 Chart

GRAPHIC ORGANIZER TRANSPARENCY/BLM 30

FORMAL ASSESSMENT

ONGOING ASSESSMENT

To test story comprehension and vocabulary, you can use the multiple choice Selection Assessment for **"The Surprise Family"** in **SELECTION AND UNIT ASSESSMENTS** for Levels 4–5.

RETEACHING

ONGOING ASSESSMENT

For additional work with analyzing character, setting, and plot, use Reteaching lessons on **page 271** or **RETEACHING BLM, page 151.**

Extend Skills In Context

Literature-Based Instruction

To provide skills and strategies instruction to meet the needs of your children, select from these lessons.

☑ These skills are tested in the Unit Progress Assessment.

Meeting Individual Needs

*To provide additional literacy experiences tailored to specific students' needs and interests, use this literature and these resources. Activities are provided on **pages 285E–285F**.*

MULTILEVEL RESOURCES FOR FLEXIBLE GROUPING

EASY	EASY AVERAGE	EASY	AVERAGE CHALLENGE

SPOTLIGHT: LITERACY SUPPORT

EARLY INTERVENTION
COMPREHENSION:
Summarize

PHONICS AND DECODING:
Long Vowels and
Phonograms: /ī/-*ice*

SPOTLIGHT: PHONICS/ DECODING

PHONICS AND DECODING
☑ LONG VOWELS AND PHONOGRAMS: /ā/-*ay*

🔘 **Also available on CD-ROM**

SPOTLIGHT: VOCABULARY/ COMPREHENSION

VOCABULARY
- everywhere
- drink
- afternoon
- swim
- farther
- nest

COMPREHENSION
☑ CHARACTER, PLOT, SETTING

TRADE BOOK LIBRARY

COMPREHENSION
☑ CHARACTER, PLOT, SETTING

Meeting Individual Needs
Multilevel Resources

BEAK-A-BOO

REREAD A FAMILIAR BOOK

Reinforce successful reading experiences by inviting children to read a familiar book, such as the **LITERACY SUPPORT BOOK** *Elephant Boy*.

READ A NEW BOOK

Preview the **LITERACY SUPPORT BOOK** *Beak-a-Boo*. Point out illustrations, using story vocabulary words such as *May* and *hides*.

Read aloud the story, emphasizing the language pattern. Encourage children to chime in as you read the repetitive phrase, *Where is May?* Model how to use summarizing. After reading **page 4**, you might say, "So far, May has hid with the pigs and the sheep. I wonder where she'll hide next. I'll have to read to find out."

BUILD WORDS

Read this sentence from **page 2:** *May likes to play hide and seek.* Ask children to think of a word that rhymes with *hide*. Have children use the **Word Building Kit** to build rhyming words with the *-ide* phonogram, such as *ride, side, slide,* and *bride*.

For a full lesson on long vowels and phonograms: /ī/-*ide,* see **pages 249G–249I.**

WRITE SENTENCES

Invite children to write sentences about the places May hides in *Beak-a-Boo*. Have children share their sentences with partners, asking each other to point out various words. Invite volunteers to share their sentences as you write them on the chalkboard or chart paper. Encourage the class to read the sentences together. Invite children to illustrate their work.

READ INDEPENDENTLY

Have children reread *Beak-a-Boo* independently. As they read aloud, note the strategies that they use successfully and point them out after their reading.

May hides with the sheep.

EASY **AVERAGE**

ACTIVITIES

PHONICS AND DECODING

MOLLY MAY

⊘ **Long Vowels and Phonograms: /ā/-*ay***

CREATE *-AY* WORDS Invite children to write the phonogram *-ay* on the chalk-board. Ask them to write the letter *b* in front of the phonogram and read the word. Have children erase the *b* and replace it with the blend *st* and again read the word. Continue this erase/replace/read procedure with the following consonants and blends: *d, h, gr, j, l, m, p, pr, sl, tr, r, s,* and *w*. **LINGUISTIC/SPATIAL**

EASY

ACTIVITIES

VOCABULARY/COMPREHENSION

JUST THE SAME

everywhere, drink, afternoon, swim, farther, nest

WORD SEARCH Divide children into groups of six. Assign one vocabulary word to each group member. Children can look through the story to find their word, copy the sentence onto a piece of paper, and illustrate it. **LINGUISTIC**

⊘ **Character, Plot, Setting**

CHARACTER PICTURES Have pairs draw the duck family, using character, set-ting, and plot details from the story. The picture might include the duck house, four little yellow ducks, one big gray duckling, and Mother Duck. **SPATIAL**

AVERAGE **CHALLENGE**

ACTIVITIES

COMPREHENSION

PET SHOW!

⊘ **Character, Plot, Setting**

WRITE A LETTER Make a list of all the characters in "Pet Show!": Archie, Peter, Susie, Roberto, and the Old Woman. Have each child choose one of the characters and write/illustrate a let-ter to a friend from that character's point-of-view. Encourage children to tell about their character's pet show adventures. **INTRAPERSONAL**
Turn to **pages 287I–287P** for more teaching ideas for "Pet Show!".

Dear Katie,
    Today I went to a pet show.
I won a ribbon for the brightest
goldfish. All of my friends won
ribbons, too!
        Your friend,
    Susie

Phonics and Decoding

☑ Long Vowels and Phonograms: /ā/-*ay*

1 DEVELOP PHONEMIC AWARENESS

READ THE LITERATURE
- Reread **page 257** of "**The Surprise Family**," emphasizing the word *day* as you read. Then read the rhyme on **page 23** of **THE BIG BOOK OF RHYMES AND CHIMES**.

SAY THE RHYME
- Invite children to recite the rhyme along with you, repeating it several times.

- Say the words *May, bay,* and *play,* and ask children if the words rhyme.

- Ask children to listen to these word pairs and say "hurray" if they rhyme, "nay" if they don't.

day/May	Molly/May	play/stay
play/spray	by/bay	Mother/day

5-STEP PLAN

DECODING STRATEGIES: RHYMING, BLENDING

1 DEVELOP PHONEMIC AWARENESS

2 DISCOVER THE SPELLING PATTERN

3 USE DECODING STRATEGIES

4 WRITING

5 READING

CONSONANT BLENDS

2 DISCOVER THE SPELLING PATTERN

SHOW THE RHYME
- Display **page 23** in the **BIG BOOK OF RHYMES AND CHIMES**. Ask a volunteer to read the word with the underlined letters.

- Read the rhyme together. Ask a child to point to each word as you read it. Frame the word *bay* and run your finger under the phonogram *-ay.*

- Have the children read the rhyme with you and raise a hand each time they hear a word with *-ay.*

*For additional lessons and practice with long ā, see **PHONICS SUPPORT BLM**, pages 24 and 81.*

BIG BOOK
OF
RHYMES
AND
CHIMES

Molly May

Molly May! Molly May!
Never would listen
When her mother would say,
"Don't play by yourself
In the bay, Molly May!"

May

BIG BOOK OF RHYMES AND CHIMES, page 23

SKILLS ▶ TRACE

LONG VOWELS AND PHONOGRAMS: /ā/-*ay*

Tested: Progress Assessment, Level 4 ,Unit 2

Introduce:	Level 4: 285G
Practice Book:	240
Reteaching BLM:	155

ACTIVITIES

③ DECODING STRATEGIES: BLENDING

MODEL THE STRATEGY
- Write the phonogram -*ay* on chart paper or on the chalkboard. Model the blending strategy by blending *b* with -*ay*.

THINK ALOUD *Now I'm going to build words with* -ay. *Let's put a* b *in front of the phonogram to make the word* bay. *Listen as I blend the letters:* b-ay. Invite volunteers to practice the blending strategy with *pl-ay, st-ay,* and *s-ay.*

MAKE A WORD WALL
- Write the phonogram -*ay* in the center of a circle.
- Give children a strip of paper, and invite them to write an -*ay* word on their paper.
- Place the strips of paper around the circle so they look like rays of the sun.

PHONOGRAM SLIDES
- Draw a slide on the chalkboard and write the phonogram -*ay* on the bottom of the slide.
- Have a volunteer write the letter *d* on a piece of paper, and bring it to the slide. Ask the class what happens when the letter *d* climbs up the stairs and slides into -*ay.*
- The class can mimic the strategy with other letters.

USE THE WORD BUILDING KIT
- Use the Word Building Kit to extend the blending activity. Insert cards with the phonogram -*ay* into the pockets of the mini-pocket chart.
- Place the letters *b, d,* and *m* in front of the phonograms. Model the blending strategy as you read the words with children.
- Invite children to build new words using single consonants and consonant blends and digraphs.

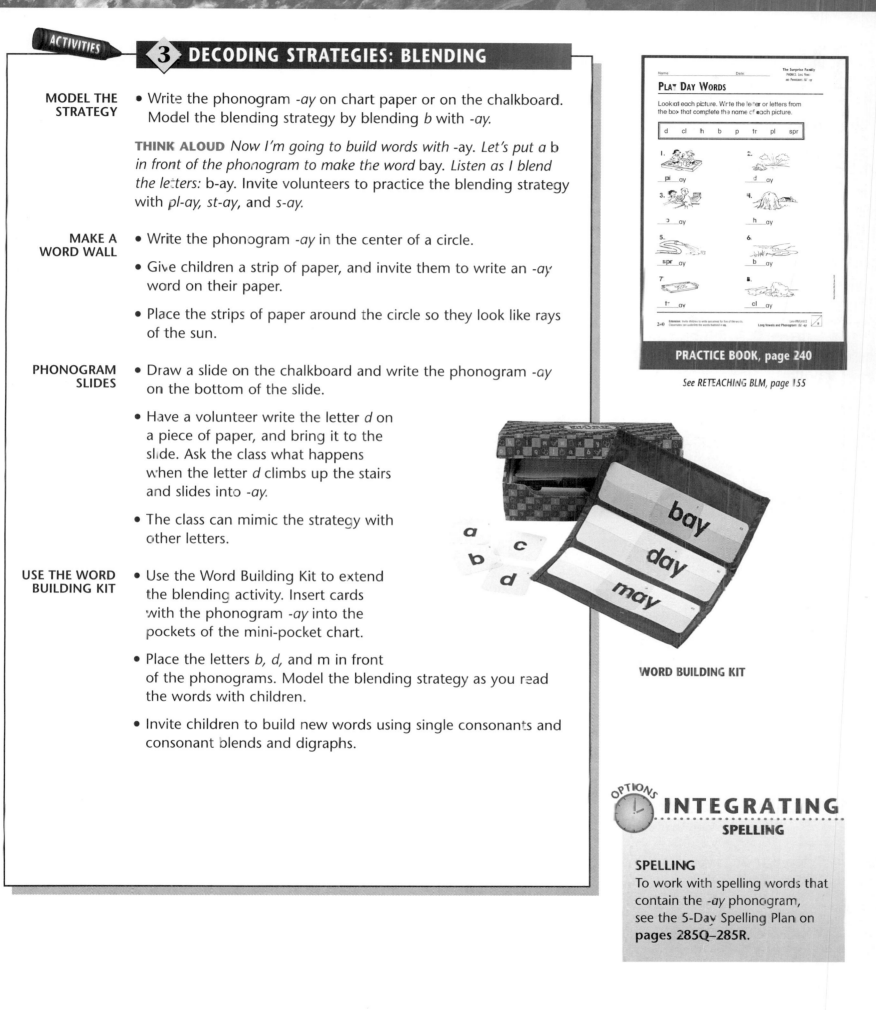

PRACTICE BOOK, page 240

See RETEACHING BLM, page 155

WORD BUILDING KIT

OPTIONS

INTEGRATING
SPELLING

SPELLING
To work with spelling words that contain the -*ay* phonogram, see the 5-Day Spelling Plan on pages 285Q–285R.

Phonics and Decoding

☑ Long Vowels and Phonograms: /ā/-*ay*

ACTIVITIES

4 WRITING

USE THE PHONOGRAM

- Ask children to work with partners to create questions and answers using the phonogram -*ay*. Children can draw pictures to go with their questions and post them side by side.

PHONICS ACTIVITY BOOK, pages 117–118

ACTIVITIES

5 READING

READ "THE SURPRISE FAMILY"
Tell children they will encounter words with the phonogram -*ay* in almost all the books they read. Reread **"The Surprise Family"** and ask children to point out words with the phonogram -*ay*.

READ "MOLLY MAY"
Children can meet in pairs or small groups to read, "Molly May." Encourage children to look for the rhyme from the **BIG BOOK OF RHYMES AND CHIMES, page 23.** They can read the rhyme together and talk about what might happen to Molly May.

'TRONIC PHONICS
"Molly May" is also available in **'TRONIC PHONICS™** on CD-ROM. Children can work independently or in pairs to read the story, engage in blending activities, and write their own story.

SPOTLIGHT: PHONICS AND DECODING
Molly May

✍ Consonant Blends: /skw/*squ*

DEVELOP PHONEMIC AWARENESS FOR /skw/*squ*

READ ALOUD
- Direct children's attention to **pages 274–275** of **"The Surprise Family."** Tell children that what the hen is doing is called squawking.

DEVELOP PRINT AWARENESS FOR /skw/*squ*

DISPLAY THE STORY STRIPS
- Write the word *squawk* on the chalkboard. Underline the phonogram *squ,* and ask children to identify the sound these letters make.

- Ask children to look around the classroom for posters, charts, books, and displays that contain words that begin with the same sound as *squawk.*

- List children's words on the chalkboard or chart paper, under a child's drawing of a squawking chicken.

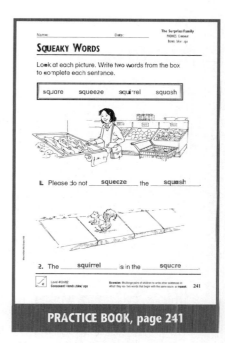

PRACTICE BOOK, page 241

See RETEACHING BLM, page 156
See PHONICS ACTIVITY BOOK, pages 119–120

READ AND WRITE

LISTEN FOR WORDS
- As children read other stories, encourage them to listen for words that begin with the /skw/ sound.

MAKE A PICTURE DICTIONARY
- Children can create their own picture dictionaries of words that have the same sound as *squawk.*

- Have them write words that begin with the /skw/ sound on separate sheets of paper.

- Tell them to draw a picture to go with each word.

- Staple pictures together to make a class picture dictionary.

SKILLS ⟩ TRACE

CONSONANT BLEND: /skw/*squ-*

**Tested: Progress Assessment,
    Level 4 Unit 2**

Introduce:	Level 4: 285J
Practice Book:	241
Reteaching BLM:	156

squeak

Vocabulary READ

ACTIVITIES

VOCABULARY REVIEW

| everywhere | drink | afternoon |
| farther | nest | swim |

WORD EGGS Number plastic eggs from 1 to 6 and place the answers to the clues below in each one. Have children write the vocabulary words on strips of paper. Read the clues and ask children to hold up the correct strip in response. Then have volunteers open the appropriate egg to check the answer.

1. Which word means all over the world? **(everywhere)**

2. Which word can answer the question "What time of day is it?" **(afternoon)**

3. Which word means the opposite of closer? **(farther)**

4. Which word describes something people and ducks can do, but not hens? **(swim)**

5. Which word describes something everyone does when they're thirsty? **(drink)**

6. Which word goes along with house, shell, and hive? **(nest)**

VOCABULARY STRATEGY   Compound Words

LINK TO LITERATURE Ask children to discuss the meaning of *nobody* on **page 258.** Write the words *no* and *body* and ask children to define each word. Compare the word *nobody* to the words *somebody* and *everybody*. Be sure children understand that each of these words is a compound word—a word made up of two smaller ones.

EXPLORE In groups, children can make stick puppets of themselves out of paper and popsicle sticks. A square of fabric can be used as a curtain to reveal *nobody, somebody, everybody,* and *anybody*.

DISCUSS Invite volunteers to search the selection for more examples of compound words. Make a list on the board and ask children what smaller words the compound words are made of.

USE DIFFERENT MODALITIES Ask children to listen and watch for compound words on television, in print, and in conversations. Create a classroom collection of compound words.

Listening, Speaking, Viewing

DRAMATIZATION

GROUP Invite groups of children to dramatize the story. Let them decide whether they want to use words or pantomimes in their dramas. You may have one group try it each way. Groups can work together to assign roles, practice, and perform.

LISTENING AND SPEAKING TIPS Remind speakers to speak slowly and clearly so the audience can understand them. Have children listen carefully so they can compare and contrast the ways each group dramatizes the selection.

VIEW ANIMAL BOOKS

PARTNER Gather books, fiction and nonfiction, about animals. Ask children to work together to skim, read, and explore the books, then categorize them as to whether they show realistic characteristics or fanciful characteristics of animals.

VIEWING TIP Try comparing two books that feature the same kind of animal to make more clear the distinction between realistic and fanciful.

ORAL LANGUAGE DEVELOPMENT

ONE **MYSTERY ANIMAL** Invite children to select an animal they are interested in. Help them find a library book that tells about the animal. Encourage them to draw a picture of the animal, and write or think of three sentences that describe it. Let them tell the sentences to the class without showing the picture or saying the name of the animal. Class members can try to guess the animals being described.

ADDITIONAL RESOURCES

GROUP **STORYTELLING** Read aloud the folktale "Lion and the Ostrich Chicks" from the book of **READ ALOUDS, PLAYS, AND CHORAL READINGS.** A recording is available on the **SONGS AND STORIES AUDIOCASSETTE.**

ONE **LISTEN TO THE STORY** If children haven't already done so, they can listen to the **LISTENING LIBRARY AUDIOCASSETTE** for a dramatic reading of "**The Surprise Family.**"

GROUP **LISTEN TO THE SONG** Invite children to listen to the song "Shaiu Ya" on the **SONGS AND STORIES AUDIOCASSETTES.**

PORTFOLIO

Photograph or videotape children's performances to include in their portfolios.

OPPORTUNITIES

Writing

Writing Process: Description

Invite children to think of a time when they were surprised. Guide them to write a descriptive paragraph that tells about the event from beginning to end. Ask them to recall how events in "**The Surprise Family**" were shown.

PREWRITING

Suggest that children draw three pictures that show the sequence of the event. Children might ask themselves, What happened first?, What was the most exciting part? and What happened at the end?

DRAFTING

As children get ready to write, guide them to use their pictures to describe each part of the event as it was when it was actually happening. They can fix spelling and punctuation later.

REVISING

As children reread their work, they can ask themselves questions such as, "Are the parts of the event presented in order? Would a reader enjoy reading about the event? Has anything important been left out of the description?"

REVISING STRATEGY: TAKE TIME OUT

Once the draft is done, ask children to put it aside and do something else. Tell them that this is something professional writers often do to enable themselves to come back to their work and look at it with fresh eyes. Suggest the following list of things to do while taking a break from writing:

• read a book

• play a game

• write in your journal

• draw a picture

• talk with someone else who's taking a break from writing

PROOFREADING

At the end of revision, children should check their spelling, grammar, and punctuation. If you have already presented the grammar lesson on **pages 285O–285P**, ask children to check their use of the verbs *was* and *were*.

PUBLISHING

Have children illustrate their descriptions. Display the illustrations and descriptions on a bulletin board entitled, "Life is Full of Surprises."

	RUBRIC FOR DESCRIPTIVE WRITING
4	**EXCELLENT** This personal narrative describes an incident clearly and in logical order. The writer makes creative choices and tells the story well.
3	**GOOD** This paper gives a satisfactory description of an incident. The sequence is logical.
2	**FAIR** This narrative fulfills the assignment but the details may be few and underdeveloped.
1	**POOR** This paper does not fulfill the assignment. It does not describe an event.

Writing Projects Tronic Phonics

The **Make a Book** section allows children to write and illustrate their own stories.

(handwritten card) your Invitd to a party!

(handwritten invitation) When? Monday Time? 7 PM Where? My House your Friend Jenna

PROJECT 1

GREETING CARD Pretend that you are giving a surprise party for a friend or relative. Draw a greeting card inviting someone to the party. In the card, tell whom you're giving the party for and why, and where and when it will take place. **EASY**

PROJECT 2

THE SURPRISE FAMILY Draw a picture of a family that looks very surprised. Write two sentences below your picture to explain why they are so surprised. Share your "surprise" family with the class. **AVERAGE**

(handwritten) They are Surprised with a new Car. They are happy!

PROJECT 3

UNEXPECTED LETTER Everyone has secrets—wonderful talents or abilities or experiences! Think of something about yourself that might be surprising to a friend. Write your friend a letter sharing your surprising secret. **CHALLENGE**

GRAMMAR, MECHANICS, AND USAGE If you have already presented the grammar lesson on **pages 285O–285P** or in the **GRAMMAR MINILESSONS, page 22,** remind children to review their writing for use of the verbs *was* and *were.*

SPELLING Children can choose words from their writing that they want to learn to spell and add these to their personal spelling list. See also the spelling lesson on **pages 285Q–285R.**

PORTFOLIO OPPORTUNITIES

Invite children to choose examples from their writing to include in their portfolios.

5-Day Plan
Grammar

WAS AND WERE

MEETING
INDIVIDUAL
NEEDS

Second-Language Support
Some English learners may have trouble identifying plural and singular subjects. Give them extra opportunities to practice, using concrete objects.

DAY 1

Daily Language Activity

Write the sentences on the chalkboard each day or use Transparency 8. Have children correct the sentences orally.

1. The egg were ready to hatch. **was**
2. The chick's mother were a boy. **was**
3. The boy and the chick was happy together. **were**

DAY 2

Daily Language Activity

Present these sentences and have children correct them aloud.

1. The boy were kind to the chick. **was**
2. She were safe in his pocket. **was**
3. Both of them was warm under the quilt. **were**

TEACH *WAS* AND *WERE*

FROM THE LITERATURE

INTRODUCE Read the third sentence on **page 279** of "**The Surprise Family**": "They were safe." Write the sentence on the chalkboard, circling the word *were*. Talk about how the sentence would be different if the hen had just one baby. **(It was safe.)**

DEFINE *WAS* AND *WERE*

DEVELOP/APPLY Write the following sentences on the chalkboard. Ask children how the verbs in each sentence are alike and different.

The hen was happy.
The ducks were happy.

Was and *were* are both verbs that tell about things that happened in the past. *Was* tells about one thing and *were* tells about more than one thing. Invite volunteers to suggest other sentences with *was* or *were*. Encourage them to explain why *was* or *were* is correct in each sentence.

SUMMARIZE

CLOSE Help children list rules for *was* and *were*.

USING WAS AND WERE

Remember
Use **was** for one.
Use **were** for more than one.

Each sentence is missing a word.
Write **was** or **were** on the line.

1. Ducks _____ swimming in the pond.

2. One duck _____ looking for food.

3. His head _____ under the water.

4. The other ducks _____ hungry, too.

106

DAY 1, GRAMMAR PRACTICE BOOK, page 106

USING WAS

Remember
Use **was** when you tell about one person, animal, or thing.

Read each sentence.
If it tells about one person, animal, or thing, write the word **was** on the line. If it tells about more than one, do not write anything.

1. Greg's new pet _____ a kitten.

2. The kitten's name _____ Fred.

3. Fred _____ cute and furry.

4. He _____ silly, too.

5. Greg and his dad _____ happy to have Fred.

107

DAY 2, GRAMMAR PRACTICE BOOK, page 107

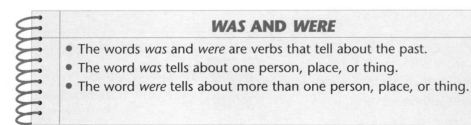

WAS AND WERE

- The words *was* and *were* are verbs that tell about the past.
- The word *was* tells about one person, place, or thing.
- The word *were* tells about more than one person, place, or thing.

DAY 3

Daily Language Activity

Present these sentences and have children correct them aloud.

1. Soon the chick were a hen. was
2. The hen were afraid to swim. was
3. Her babies was all good swimmers. were

WRITING APPLICATION

A NEWS STORY

Have children write a news story about the hatching of the ducklings. They may want to tell how the hen and the babies looked and how they felt when they saw each other. Have children identify the words *was* and *were* in their writing.

GRAMMAR/MECHANICS CHECKLIST

In evaluating their writing, children may want to check that
- correct forms of *was* and *were* are used to match subjects.
- sentences begin with a capital letter and end with a punctuation mark.

DAY 4

Daily Language Activity

Present these sentences and have children correct them aloud.

1. The hen's babies was ducklings. were
2. Their beaks was not pointed. were
3. Their feet was webbed. were

QUICK WRITE

PERSONAL NARRATIVE

Invite children to imagine being a duckling or chick inside an egg. Ask them to write about their feelings before, during, and after hatching.

DAY 5

Daily Language Activity

Present these sentences and have children correct them aloud.

1. The babies was not chicks. were
2. The hen were surprised. was
3. The hen and the ducks was a family. were

See page 22 of the GRAMMAR MINILESSONS for more information on was and were.

USING WERE

Remember

Use the verb **was** for one.   One child **was** the baker.

Use the verb **were** for more than one.   Two children **were** helpers.

Draw a line under each verb.
Write the subject that names more than one.

1. Three eggs were fresh.

2. One dozen muffins were ready.

3. Two jars of jelly were on the table.

4. Four children were hungry.

DAY 3, GRAMMAR PRACTICE BOOK, page 108

CHOOSING WAS OR WERE

Remember

Use **was** to tell about one.
Use **were** to tell about more than one.

Each sentence tells about one or one more than one.
Write **was** or **were** on the line.

1. The dog _____ swimming.

2. The flowers _____ pretty.

3. The frogs _____ jumping.

4. The cat _____ in the tree.

DAY 4, GRAMMAR PRACTICE BOOK, page 109

USING WAS AND WERE

Remember

Use **was** and **were** to tell about the past.
Use **was** for one.
Use **were** for more than one.

Answer the questions to complete the story.
Use **was** and **were** in your sentences.

It was a day like any other. Then I saw the egg. It cracked open.

What came out?

Where did it come from?

What color was it?

What happened next?

DAY 5, GRAMMAR PRACTICE BOOK, page 110

5-Day Plan
Spelling

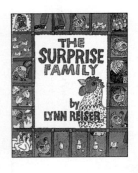

THE SURPRISE FAMILY by LYNN REISER

DAY 1

BEGIN WITH A PRETEST

ASSESS PRIOR KNOWLEDGE: WORDS WITH /ā/-ay

Use the dictation sentences below and **page 106** of the **SPELLING ACTIVITY BOOK** for the pretest. A Student Record form is provided.

Allow children to correct their own papers. Ask them to pay special attention to the words they misspelled.

SPELLING WORDS /ā/-ay			CHALLENGE WORDS	
away	bay	say	every	only
anyway	day			

Note: Words in **dark type** are from the story.

DICTATION SENTENCES

SPELLING WORDS

1. The boy would not let the egg roll <u>away</u>.
2. The hen loved the ducklings <u>anyway</u>.
3. Can ducklings swim in the <u>bay</u>?
4. The boy and the hen had a nice <u>day</u>.
5. What did the boy <u>say</u> to the hen?

CHALLENGE WORDS

6. We saw the ducklings <u>every</u> day.
7. The hen saw <u>only</u> one come back.

DAY 2

EXPLORE THE SPELLING PATTERN

IDENTIFY THE PHONOGRAM -ay

Write the Spelling Words on the chalkboard, reading them aloud with the class. Provide pairs of children with five index cards each, and invite them to write a spelling word on each card. Encourage them to lay the cards in a vertical column and identify what is the same in each word. Invite them to highlight the phonogram -ay on each card by circling the letters with a colored crayon.

aw (ay)   b (ay)

anyw (ay)   d (ay)   s (ay)

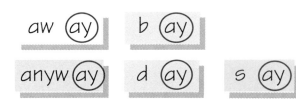

DAY 1, SPELLING ACTIVITY BOOK, page 106

Name: _____ Date: _____ The Surprise Family
Pretest

/ā/-ay

Pretest Directions
Fold back the paper in half. Use the blanks to write each word as it is read aloud. When you finish the test, unfold the paper. Use the list at the left to correct any spelling mistakes. Practice the words you missed for the Final Test.

To Parents
Here are the results of your child's weekly spelling Pretest. You can help your child study for the Final Test by following these simple steps for each word on the list:

1. Read the word to your child.

1. away
2. anyway
3. bay
4. day
5. say

Challenge Words
every
only

2. Have your child write the word, saying each letter as it is written.
3. Say each letter of the word as your child checks the spelling.
4. If a mistake has been made, have your child read each letter of the correctly spelled word aloud and then repeat steps 1–3.

Parent/Child Activity
Ask your child to tell you the two letters that are the same in each word.

1. _____
2. _____
3. _____
4. _____
5. _____

Challenge Words
_____

106

DAY 2, SPELLING ACTIVITY BOOK, page 107

Name: _____ Date: _____ The Surprise Family
Spelling Pattern

/ā/-ay

Write the rest of the spelling words so they are in ABC order. Circle the two letters that are in every word.

1. anyw(ay)   2. aw(ay)   3. b(ay)
4. d(ay)   5. s(ay)

Circle the spelling word in these longer words.

6. birth(day)   7. week(day)   8. holi(day)
9. Mon(day)   10. (bay)berry   11. Wednes(day)
12. (say)ing   13. Fri(day)

Change the **b** of bay to **pl**, **gr**, and **tr** to make new words. Write the words.

14. play   15. gray   16. tray

Note: The Challenge Words do not follow the pattern and are not included here.

107

DAY 3

CONSTRUCTING WORDS

MAKE A LETTER CUBE

Help small groups make a letter cube: Tape down the top of a small, empty milk carton and cover it with construction paper. Write one of the following letters or letter combinations on each side: *aw, anyw, b, d, s* Then write *ay* on a sheet of paper. The groups can take turns rolling the cube and pairing the letter(s) they roll with the phonogram *ay* to create Spelling Words.

WORK WITH MEANING

DEFINE THE WORDS

Invite children to make up their own definitions for the Spelling Words and write them. Have a group sharing time where children read and discuss their definitions.

The optional extension activity for the Challenge Word on **page 108** of the **SPELLING ACTIVITY BOOK** may be assigned on Day 3.

DAY 4

SPELLING AND WRITING

CREATING A STORY

Encourage children to create a story using "A Great Day" as the title. Tell them you will award them one point each time they use a Spelling Word. Tell them you will give them four points if they use more than one Spelling Word in the same sentence. The object is to see who can gather the most points.

One day, two kids wanted to go away fishing by the bay. So they waited for a bus. They waited and waited until it was dark. One said to the other,"I say, the bus is quite late, should we go home?" The other one said,"We might as well go home anyway since we missed daylight."

DAY 5

END WITH A POSTTEST

REASSESS CHILDREN'S KNOWLEDGE

Use **page 110** of the **SPELLING ACTIVITY BOOK** or the dictation sentences on **page 285Q** for the posttest. Children should record their scores on the Student Record form provided.

DAY 3, SPELLING ACTIVITY BOOK, page 108

DAY 4, SPELLING ACTIVITY BOOK, page 109

DAY 4, SPELLING ACTIVITY BOOK, page 110

Reading Resources
Study Skills

DIRECTIONS

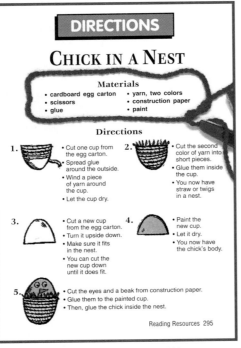

DIRECTIONS

CHICK IN A NEST

Materials
- cardboard egg carton
- scissors
- glue
- yarn, two colors
- construction paper
- paint

Directions

1. • Cut one cup from the egg carton.
   • Spread glue around the outside.
   • Wind a piece of yarn around the cup.
   • Let the cup dry.

2. • Cut the second color of yarn into short pieces.
   • Glue them inside the cup.
   • You now have straw or twigs in a nest.

3. • Cut a new cup from the egg carton.
   • Turn it upside down.
   • Make sure it fits in the nest.
   • You can cut the new cup down until it does fit.

4. • Paint the new cup.
   • Let it dry.
   • You now have the chick's body.

5. • Cut the eyes and a beak from construction paper.
   • Glue them to the painted cup.
   • Then, glue the chick inside the nest.

Reading Resources 295

For PUPIL EDITION, see page 291

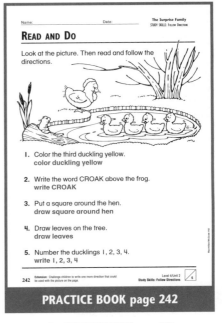

Name: _____ Date: _____   The Surprise Family
STUDY SKILLS: Follow Directions

READ AND DO

Look at the picture. Then read and follow the directions.

1. Color the third duckling yellow.
   color duckling yellow

2. Write the word CROAK above the frog.
   write CROAK

3. Put a square around the hen.
   draw square around hen

4. Draw leaves on the tree.
   draw leaves

5. Number the ducklings 1, 2, 3, 4.
   write 1, 2, 3, 4

Extension: Challenge children to write one more direction that could
be used with the picture on the page.

242   Level 4/Unit 2
                        Study Skills: Follow Directions

PRACTICE BOOK page 242

See RETEACHING BLM, page 157

⌾ Follow Directions

INTRODUCE Ask children to recall where the baby chick in **"The Surprise Family"** found herself just after she hatched. Discuss where baby chicks are usually located when they hatch. Invite children to make their own baby chicks to put anywhere they want.

DEVELOP/APPLY Have children turn to **page 295** in their anthologies. Ask what the page tells them how to do. Discuss that **directions** help a reader do or make something.

Point out that it's a good idea to read through all steps before beginning to follow directions. Have children read the list of materials and each step of the directions. Ask how pictures help make directions clearer. Discuss what might happen if steps were done out of order. Have children refer to the directions to answer questions like these:

- What materials are needed to make a chick in a nest? Do we already have the materials and tools needed? Which ones? Which ones do we need to get?

- What is the chick's body made out of?
- What do you do first, cut out the eyes and beak or paint the chick's body?

CLOSE Gather materials and invite children to make their own chicks in a nest following the directions. When finished, they can brainstorm ideas about where their chicks were when they hatched and who or what the chicks saw first.

Multicultural Perspectives

WHAT MAKES A FAMILY?

It takes more than Mom and Dad to make a family. In most nations, children benefit from the nurturing influence of a number of people other than their mothers and fathers. Some families have two parents, others just one. Still other families include relatives such as grandparents, aunts, and uncles. Like the animals in **"The Surprise Family,"** people need not be related by blood to be a family. It is the closeness that people share that defines them as family. Foster and adopted children are not related to their parents by birth, yet they live with their guardian parents and are dearly loved by them.

Egyptian households consist of an extended family: parents and children, as well as grandparents, aunts, and uncles. Grandparents help to raise the youngsters while mothers and fathers are at work.

It is the closeness that people share that defines them as family.

The extended family is also important in Ethiopia, where relatives help rear youngsters. Often, the extended family lives with a child and the parents. Each relative shares all belongings with the family.

Tribal elders in Africa share the past with children through stories told in the village square. Tribal elders in Native American communities in North America hold a similar role, imparting values and traditions through folk tales.

The Kikuyu of Kenya have special ties to their "age set," a group of people who were all born in the same year. Each group protects and teaches its members. Rural Nigerians have similar support systems. Older children from different families share chores with each other and look after the village youngsters.

Meet My Family

Have children create a family tree of family members with whom they live or people who are important to them. Invite children to tell the role played by each family member.

Across the Curriculum

MATH

PARTNER

ADDITIONAL EGGS
30 minutes

Materials: construction paper; scissors; markers

SOLVING PROBLEMS

Children can use egg cutouts to help them solve math problems.

- Have each child trace several egg shapes onto construction paper and cut them out. Then have them cut each egg in half with zigzag cuts.

- Help children put the eggs back together, and write a math problem on one half of each egg, and the answer on the other half.

- Children can exchange eggs with a partner and try to solve each other's problems by putting together the correct egg halves.

LOGICAL/MATHEMATICAL

SCIENCE/ART

ONE

POND LIFE
1 hour

Materials: construction paper; old magazines; fabric

COLLAGING AND PAINTING

Children can create a collage of pond life.

- Ask children to brainstorm a list of creatures that live in or near a pond. Have them draw a line across their construction paper to show the surface of their pond.

- Guide them to show which creatures live above the surface and which live below. Children can cut animals from old magazines, make cutouts, or draw directly onto their papers.

SPATIAL

SCIENCE

GROUP

WHAT THEY NEED

2 days

Materials: children's picture reference books; cardboard box; art supplies

CREATING A HABITAT

Children can work together to make models of animal habitats.

- Ask small groups of children to choose an animal that wouldn't typically be a pet, such as a giraffe or a water buffalo. Children can work together to learn about the animal's habitat.

- Have children use what they learn to build and label a model of a habitat for their animal. Habitats should include the terrain the animal is used to, and provision should be made for giving the animal the food and shelter it needs.

- Invite children to display and explain their habitat models.

SPATIAL

Water Buffalos Live Here

MUSIC/MOVEMENT

GROUP

A STORY DANCE

1 hour

Materials: various instrumental audiotapes; audiotape player; "The Surprise Family"

DANCING

Children can create a dance based on the story of **"The Surprise Family."**

- Invite children to listen to a variety of taped music while looking over the story. Small groups can choose different tapes to accompany the dances they create.

- To get children started, ask questions such as, Who is on stage first? What happens next? How would the hen move? the ducks? the boy? and How can you show swimming in dance form?

- Invite groups to perform their dances for each other.

MUSICAL/KINESTHETIC

Poetry

READING THE POEM

TEACHER READ ALOUD Before reading the poem, invite children to share their experiences with surprises. Encourage them to tell how the surprise made them feel. Then read the poem aloud, encouraging children to listen for details. If you wish, you may play **LISTENING LIBRARY AUDIOCASSETTE**.

SOFT AND LOUD Model dramatic presentation of the poem by softly reading aloud the first three stanzas. For the final stanzas, surprise your listeners by shouting out the line "I Like Surprises." Invite children to read the poem aloud with you in a similar fashion! They might even enjoy springing up from their seats as they chorus the final line.

LITERARY DEVICES AND TECHNIQUES

RHYTHM/RHYME PATTERNS Point out to children the *abcb* rhyme pattern in the poem, helping them to see that the final words in the second and fourth lines of each stanza rhyme. Invite children to identify the rhyming words in each stanza. Then read aloud the poem, clapping after each beat to emphasize the rhythm. Invite children to clap along. Help them see that when rhyme and rhythm are both used in a poem, a musical quality results.

286

Surprises are round
Or long or tallish.
Surprises are square
Or flat or smallish.

Surprises are wrapped
With paper and bow,
And hidden in closets
Where secrets won't show.

Surprises are often
Good things to eat;
A get-well toy or
A birthday treat.

Surprises come
In such interesting sizes—

I LIKE
SURPRISES!

Jean Conder Soule

287

POETRY TALK

Children can discuss their personal responses to the poem and talk about these and other questions in small groups.

- Why do you think the poet likes surprises?

- What special surprises have you gotten? What shape was the surprise—long, tall, flat, small?

- Have you ever gotten a surprise that you didn't like? What was it?

- What would the child in **"The Surprise Family"** say if he heard this poem?

MEET THE POET

ABOUT JEAN CONDER SOULE Jean Conder Soule grew up in a small town in Massachusetts. She still remembers the happy times she had playing in the countryside. Jean draws upon her memories to write both stories and poems for children. She began writing for youngsters after her children were born. Sometimes her children even helped. Jean explains, ". . . when we took walks with the dog, we'd write verses as we walked along."

AT THE EASEL

Invite children to draw a picture of something special they got as a surprise. Have them dictate a line or two about their surprise. Children can copy the sentences onto their pictures.

The Cow That Went OINK

written and illustrated

by Bernard Most

Harcourt Brace and Company, 1990

BOOK SUMMARY

In this book, a cow that oinks and a pig that moos teach each other a new sound. Along the way, they become great friends and have the last laugh on the barnyard animals that once ridiculed them.

WRITER

ILLUSTRATOR

BERNARD MOST

Bernard Most is the author and illustrator of many books for children, including *If the Dinosaurs Came Back, My Very Own Octopus,* and *The Littlest Dinosaurs.* His clear and clever line work is what makes his animal characters so appealing.

Prepare to Read

PREVIEW THE BOOK

Show children the book and read the title and the author's name.
Then encourage children to describe what they see on the front cover.
What is the cow doing? What do the other cows think of him? What
do they think the story will be about?

BUILD BACKGROUND

BARNYARD DISCUSSION Let children know that this story is about a
cow that oinks and a pig that moos. Encourage children to discuss
why this is unusual. What sort of problems might these animals face?
Students can write their ideas on the chalkboard.

SOUND CHART Tell children that cows and pigs are typical farm animals. Encourage children to brainstorm other farm animals and the
sounds they make. Record children's suggestions on a chart like the
one below.

Animal	Sound It Makes
sheep	baa
mouse	squeak
cat	meow
horse	neigh

Read the Book

COMPREHENSION: MAKE, CONFIRM, OR REVISE PREDICTIONS

This story tells about a pig that moos and a cow that oinks. Making predictions about how the pig and cow can help each other will reinforce children's understanding of the story.

SUGGESTIONS FOR READING

INDEPENDENT READING

As children read the story, they can stop at intervals to make predictions and confirm or revise them as needed. Children can use the **BLM** on **page 287G** to record their responses

READ TOGETHER

Invite small groups of children to complete a prediction chart. Children can use the **BLM** on **page 287H** to make predictions about the story.

READ AND TEACH

You may wish to read the book with small groups of children to teach them about making predictions. Use the Strategic Reading questions on **page 287D** to model how a strategic reader makes predictions while reading a story. You may also use the Strategic Reading questions with the preceding Suggestions for Reading.

STRATEGIC READING

As children read **"The Cow That Went OINK,"** have them concentrate on making predictions about the characters in the story. The questions below will help guide children's reading and help them use the strategy to assist in story comprehension.

AFTER PAGE 11
- Who is making the friendly "moo" sound? Was your prediction correct?
- How does the cow feel about making the wrong sound?

AFTER PAGE 16
- How does the pig who moos feel? Was your prediction correct?
- What would you do if you heard a pig "moo"?

AFTER PAGE 32
- Invite children to act out how the pig and cow feel when they learn to "oink" and "moo."
- How did the other animals feel about the cow's and pig's success?

The cow that went OINK was very sad.

The pigs that went OINK laughed at the pig that went MOO.

The pig could OINK. Now she would teach the cow to MOO.

RESPOND TO THE LITERATURE

Invite children to respond to the selection by choosing from among these suggestions:

ONE In their journals, children can write or draw about which part of the story they liked best.

PARTNER Invite pairs of children to look through the book and draw a picture together illustrating their favorite scene from the book.

GROUP Have groups of children read together to discuss how they liked the book. You might wish to begin your discussion with the following questions:

- How did the cow and pig teach each other? What do you think of the way they taught each other?

- What would you tell a friend about this book?

Writing

WRITING ABOUT THE THEME

CRITICAL THINKING After reading **"The Cow That Went Oink,"** children will see how the book relates to the unit theme, Surprise Along the Way. The story tells of a cow and a pig that make some surprising sounds.

QUICK WRITE Ask children to write a few sentences about an unusual animal that they know.

WRITING PROJECTS

PROJECT 1 **MAKE A LIST** Write a list of instructions for cow and pig to help them remember how to make both moo and oink sounds. **EASY**

PROJECT 2 **DESCRIPTION** Describe a farm scene that includes some of the animals in the story. You may wish to illustrate your description. **AVERAGE**

PROJECT 3 **CONTINUE THE STORY** Imagine what might happen if the cow and pig decided to teach some of the other farm animals some new sounds. What would happen? Continue the story. **CHALLENGE**

Across the Curriculum

ART

Pig and Cow Art

Materials: drawing paper, markers, crayons, water colors

Partners can draw pictures of cow and pig engaged in some farm activities. What do they eat? Where do they sleep? Do they continue to play and learn with each other? Encourage children to share their drawings with the class.

SOCIAL STUDIES

What Farms Do for Us

Materials: paper, pencils, markers

Farms are very important to all of us. Farms produce our food and other crops, such as cotton, which is used to make clothing. Invite children to find books in the library about farms and farm life. Then encourage them to write a short report and share their findings with the class.

MUSIC

Barnyard Sounds

Materials: tapes and tape recorders

Small groups can create tape recordings of barnyard sounds. The groups should first make a list of the animals they wish to include. Then they should practice making the sounds before actually recording. Assist children in making their recordings. Then have children play the recordings for the class and have the class guess which animals the sounds belong to.

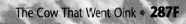

WHAT WILL HAPPEN NEXT?

Stop at the end of the page that has these words. What will happen next? Write what you think will happen next.

....

One day the cow heard a friendly MOO.

What will happen next?_____

_____

_____

And all the other animals laughed at her, too.

What will happen next?_____

_____

_____

**The cow and pig were very happy.
Each of them could MOO and OINK.**

What will happen next?_____

_____

_____

....

Did you predict what would happen? How many times?

_____

_____

PREDICTION CHART

Did you figure out what would happen next in the story? Check the boxes to show how you did.

Event	Prediction	Yes	No
One day the cow heard a friendly MOO.	It was a pig that said MOO.		
All the other animals laughed at her, too.	The pig that said MOO was very sad.		
The pig that went MOO tried to go OINK.	She will learn to OINK.		
The cow that went OINK tried to go MOO	He will learn to MOO.		
Each of them could MOO and OINK.	They had the last laugh.		

Pet Show!

written and illustrated

by Ezra Jack Keats

Macmillan, 1972

BOOK SUMMARY

Archie, the main character in **"Pet Show!"** wants to enter his cat in the neighborhood pet show. There is only one problem. Archie's cat has vanished. Though all of his friends help him search for his cat, Archie is unable to find it. Archie doesn't give up. And the pet he finally brings to the show is a very surprising one indeed.

EZRA JACK KEATS

Ezra Jack Keats was born in Brooklyn, New York, and was a child of the city. He illustrated nearly a dozen books before writing his first, *The Snowy Day,* which won the 1963 Caldecott Medal. With solid and patterned paper as wedges of color, combined with illustrations thick with paint, Keats portrays a world of endearing characters and energetic cityscapes. His other books include: *Goggles! Hi, Cat!* and *Dreams.*

Prepare to Read

PREVIEW THE BOOK

Show children the book and read the title and the author's name. Point out that this book was written and illustrated by the same person. Then encourage children to describe what they see on the front cover. What does the sign say? What are the boys thinking? What do they think the story will be about?

BUILD BACKGROUND

CITY TALK Point out that this story takes place in the city—in a neighborhood that includes lots of people who help and look out for each other. Encourage children to discuss what they know about city neighborhoods. If you do not live in an urban area, you may wish to bring in pictures from magazines and books that show city neighborhoods. What sights do children see? Who are the people? Where do they live?

PET SHOW WEB Let children know that the main event in this story is a neighborhood pet show. Guide children to brainstorm the kinds of animals that usually participate in pet shows and other things about pet shows that they know. Record their responses in a word web like the one below.

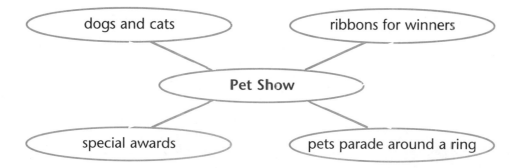

Read the Book

COMPREHENSION: CHARACTER, PLOT, SETTING

This story tells about Archie, a very clever boy, who comes up with an unusual pet to enter in the show. Thinking about character and setting will help children understand why the events in the story unfold as they do.

SUGGESTIONS FOR READING

INDEPENDENT READING

As children read the story, they can stop at intervals to record important events in the story. Children can use the **BLM** on **page 287O** to write down their responses.

READ TOGETHER

Invite small groups of children to read the story. They can use the **BLM** on **page 287P** to create a story map together.

READ AND TEACH

You may wish to read the book with small groups of children to teach them about character, plot, and setting. Use the Strategic Reading questions on **page 287L** to model how a strategic reader thinks about character, plot, and setting while reading a story. You may also use the Strategic Reading questions with the preceding Suggestions for Reading.

STRATEGIC READING

As children read "**Pet Show!**" have them concentrate on character, plot, and setting. Tell children that by concentrating on plot and setting, they will be able to understand what happens to the characters in the story. The questions below will help guide children's reading and help them use the strategies to assist in story comprehension.

AFTER PAGE 19
- Where does the story take place? How can you tell it is a city?
- What is everyone so excited about?
- Who can tell us what problem Archie is having?

AFTER PAGE 17
- Everyone won a prize. What was your favorite prize for? Handsomest frog? Busiest ants?

AFTER PAGE 33
- What did Archie bring to the show? What is a germ?
- Why do you think Archie let the old woman keep the ribbon? What does this tell you about Archie?
- Imagine that you are having a pet show in your neighborhood. Tell us about what animal you will bring.

RESPOND TO THE LITERATURE

Invite children to respond to the selection by choosing from among these suggestions:

ONE In their journals, children can write or draw about which part of the story they liked best.

PARTNER Invite pairs of children to draw a picture together of what a pet show in their neighborhood would look like.

GROUP Have groups of children discuss how they liked the book. You might choose to begin your discussion with the following questions:

- What did you think when Archie showed up with a germ? Was this a good idea?
- What would you tell a friend about Archie?

Writing

WRITING ABOUT THE THEME

CRITICAL THINKING After reading **"Pet Show!"** children will see how the book relates to the unit theme, Surprise Along the Way. In the story the main character brings quite a surprise to the pet show.

QUICK WRITE Ask children to write a few sentences about a time they were surprised by something.

WRITING PROJECTS

PROJECT 1 **CREATE AN AWARD** Make an award for Archie and his quick thinking. On the award tell why Archie is getting the award. `EASY`

PROJECT 2 **LOST AND FOUND POSTER** Make a lost and found poster for Archie's missing cat. Describe the cat and tell why Archie needs the cat returned. Tell if there is a reward and what it is. `AVERAGE`

PROJECT 3 **DESCRIPTION** Describe the neighborhood where Archie lives. Use the illustrations in the story to help you with your description. Read your description to the class. `CHALLENGE`

Across the Curriculum

SCIENCE

Cat Characteristics

Materials: paper, pencils, construction paper

Archie couldn't find his cat in the story. Invite children to write a short report telling everything they know about cats. Children might include information about kinds of cats and what some of their habits and characteristics are. Partners can share their reports with the class.

SOCIAL STUDIES/ART

Life in the City

Materials: shoe box, clay, construction paper, scissors

Children can make a diorama of a city neighborhood like the one in the story. They can create the buildings of the neighborhood from construction paper and use clay to make some people in the neighborhood.

DRAMA

Stage the Pet Show

Materials: simple props to indicate animal participants

Small groups can reenact the pet show. Children can make and carry simple drawings of their animals and be prepared to tell the judges why their animal should win a prize. Groups should stage their show for the class.

THE MAIN EVENTS

As you read the story, write the main events.

The neighborhood is having a pet show.

Archie decides _____

Archie's cat is missing.

Archie's friends _____

No one can find the cat.

Archie is _____

Everyone goes to the pet show.

Everyone _____

Archie brings a surprise to the show.

The surprise is _____

At the end, Archie _____

_____

A STORY MAP

As you read the story, fill in the story map.

The characters were:

_____

_____

The main character's problem:

_____

_____

The main character solved his problem:

_____

_____

At the end of the story:

_____

_____

Looking Back

THEME REVIEW

Review the theme focus with children: Life is full of surprises.

Invite children to discuss the stories they've read, recalling the surprises they encountered.

COOPERATIVE PROJECT

Skits About Surprises Review the steps that each group took to complete their Skits About Surprises. Discuss the importance of each role to the group project. Encourage children to evaluate things that went smoothly and things that did not.

ONGOING ASSESSMENT (INFORMAL) Use the scoring rubric to assess children's cooperative projects.

SCORING RUBRIC

CRITERION	Skit tells the story of a surprising event that happens to people.	Skit includes essential elements: characters, dialog, props.
4	Skit depicts a surprising event in a clear, logical sequence.	Skit includes all essential parts. Story characters are clear; dialog is cohesive; speech is clear and audible.
3	Surprising event is presented in a somewhat logical sequence.	Skit includes all essential parts; some characters may be unnecessary; speech may be unclear.
2	Surprising event appears disjointed and out of order.	Skit includes two essential parts.
1	Event does not involve a surprise.	Skit includes only one essential part.

LINKS ACROSS THE LITERATURE

Encourage children to make connections among the selections by asking **WHAT IF** questions, such as

WHAT IF the boy in **"One Monday Morning"** had seen the strange Something in **"Seven Blind Mice"?** Would the boy have been surprised?

WHAT IF the characters in **"The Surprise Family"** appeared by the pond in **"Seven Blind Mice"?**

WHAT IF the king, the queen, and the little prince in **"One "Monday Morning"** visited Titch in **"You'll Soon Grow Into Them, Titch"?**

WRITING ABOUT THE THEME

Invite children to think about a surprise that has involved them. Did they do something to surprise someone? Did something happen to surprise them? Encourage children to draw a picture and write one or more sentences about a surprise that involved them.

VOCABULARY REVIEW

Write the instructional vocabulary words for Unit 2 on the chalkboard. Read them aloud, then have children work in groups of three to play a game of "Vocabulary Go Fish."

- Provide each group with a set of index cards on which to write the vocabulary words (two cards for each word).

- Children in each group decide who will be the dealer and who will go first, second, and third. The dealer shuffles the cards and deals five cards to each player. The remaining cards are placed face down in a deck.

- Children look at their cards and pull out any pairs. Then player 1 begins by asking player 2: Do you have the word *queen*? (or any vocabulary word in the player's hand) If yes, player 2 gives player 1 the card and he or she makes a pair. If no, player 1 draws a card from the deck. Then player 2 questions player 3, player 3 questions player 1, and so on until all the cards have been paired.

- Players take turns challenging one another to make up sentences using the vocabulary words on the cards they acquired.

VOCABULARY WORDS

ONE MONDAY MORNING

cook	knight	prince
queen	return	visit

YOU'LL SOON GROW INTO THEM, TITCH

brother	clothes	pair
pants	sister	socks

SEVEN BLIND MICE

agree	elephant	great
strange	turn	whole

THE SURPRISE FAMILY

afternoon	drink	everywhere
farther	nest	swim

Use **page 243** of the **PRACTICE BOOK** for additional vocabulary practice.

GRAMMAR REVIEW

Review the skills covered in the Grammar Lessons: special forms of present and past-tense verbs. Write sentences on the chalkboard using these words: *come, came, say, said, go, went, was, were.* Have volunteers read the sentences aloud and tell if each sentence relates to the present or the past. Invite volunteers to underline the verb in each sentence that tells if it is in the present or the past. You may wish to refer to **pages 21–22** of the **GRAMMAR MINILESSONS**.

SPELLING REVIEW

Give each child four blank word cards. Review the spelling patterns on the chalkboard, writing the letters for each of the patterns as a category label. After each pattern has been reviewed, invite the children to write a word using the pattern. Have volunteers affix their words under the appropriate labels.

GRAMMAR MINILESSONS

Assessment

Use the results of the informal and formal assessment opportunities in the unit to help you make decisions about future instruction.

SKILLS/STRATEGIES THROUGH EXPLICIT INSTRUCTION

Revisit activities in the unit to address the specific needs of children.

Comprehension

Make, Confirm, or Revise Predictions 140, 157, 177B, 212, 221, 249B
Character, Plot, Setting 180, 203, 207B, 256, 271, 285B
  Practice Book 201, 216, 223, 235
  Reteaching BLM 123, 136, 141, 151

Phonics and Decoding

Long Vowels and Phonograms 177G, 207G, 249G, 285G
Consonant Blends and Digraphs 177J, 207J, 249J, 285J
  Practice Book 204, 206, 207, 218, 219, 221, 228, 229, 233, 236, 240, 241
  Reteaching BLM 127, 128, 137, 138, 139, 145, 146, 149, 155, 156

SEE MACMILLAN/McGRAW-HILL STAFF DEVELOPMENT GUIDE.

SKILLS/STRATEGIES IN A NEW CONTEXT

Opportunities to teach skills covered in this unit are provided in the units that follow.

Comprehension

Make, Confirm, or Revise Predictions
Level 5 197
Character, Plot, Setting Level 5 47, 127
  Practice Book Level 5 256, 310
  Reteaching BLM Level 5 167, 212

Phonics and Decoding

Long Vowels and Phonograms Level 5 37G
Consonant Blends Level 5 37J
  Practice Book Level 5 245, 247
  Reteaching BLM Level 5 158, 160

See Unit Overview pages for additional skills:
Level 5 8/9H–8/9I, 136/137H–136/137I.

FLEXIBLE GROUPING SUGGESTIONS

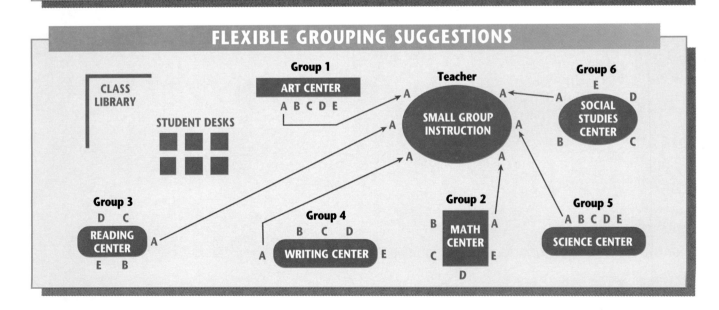

Glossary

INTRODUCTION

Introduce children to the Glossary by inviting them to look through the pages, describing and discussing what they see there.

Explain that the **Glossary** will help them find out the meanings of words. Explain that the Glossary is a special kind of dictionary just for this book. You will probably want to give a simple **definition** of **dictionary**, such as: "a book that shows how words are spelled and what they mean."

ALPHABETICAL

Point out that words in a glossary, like words in a dictionary, are listed in **alphabetical order**. Have children note the order of the large capital letters, and have them note all the words listed below a particular letter begin with that letter. Have a volunteer name a letter, then have children turn to that letter in the Glossary. Read aloud with children the words listed under the letter.

Point out the **guide words** at the top of each page and explain that these words tell the first word and the last word that appear on the page. Have children match entry words and guide words on one of the Glossary pages.

ENTRIES

Point out the **entry words.** Ask children to note that each entry word is printed in heavy black type and that it appears on a line by itself. Explain that the meaning, or **definition,** of the word as it is used in this book is given in the first sentence below. Explain that the second sentence is an example of how the word (or some form of it) can be used correctly. Give each child an opportunity to identify either a definition or an example sentence.

Explain that the words following the small triangles are different forms of the entry word. Find examples of a plural noun, verb forms, and adjective forms, and discuss the use of each with the class.

Finally, point out the illustrations that help make the definitions clearer. Draw attention to the boldfaced word in the caption that explains what is being illustrated.

Give children time to study the Glossary and discover what information it includes.

GLOSSARY

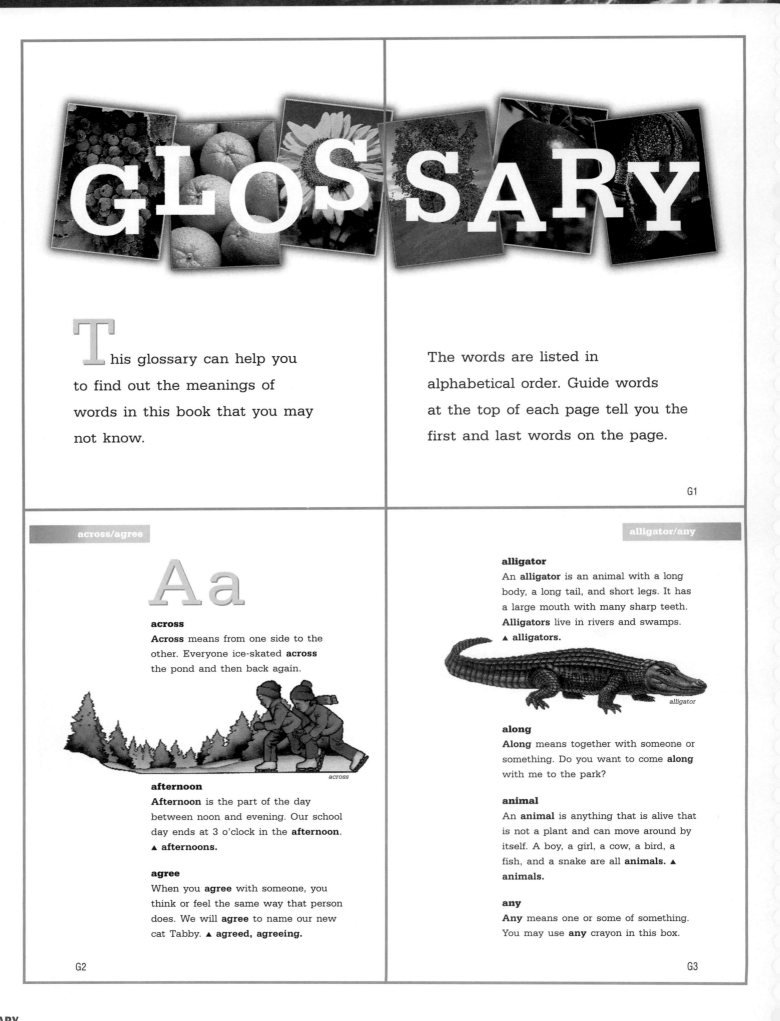

This glossary can help you to find out the meanings of words in this book that you may not know.

The words are listed in alphabetical order. Guide words at the top of each page tell you the first and last words on the page.

G1

Aa

across
Across means from one side to the other. Everyone ice-skated **across** the pond and then back again.

across

afternoon
Afternoon is the part of the day between noon and evening. Our school day ends at 3 o'clock in the **afternoon**. ▲ **afternoons.**

agree
When you **agree** with someone, you think or feel the same way that person does. We will **agree** to name our new cat Tabby. ▲ **agreed, agreeing.**

G2

alligator
An **alligator** is an animal with a long body, a long tail, and short legs. It has a large mouth with many sharp teeth. **Alligators** live in rivers and swamps. ▲ **alligators.**

alligator

along
Along means together with someone or something. Do you want to come **along** with me to the park?

animal
An **animal** is anything that is alive that is not a plant and can move around by itself. A boy, a girl, a cow, a bird, a fish, and a snake are all **animals**. ▲ **animals.**

any
Any means one or some of something. You may use **any** crayon in this box.

G3

Bb

barber

barber
A **barber** is a person who cuts hair. Mom took me to the **barber** because my hair was too long. ▲ **barbers.**

beautiful
When something is **beautiful**, it is very pretty to look at or listen to. The sunset last night was **beautiful.**

body
A **body** is all of a person or an animal. An elephant has a huge, heavy **body.** ▲ **bodies.**

brother
Your **brother** is a boy who has the same mother and father as you do. My **brother** feeds the dog when he gets home from school. ▲ **brothers.**

G4

bush
A **bush** is a plant that is smaller than a tree. A **bush** has many branches. Roses and some kinds of berries grow on **bushes.** ▲ **bushes.**

butterfly
A **butterfly** is an insect that has four large wings with bright colors. A **butterfly** landed on the flower. ▲ **butterflies.**

butterfly

Cc

call
Call means to say something in a loud voice. Dad will **call** us when dinner is ready. ▲ **called, calling.**

caterpillar
A **caterpillar** is a baby butterfly that has a soft, long, round body, no wings, many legs, and is often furry. The **caterpillar** crawled onto her finger. ▲ **caterpillars.**

caterpillar

G5

clothes
People wear **clothes** to cover their bodies. Coats, dresses, pants, and jackets are kinds of **clothes.**

cook
A **cook** is a person who makes food ready to eat. My mom is a good **cook.** ▲ **cooked, cooking.**

count
Count means to find out how many of something there are. Let's **count** how many apples we picked. ▲ **counted, counting.**

count

Dd

danger
Danger means that something could happen to hurt you. The bird escaped **danger** by flying away from the cat. ▲ **dangers.**

G6

drink
A **drink** is a liquid you put in your mouth and swallow. Tim's favorite **drink** is milk. ▲ **drinks.**

ear

Ee

ear
An **ear** is the part of the body that you hear with. There is one **ear** on each side of your head. ▲ **ears.**

elephant
An **elephant** is the biggest and strongest animal that lives on land. It has thick gray skin and a long nose called a trunk. We saw an **elephant** at the zoo. ▲ **elephants.**

everywhere
Everywhere means in all places. Betty looked **everywhere** in the house for her shoes.

G7

eye
An **eye** is the part of the body that you see with. The baby closed his **eyes** and went to sleep. ▲ **eyes.**

F f

fall
Fall means to come down from a place. I like to watch the rain **fall** from the sky. ▲ **fell, fallen, falling.**

fall

farther
When something is **farther** away it means that it is a greater distance away. Rae's paper plane flew **farther** than Tommy's did.

G8

food
Food is what we eat. Everything that lives needs **food** to grow. ▲ **foods.**

G g

give
Give means to let someone have something to keep. Suzy **gives** toys to her little sister. ▲ **gave, given, giving.**

great
Great means large or a lot. A **great** number of people voted in the election. ▲ **greater, greatest.**

H h

head
The **head** is the part of the body above the neck. Eyes, ears, nose, and mouth are all parts of the **head.** ▲ **heads.**

head

G9

J j

jester
A **jester** was a person long ago who played jokes and made people laugh. The king and queen laughed at the silly **jester.** ▲ **jesters.**

K k

kind
Kind means a group of things that are alike in some way. Apples are a **kind** of fruit. ▲ **kinds.**

king
A **king** is a man who rules a country. I like the story about a **king** and a queen who live in a castle. ▲ **kings.**

king

G10

knight
Long ago, a **knight** was a soldier for a king or queen. **Knights** wore armor and rode horses. ▲ **knights.**

knight

L l

leg
A **leg** is a part of the body that you stand or walk on. People and animals stand and walk on their **legs.** ▲ **legs.**

M m

morning
Morning is the part of the day before noon. I like to wake up early in the **morning** when the sun shines through my window. ▲ **mornings.**

G11

Nn

nest

A **nest** is a bird's house. Birds build their **nests** with leaves, sticks, and mud. ▲ **nests.**

nest

nice

When something is **nice**, it makes you feel good. The sun was shining, and it was a **nice** day. ▲ **nicer, nicest.**

nose

Your **nose** is in the center of your face. You breathe and smell things through your **nose.** ▲ **noses.**

G12

Pp

pair

A **pair** means two things that go together or something that has two legs or two parts. I need a new **pair** of socks. ▲ **pairs.**

pants

Pants are clothes that you wear on the bottom half of your body. Pants cover each leg separately. Jamie wore new **pants** to the party.

pond

A **pond** is a small lake with land all around it. The **pond** in back of my house has fish and frogs in it. ▲ **ponds.**

pond

prince

A **prince** is the son of a king or queen. Someday the **prince** will become a king. ▲ **princes.**

Qq

queen

A **queen** is a woman who rules a country. The **queen** waved to the people as she rode in the carriage. ▲ **queens.**

queen

Rr

return

Return means to come back or to go back. My cousin will **return** to France after visiting us. ▲ **returned, returning.**

G14

Ss

silly

When someone or something is **silly**, it makes us laugh. That **silly** clown did such funny things. ▲ **sillier, silliest.**

silly

sister

Your **sister** is a girl who has the same mother and father as you do. My **sister** and I both have blue eyes. ▲ **sisters.**

sock

A **sock** is a soft cover for your foot. **Socks** are worn inside shoes. ▲ **socks.**

G15

strange

Strange means very different from what you expect. Joseph drew a picture of a **strange** animal with red ears.
▲ **stranger, strangest.**

swim

Swim means to move in the water by using arms, legs, fins, or a tail. People **swim** using their arms and legs. ▲ **swam, swum, swimming.**

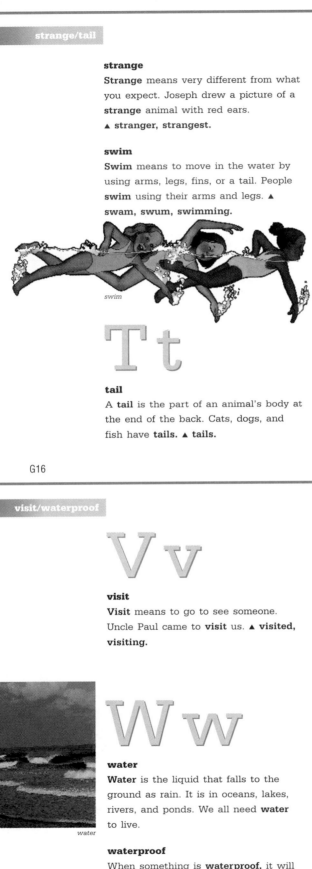

swim

Tt

tail

A **tail** is the part of an animal's body at the end of the back. Cats, dogs, and fish have **tails.** ▲ **tails.**

G16

trouble

Trouble means that something is hard to do or might even be dangerous. Pat had **trouble** putting on his boots.
▲ **troubles.**

trunk

A **trunk** is the long nose of an elephant. Elephants use their **trunks** to pick things up. ▲ **trunks.**

trunk

turn

A **turn** is a person's time to do something. It is Dan's **turn** to hit the ball. ▲ **turns.**

G17

Vv

visit

Visit means to go to see someone. Uncle Paul came to **visit** us. ▲ **visited, visiting.**

Ww

water

Water is the liquid that falls to the ground as rain. It is in oceans, lakes, rivers, and ponds. We all need **water** to live.

water

waterproof

When something is **waterproof,** it will not let water go through it. Billy's raincoat was **waterproof.**

G18

whole

When something is **whole,** it has no parts missing from it. Myra read the **whole** book in just two days.

wing

A **wing** is the part of a butterfly or insect that helps it to fly. The **wings** of the butterfly are very beautiful.
▲ **wings.**

woods

An area with a lot of trees and other plants is called a **woods.** We walked through the **woods.**

woods

G19

ACKNOWLEDGMENTS

The publisher gratefully acknowledges permission to reprint the following copyrighted material:

Entire text, art, and cover of ANY KIND OF DOG by Lynn Reiser. Copyright (c) 1992 by Lynn Whisnant Reisner. By permission of Greenwillow Books, a division of William Morrow and Company.

"Anybody Home?" by Aileen Fisher. By permission of the author, who controls the rights..

"The Cloud" by Emma Pérez. Reprinted by permission.

"The Elephant's Trunk" reprinted from the September, Series II issue of *YOUR BIG BACKYARD*, with the permission of the publisher, the National Wildlife Federation. Copyright 1981 by the National Wildlife Federation.

"The Family Circus" by Bil Keane, from THROUGH THE YEARS WITH THE FAMILY CIRCUS. Copyright © 1992 by Bil Keane Inc., published by Ballantine Books, a division of Random House, Inc. Reprinted by permission.

"First Snow" by Marie Louise Allen. Reprinted by permission.

"The Folk Who Live in Backward Town" reprinted by permission of Gina Maccoby Literary Agency. Copyright © 1959 by Mary Ann Hoberman. renewed 1987.

"Hattie and the Fox" is the entire text and all artwork from HATTIE AND THE FOX by Mem Fox. Text copyright (c) 1986 by Mem Fox. Illustrations copyright (c) 1986 by Patricia Mullins. Reprinted with permission of Simon & Schuster Books For Young Children, Simon & Schuster Children's Publishing Division.

The book cover of LON PO PO: A RED RIDING HOOD STORY FROM CHINA by Ed Young. Copyright © 1989 by Ed Young. Published by the Putnam Publishing Group. Reprinted by permission.

"Magic in Mother Gooseland" by Sally Lucas is from HIGHLIGHTS FOR CHILDREN July/August 1993 issue. Copyright © 1993 by Highlights for Children, Inc., Columbus, Ohio.

"One Monday Morning" by Uri Shulevitz. Copyright (c) 1974 by Uri Shulevitz. Reprinted with permission of Atheneum Books for Young Readers, Simon & Schuster Children's Publishing Division.

"Open" by Chikaoka Saori. Reprinted by permission.

"Seven Blind Mice" by Ed Young. Copyright© 1992, by Ed Young, published by Philomel Books. Reprinted by permission of the publisher.

"Seven Sillies" by Joyce Dunbar, illustrated by Chris Downing, Copyright © 1993, by Joyce Dunbar and Chris Downing. Reprinted by permission of Andersen Press, Ltd.

Text of "Something Big Has Been Here" from SOMETHING BIG HAS BEEN HERE by Jack Prelutsky. Text copyright © 1990 by Jack Prelutsky. By permission of Greenwillow Books, a division of William Morrow and Company, Inc.

Entire text, art, and cover of THE STORY OF CHICKEN LICKEN by Jan Ormerod. Copyright (c) 1985 by Jan Ormerod. By permission of Lothrop, Lee & Shepard Books, a division of William Morrow and Company. Inc.

"Surprises" by Jean Conder Soule. Reprinted by permission.

Entire text, art, and cover of THE SURPRISE FAMILY by Lynn Reiser. Copyright (c) 1994 by Lynn Whisnant Reiser. By permission of Greenwillow Books, a division of William Morrow and Company.

"Things That Happen" by Felice Holman, reprinted by permission of the author from AT THE TOP OF MY VOICE AND OTHER POEMS, Charles Scribner's Sons. Copyright © 1970 Felice Holman.

"A Wild Alphabet" reprinted from the June, Series I issue of Your Big Backyard, with the permission of the publisher, the National Wildlife Federation. Copyright (c) 1980 by the National Wildlife Federation.

"You'll Soon Grow into Them, Titch" Text & Art from YOU'LL SOON GROW INTO THEM TITCH by Pat Hutchins. Copyright © 1983 by Pat Hutchins. By permission of Greenwillow Books, a division of William Morrow & Company, Inc.

COVER DESIGN: Carbone Smolan Associates
COVER ILLUSTRATION: Steve Johnson & Lou Fancher (front - rabbit and boy, and back), Kathleen O'Malley (front - butterflies)

DESIGN CREDITS
Carbone Smolan Associates, front matter 138-139
Bill Smith Studio, 208-209, 250-253
Function Thru Form, Inc., 288-293

ILLUSTRATION CREDITS
Steve Johnson & Lou Fancher, 138-139; Jeff Shelly, 208-209 (bkgd.); Mary King 250-251 (bkgd.); Kevin Sprouls, 250; June Sobel, 254-255. **Reading Resources:** Nelle Davis, 288, 290-291; Randy Chewning, 292; Felicia Telsey, 293. **Glossary:** Bob Pepper, G2, G6, G9, G10, G14, G16; Will and Cory Nelson, G3, G4-G5, G12.

PHOTOGRAPHY CREDITS

All photographs are by the Macmillan/McGraw-Hill School Division (MMSD) except as noted below.

207: Courtesy of Pat Hutchins. 213: Moninca Stevenson for MMSD. 250: b. Ralph A. Reinhold/Animals Animals. 251:b Johnny Johnson/DRK Photo; t Gerard Lacz/Animals Animals. 252-253: John Curtis/The Stock Market 285: William Morrow & Company; 288: Art Wolf/Tony Stone Images. 289: David Muench/Tony Stone Images. 293: t.l. Monica Stevenson for MMSD. **Glossary:** GO: Inga Spence/Tom Stack & Associates; Superstock; Comstock. G1: Jack Van Antwerp/The Stock Market; Craig Tuttle/The Stock Market; Richard Gross/The Stock Market. G11: t.l. Charles Mahaux/The Image Bank. G13: b. Arthur Meyerson/The Image Bank. G15: t Ted Horowitz/The Stock Market. G17: Tim Davis/Tony Stone Images. G18: m. Uniphoto, Inc. G19: b. John Eastcott/The Image Works.

Acknowledgments

The publisher gratefully acknowledges permission to reprint the following copyrighted material:

Cover Design: Carbone Smolan Associates

Cover Illustration: Steve Johnson & Lou Fancher

Production: Textart, Inc.

Illustrations: Bernard Adnet, Batelman Illustration, Stephanie Britt, Eileen Elterman, Elisa, Anthony, Janet and Tom Gagliano, Myron Grossman, Andy Levine, Steve Sullivan, Paul Turzio, Michael Woo

Photography: All photographs are by the Macmillan/McGraw Hill School Division (MMSD) and Ken Karp for MMSD, David Mager for MMSD, Anne Neilson for MMSD, Clara von Aich for MMSD, except as noted below.

Level 2 58; I.S. Nielsen/Bruce Coleman Inc. pg. 111; r. Max Schneider/The Image Bank, Level 5 229U; I. Lynda Richardson/Peter Arnold, Inc.. 229; r. Elizabeth Lemoine-Jacana/Photo Researchers, Inc., 261U; r. Hal Yeager/FPG International. Level 6 199S; I. Joseph Van Ox/The Image Bank. 321S; I. Kelvin Aitkes/eter Arnold, Inc. Level 7 225T; I. UPI/Bettmann. 287S; I. Peter Arnold, Inc. Level 8 79R; I. W. Hill/ The Image Works. 149R; r. Stuart L. Craig Jr./Bruce Coleman, Inc. Level 9 46H; James Lemass/The Picture Cube, Inc. 173H; Eric Meola/The Image Bank. 297R; I. Carl M. Purcell/Uniphoto Picture Agency. Level 10 43Q; r. Jean-Marc Truchet/Tony Stone Worldwide. 317R; r. Kevin Schafer/Peter Arnold, Inc. 411R; r. ProFiles West. 521R; I. Phyllis Picardi/Stock, Boston. 545R; I. Dany Krist/Uniphoto Picture Agency. Level 11 71Q; I. Superstock. 41R; I. W. E. Finch/Stock, Boston. 179R; r. George A. Dillon/Stock, Boston. 207R; I. Freeman Patterson/ Masterfile. 245R; r. F. Pedrick/The Image Works. 263R; t.r. Gary Gay/The Image Bank. 263R; r. Charles Gupton/Uniphoto. 263R. 285Q; r. Alex Stewart/The Image Bank. 317R; I. Bettmann Archive. 351R; I. Nathan Benn/Woodfin Camp & Assoc. 441Q; I. The Bettmann Archive. 419Q; r. Hans Blohm/Masterfile. 481R; r. Anthony Mercieca/Photo Researchers, Inc.

Teacher's Resources

CONTENTS

READER CARD 1 RESPONSE

One Monday Morning
pages 140–177

With a group or partner, share your thoughts about the selection. Talk about these questions and any other ideas you may have.

- Did any of the characters remind you of people you know?

- How are you like the little prince? How are you different from him?

- Would you have acted the same way as the little boy did when all of the visitors dropped in?

- What would you tell a friend about this story?

READER CARD 2 RESPONSE

You'll Soon Grow Into Them, Titch
pages 180–207

With your partner or small group, share your responses to the selection. Discuss these questions or ideas of your own.

- Which thoughts would you like to share from your journal?

- Have you ever been in a situation similar to Titch? Describe what it was like.

- Do you or does anyone you know have a new baby brother or sister? How does it feel?

- How many brothers or sisters do you have in your family? Are you the youngest or oldest?

- This unit is about surprises. What surprised you the most in this story?

READER CARD 3 RESPONSE

Seven Blind Mice
pages 212–249

Share your thoughts and feelings about the story. Talk about these questions with a partner or group.

- Did you see the strange Something the same way any of the mice did?

- Why do you think each mouse saw the Something as he did?

- What did you notice about the use of color in the story?

- What other stories do you know that teach a lesson?

- How does this story fit with the theme, Surprises Along the Way?

READER CARD 4 RESPONSE

The Surprise Family
pages 256–285

With a group, share your ideas about the story. You can talk about what you liked most. You can also talk about these questions.

- Check your journal entry for this selection. Which idea do you want to share?

- Why do you think the boy wants to take care of the hen? Why does the hen want to take care of the ducklings?

- How do people in families take care of each other?

- What did "The Surprise Family" teach you about dealing with something unexpected?

Theme Matrix

GRADES K, 1, 2

	COMMUNITY	PROBLEM SOLVING	COOPERATION	SAVING THE ENVIRONMENT	THE NATURAL WORLD	CHALLENGES	STORYTELLING	YOURSELF AND OTHERS	PICTURES OF AMERICA	JOURNEYS	FRIENDS AND FAMILIES	DISCOVERIES	IMAGINATION	OBSERVATION	PERSPECTIVES
KINDERGARTEN															
Getting Together	•		•				•	•		•			•		
Frog in the Middle		•	•	•			•			•				•	
"Paddle," Said the Swan				•									•		
Rain Talk				•				•					•		
Oh, A-Hunting We Will Go	•		•	•	•			•	•						
Who Said Red?				•				•			•		•		
Bread, Bread, Bread	•		•				•					•	•		
Changes, Changes				•			•					•	•		
Titch		•	•	•	•		•					•	•		
I Had a Cat	•	•		•											
Handtalk Zoo	•			•		•		•		•		•	•		
White Is the Moon				•								•	•		
What Do You See?		•		•								•	•	•	
Hi, Cat!	•		•					•			•				
All I Am							•	•			•	•			
As the Crow Flies	•						•	•						•	
GRADE 1 • LEVEL 1															
I Went Walking				•		•	•			•		•	•		
Rain				•				•				•	•		
Five Little Ducks				•		•				•	•	•			
The Chick and the Duckling				•	•		•				•	•			
The Good Bad Cat		•		•	•							•			
My Friends	•		•	•			•				•	•		•	
GRADE 1 • LEVEL 2															
Bet You Can't		•	•			•					•		•		
Coco Can't Wait!										•	•				
Down by the Bay				•		•				•		•	•		
Jasper's Beanstalk				•	•							•	•		
GRADE 1 • LEVEL 3															
An Egg Is An Egg				•			•					•		•	•
Whose Baby?				•							•	•		•	
Everything Grows				•			•	•			•	•		•	
White Rabbit's Color Book		•		•								•			
GRADE 1 • LEVEL 4															
Hattie and the Fox, p. 10	•	•		•			•						•	•	
Any Kind of Dog, p. 46		•		•			•				•				
Seven Sillies, p. 74	•			•			•				•	•		•	•
The Story of Chicken Licken, p. 108	•			•		•	•			•	•				

Title	COMMUNITY	PROBLEM SOLVING	COOPERATION	SAVING THE ENVIRONMENT	THE NATURAL WORLD	CHALLENGES	STORYTELLING	YOURSELF AND OTHERS	PICTURES OF AMERICA	JOURNEYS	FRIENDS AND FAMILIES	DISCOVERIES	IMAGINATION	OBSERVATION	PERSPECTIVES
GRADE 1 • LEVEL 4 cont'd															
One Monday Morning, p. 140							●			●			●		
You'll Soon Grow Into Them, p. 180		●	●				●	●		●					
Seven Blind Mice, p. 212		●	●		●	●						●	●	●	●
The Surprise Family, p. 256	●			●	●		●				●	●			
GRADE 1 • LEVEL 5															
In the Attic, p. 10		●								●		●	●	●	
Julieta and Her Paintbrush, p. 40				●			●					●	●	●	
Jimmy Lee Did It, p. 76		●				●					●		●		●
New Shoes for Silvia, p. 104		●									●		●	●	
Just a Little Bit, p. 138		●	●			●					●				
A Birthday Basket for Tía, p. 170		●					●				●				
Guinea Pigs Don't Read Books, p. 206				●								●		●	
A Letter to Amy, p. 232							●				●				
GRADE 2 • LEVEL 6															
Charlie Anderson, p. 12		●					●				●	●			
Henry and Mudge, p. 40							●				●				
Luka's Quilt, p. 62	●	●	●				●	●			●			●	
Carry Go Bring Come, p. 94			●								●				
The Sun Is Always Shining, p. 122				●								●		●	
Willie's Not the Hugging Kind, p. 150							●	●			●	●		●	
Nine-in-One, Grr! Grr! p. 178		●		●	●		●			●					
The Wednesday Surprise, p. 206		●				●	●				●	●			
The Mysterious Tadpole, p. 236		●	●			●	●				●	●			
The Goat in the Rug, p. 268		●								●	●		●		
Henry's Wrong Turn, p. 300	●			●		●	●		●				●		
Swimmy, p. 326	●	●	●	●						●				●	
GRADE 2 • LEVEL 7															
Dear Daddy..., p. 12						●					●	●			
Best Wishes, Ed, p. 40	●	●	●	●							●		●		
Puff...Flash...Bang! p. 68	●	●					●	●					●		
Angel Child, Dragon Child, p. 98	●	●	●		●		●	●		●			●		
Jamaica Tag-Along, p. 126			●				●				●	●			
The Best Friends Club, p. 154			●				●				●	●			
Our Soccer League, p. 176			●			●	●				●				
Princess Pooh, p. 202							●				●	●		●	
Come a Tide, p. 230	●	●		●	●		●				●				
The Sun, the Wind, and the Rain, p. 262				●								●		●	●
Llama and the Great Flood, p. 292	●			●		●					●				
A Curve in the River, p. 318		●		●			●	●	●	●	●				

Directory of Resources

Addison-Wesley Longman Publishing Co.
One Jacob Way
Reading, MA 01867-3999
617-944-3700 • 800-552-2259
800-358-4566 • Fax: 617-944-9338

Aladdin Paperbacks
(Imprint of Simon and Schuster
Children's Publishing Division)

Alfaguera
(See Santillana Publishing Co., Inc.)

Altea (Altea, Taurus, Alfaguera SA)
Juan Bravo 38, 28006 Madrid, Spain
(91) 5783159 • Fax: (91) 5783220

Anaya (Ediciones Anaya SA)
Aragó 237, 08007 Barcelona, Spain
(93) 2037652 • Fax: (93) 2037738

AP (Lectorum)
(See Lectorum Publications, Inc.)

**Artists & Writers Guild Books/
Golden Books**
(Imprint of Western Publishing Co., Inc.)
1220 Mound Ave., Racine, WI 53404
414-633-2431 • 212-753-8500
800-558-5972 • Fax: 414-631-1966

Astor Books
(Subsidiary of Astor Music, Inc.)
62 Cooper Square, New York, NY 10003
212-777-3700 • Fax : 212-477-4129

Atheneum Books for Young Readers
(Division of Simon & Schuster)
866 Third Avenue, New York, NY 10022
212-698-7200

Atlántida (Editorial Atlántida SA)
Azopardo 579
1307 Buenos Aires, Argentina
(01) 77156221/7748203
Fax: (01) 5413313341

Avon Books, Avon/Camelot Books
(Division of The Hearst Corp.)
1350 Avenue of the Americas
New York, NY 10019
212-261-6800 • 800-238-0658
Fax (NY): 212-261-6895 • 800-223-0239

Bantam Books
(Division of Bantam Doubleday
Dell Publishing Group, Inc.)

Bantam Little Rooster Books
(Bantam Books; division of Bantam
Doubleday Dell Publishing Group, Inc.)

Blue Sky Press
(Imprint of Scholastic; See Scholastic Inc.)

Boyds Mills Press
815 Church St., Honesdale, PA 18431
717-253-1164
(See also, St. Martin's Press, distributor)

Bradbury Press
(See Macmillan)

Bruño (Editorial Bruño)
Maestro Alonso, 21, 28028 Madrid, Spain
(91) 3610448 • Fax: (91) 3613133

Camelot Publishing, Co.
Box 1357, Ormond Beach, FL 32175-1357
904-672-5672

Candlewick Press
(Sister company of Walker Books, Ltd., London)
2067 Massachusetts Avenue
Cambridge, MA 02140
617-661-3330 • Fax: 617-661-0565

Carolrhoda
Lerner Publications Co.
241 First Avenue North
Minneapolis, MN 55401
612-332-3344 • 800-328-4929
Fax: 612-332-7615
(See also, Lucent Books, Inc., distributor)

Charlesbridge Publishing
85 Main St., Watertown, MA 02172
617-926-0329 • 800-225-3214
Fax: 617-926-5720; 800-926-5775

Children's Book Press
6400 Hollis Street, Suite 4
Emeryville, CA 94608
510-655-3395 • Fax: 510-655-1978

Children's Press
(A Grolier Company)
Sherman Turnpike, Danbury, CT 06816
203-797-3500 • Fax: 203-797-3197

Chronicle Books
(Division of Chronicle Publishing Co.)
275 Fifth St., San Francisco, CA 94103
415-777-7240 • Fax: 415-777-8887
800-722-6657 (orders)

Clarion Books
(Division of Houghton Mifflin Co.)
215 Park Avenue South, New York, NY 10003
212-420-5800 • Fax: 212-420-5855

Cobblehill Books
(See Penguin USA)

Collier (P.F. Collier)
919 Third Ave., New York, NY 10022
212-702-3217 • Fax: 212-605-4896

Crowell Junior Books
(Thomas J. Crowell) • (See HarperCollins)

Crown Publishing Group
201 East 50 St., New York, NY 10022
212-572-6117 • Fax: 212-572-6161

Delacorte Press
(Subsidiary of Dell Publishing;
Division of Bantam Doubleday)
(See Dell Publishing)

Dell Publishing
(Division of Bantam Doubleday
Dell Publishing Group, Inc.)
1540 Broadway, New York, NY 10036
212-354-6500 • 800-223-6834
Fax: 212-302-7985

Destino (Ediciones Destino SA)
Consell de Cent 425, E 08009 Barcelona, Spain
(93) 2652305 • Fax: (93) 2657537

Dial Press
(Subsidiary of Dell Publishing/Division of
Bantam Doubleday Dell Publishing Group)
1540 Broadway, New York, NY 10036
212-354-6500 • 800-223-6834
Fax: 212-302-7985

Doubleday
(Division of Bantam Doubleday
Publishing Group, Inc.)
1540 Broadway, New York, NY 10036
212-354-6500 • 800-223-6834
Fax: 212-492-9862 (orders);
212-302-7985

Dragonfly Books
(See Alfred A. Knopf, Inc.)

E.P. Dutton
(Dutton/Signet; a division of Penguin USA)
375 Hudson St., New York, NY 10014
212-366-2000

Ekaré (Ediciones Ekaré)
Av Luis Roche, Edif del Libro
Altamira Sur, Caracas, Venezuela 1062
(02) 263-00-91 • Fax: (02) 263-32-91

Ekaré- Banco del Libro
(See Ekaré)

Espasa-Calpe (Editorial Espasa-Calpe SA)
Apdo 547, Carretera de Irún, Km 12,200
(variante de Fuencarral), 28049 Madrid, Spain
(91) 358-9689 • Fax: (91) 358-9505

Everest (Editorial Everest SA)
Carretera Léon-Coruña, Km 5
POB 339, 24080 León, Spain
(987) 802020 • Fax: (987) 801251

Farrar, Straus, & Giroux, Inc.
19 Union Square West
New York, NY 10003
212-741-6900 • Fax: 212-633-6973

Fher (Publicaciones Fher SA)
Carretera Léon-Coruña, KM5
P.O.B. 339, 24080 Léon, Spain
(987) 802020 • Fax: (987) 801251

Four Winds Press
(See Macmillan)

Franklin Watts
Franklin Watts, Inc. (A Grolier Company)
Sherman Turnpike, Danbury, CT 06816
203-797-3500 • Fax: 203-797-3197

W. H. Freeman and Co.
(Subsidiary of Scientific American, Inc.)
41 Madison Ave., New York, NY 10010
212-576-9400 • Fax: 212-481-1891

Laura Geringer Books
(See HarperCollins Children's Books)

Greenwillow Books
(Division of William Morrow & Co., Inc.)
1350 Avenue of the Americas
New York, NY 10019
212-261-6500 • 800-631-1199
Fax: 212-261-6619

Grijalbo (Ediciones Grijalbo SA)
Aragó 385, 08013 Barcelona, Spain
(93) 4587000 • Fax: (93) 458-0495

Grijalbo Puerto Rico, Inc.
Apdo 23025 UPR, Río Piedras 00931
809-765-5065 (voice and fax)

Gulliver Green Books
(Imprint of Harcourt Brace Trade
Division/Division of Harcourt Brace & Co.)
525 "B" Street, Suite 1900
San Diego, CA 92101
619-231-6616 • 800-543-1918
New York address:
15 East 26 Street, New York, NY 10010
212-592-1000

Hampton-Brown Co., Inc
26385 Carmel Rancho Boulevard
Suite 200, Carmel, CA 93923
408-625-3666 • 800-933-3510
Fax: 408-625-8619

Harcourt Brace & Company
(A Harcourt Brace Trade Division)
525 "B" Street, Suite 1900
San Diego, CA 92101
619-231-6616 • 800-543-1918
New York address:
15 East 26 Street, New York, NY 10010
212-592-1000

Harcourt Brace Jovanovich
(See Harcourt Brace & Company)

HarperCollins Children's Books
10 East 53rd St., New York, NY 10022
212-207-7000 • 800-242-7737
Fax: 212-207-7192

Harper and Row
(See HarperCollins)

Harper Trophy
(See HarperCollins Children's Books)

Heian International, Inc.
1815 West 205 Street, Suite 205
Torrance, CA 90501
310-782-6228 • Fax: 310-782-6269

Henry Holt & Co., Inc.
115 West 18 St., New York, NY 10011
212-886-9200 • 800-488-5233
Fax: 212-633-0748

Holiday House, Inc.
425 Madison Ave., New York, NY 10017
212-688-0085 • Fax: 212-421-6134

Houghton Mifflin Co.
222 Berkley St., Boston, MA 02116
617-351-5000 • 800-225-3362
Fax: 617-351-1125

Hyperion Books for Children
(Division of Disney Book Publishing, Inc.,
a Walt Disney Co.)
114 Fifth Ave., New York, NY 11011
212-633-4400

Caroline House
(See Boyds Mills Press)

JACP, Inc.
414 East 3rd Ave., San Mateo, CA 94401
415-343-9408

Joy Street Books
(Imprint of Little, Brown & Co.
See Little, Brown)

Júcar (Ediciones Júcar)
Alto Atocha, 7, 33201 Gijón, Spain
(98) 5357413 • Fax: (98) 5356879

Juventud (Editorial Juventud SA)
Provenza 101, 08029 Barcelona, Spain
(93) 439-2000/3212100 • Fax: (93) 4398383

Jean Karl Books
(See Atheneum)

Kids Can Press, Ltd.
29 Birch Avenue
Toronto, ON M4V 1E2, Canada
416-925-KIDS (voice and fax)
800-265-0884

Kingfisher Books
(Larousse Kingfisher Chamber, Inc.,
subsidiary of Groupe de la Cité)
95 Madison Avenue, 12th Floor
New York, NY 10016
212-686-1060 • 800-497-1657
Fax: 212-686-1082

Alfred A. Knopf, Inc.
(Subsidiary of Random House, Inc.)
201 East 50th St., New York, NY 10022
212-751-2600 • 800-638-6460
Fax: 212-572-2593

Learning Links, Inc.
2300 Marcus Ave., New Hyde Park, NY 11042
516-437-9071 • 800-724-2616
Fax: 516-437-5392

Leef
(Lee Lectorum Publisher, Inc.)

Lectorum Publications, Inc.
111 Eighth Ave., New York, NY 10011
212-929-2833 • 800-345-5946
Fax: 212-727-3035

Lee & Low Books, Inc.
95 Madison Ave., Rm. 606
New York, NY 10016
212-779-4400 • Fax: 212-683-1894

Lerner Publications Co.
241 First Avenue North
Minneapolis, MN 55401
612-332-3344 • 800-328-4929
Fax: 612-332-7615

Lipincott-Raven Publishers
227 East Washington Square
Philadelphia, PA 19106
215-238-4200 • 800-638-3030
Fax: 215-238-4227

Little, Brown & Company
(Subsidiary of Time, Inc.)
34 Beacon St., Boston, MA 02108
617-227-0730 • 800-343-9204
Fax: 617-227-4633

Lodestar Books
(See Penguin USA)

Lothrop, Lee, & Shepard Books
(Division of William Morrow & Co., Inc.)
1350 Avenue of the Americas
New York, NY 10019
212-261-6500 • 800-843-9384

Lucent Books, Inc.
(Affiliate of Greenhaven Press, Inc.)
Box 289011, San Diego, CA 92198-9011
619-485-7424 • 800-231-5163
Fax: 619-485-9549

Lumen (Editorial Lumen SA)
Ramón Miquel i Planas 10
E 08034 Barcelona, Spain
(93) 2043496 • Fax: (93) 2055619

Macmillan Children's Book Group
(See Simon & Schuster Children's
Publishing Division)

**Magisterio Español
(Editorial Magisterio Español SA)**
Tutor 27 • 28008 Madrid, Spain
(91) 5429838 • Fax: (91) 542-7145

Margaret K. McElderry Books
(See Simon & Schuster Children's Publishing Division)

Miñon
(See Susaeta)

Morrow Junior Books
(Division of William Morrow & Co., Inc.)
1350 Avenue of the Americas
New York, NY 10019
212-261-6500 • 800-843-9389
Fax: 212-261-6689

Mulberry Books
(Division of William Morrow & Co., Inc.)
1350 Avenue of the Americas
New York, NY 10019
212-261-6500 • 800-843-9389

Thomas Nelson, Inc.
Nelson Place at Elm Hill Pike
Nashville, TN 37214
Mailing address:
Box 141000, Nashville, TN 37214
615-889-9000 • 800-251-4000

New England Aquarium Books
(See Franklin Watts)

New Readers Press
(Division of Laubacti Literacy International)
Box 131, Syracuse, NY 13210
315-422-9121 • 800-448-8878

Orchard Books (A Grolier Company)
95 Madison Ave., New York, NY 10016
212-951-2600 • 800-433-3411
Fax: 212-213-6435

Oxford University Press
198 Madison Ave., New York, NY 10015
212-726-6000 • 800-451-7556
Fax: 212-726-6455

Paraninfo (Editorial Paraninfo SA)
Magallanes 25, 28015 Madrid, Spain
(91) 4463050 • Fax: (91) 4456218

Parramon (Ediciones Parramon SA)
Gran Vía de les Corts
Catalanes 332, 6th fl, Apdo 2001
08004 Barcelona, Spain
(93) 4261819 • Fax: (93) 4263628

Pantheon
(Imprint of Random House, Inc.)
201 East 50th St., New York, NY 10022
212-751-2600 • 800-638-6460
Fax: 212-572-6030

Peisa (Promoción Editorial Inca SA)
Emilio Althaus 460, Oficina 202
Apdo 11155, Lima 14, Peru
(014) 718884 • Fax: (014) 705205

Penguin USA
375 Hudson St., New York, NY 10014
212-366-2000 • Fax: 212-366-2666

Willa Perlman Books
(See Simon & Schuster Children's Publishing Division)

Philomel Books
(Imprint of Putnam; See Putnam Books)

Picture Books
(See Simon & Schuster Children's Publishing)

Clarkson Potter Publisher
(See Random House/Crown Publishers, Inc.)

Prentice-Hall
(See Simon & Schuster)

Preservation Press
(Subsidiary of National Trust for Historic Preservation)
1785 Massachusetts Avenue NW
Washington, DC 20036
202-673-4058 (orders) • 800-766-6847
Fax: 202-673-4172

Puffin Books
(Imprint of Penguin Books, Ltd.)
27 Wright's Lane, London W8 5TZ, England
(0171) 4163000 • Fax:(0171) 4163099

Putnam & Grosset (Grosset/Putnam)
(See G.P. Putnam's Sons)

G.P. Putnam's Sons
(Trade Books Division, The Putnam Berkley Group, Inc.)
200 Madison Ave., New York, NY 10016
212-951-8400 • 800-631-8571

Random House, Inc.
201 East 50th St., New York, NY 10022
212-751-2600 • 800-726-0600
Fax: 212-572-8700

Red Feather Books
(See Henry Holt & Co., Inc.)

Runestone Books
(Division of Lerner Group)
241 1st Ave. North, Minneapolis, MN 55401
612-332-3344 • 800-328-4929
Fax: 612-332-7615

Sandpiper
(See Houghton-Mifflin)

Santillana Publishing Co., Inc.
855 W. Walnut St., Compton, CA 90220
310-763-0455 • 800-245-8584
Fax: 310-763-4460

Scholastic, Inc.
555 Broadway, New York, NY 10012
212-243-6100 • 800-392-2179
Fax: 212-343-6930

Charles Scribner's Sons
(Imprint of Simon & Schuster Trade Division)
1230 Avenue of the Americas
New York, NY 10020
212-702-2000 • Fax: 212-605-9375

Scroll Press, Inc.
2858 Valerie Court, Merrick, NY 11566
516-379-4283

Shen's Books and Supplies
821 South First Ave., Arcadia, CA 91006
818-445-6958 • 800-456-6000
Fax: 818-445-6940

Sierra Club Books for Children
100 Bush St., San Francisco, CA 94104
415-291-1600 • Fax: 415-291-1602

Silver Burdett Ginn
(Division of Simon & Schuster Education Group)
299 Jefferson Rd., Parsippany, NJ 07054-0480
201-739-8000

Simon & Schuster Books for Young Readers
(See Simon & Schuster Children's Publishing Division)

Simon & Schuster Children's Publishing Division
(Division of Simon & Schuster Consumer Group)
1230 Avenue of the Americas
New York, NY 10020
212-698-7200

Sitesa (Sistemas Tecnicos de Edición SA de CV)
San Marcos No. 102, Col Tlalpan, 14000
Mexico, DF
(05) 655-9144 • Fax (05) 573-9412

SM (Ediciones SM)
Joaquin Turina 39, 28044 Madrid, Spain
(91) 2085145 • Fax: (91) 2039927

Smithsonian Institution Press
470 L'Enfant Plaza, Room 7100
Washington, DC 20560
202-287-3738 • 800-782-4612
Fax: 202-287-3184/3637

Soundprints
(Subsidiary of Trudy Management Corporation)
165 Water St., Norwalk, CT 06856
203-838-6009 • 800-228-7839
Fax: 203-866-9944

St. Martin's Press
175 Fifth Ave., New York, NY 10010
212-674-5151 • 800-221-7945
Fax: 212-420-9314

Stemmer House Publishers, Inc.
2627 Caves Road
Owings Mills, MD 21117
410-363-3690 • Fax: 410-363-8459

Gareth Stevens Children's Books
(Imprint of Gareth Stevens, Inc.)
555 North River Center Drive, Suite 201
Milwaukee, WI 53212
414-225-0333 • 800-341-3569
Fax: 414-225-0377

Sudamericana (Editorial Sudamericana SA)
Humberto 531/55
1103 Buenos Aires, Argentina
(01) 362218/362-1222/3621616
Fax: (01) 362-7364

Susaeta (Ediciones Susaeta SA)
Calle Campezo s/n, 28022 Madrid, Spain
(01) 7472111 • Fax (01) 7479295

Ediciones Susaeta
Calle 9 No. 79-35, Apdo Aéreo 1742-598
Santafé de Bogotá de Cundinamarca, Colombia
(01) 2125485 • Fax: (01) 2872413

Tambourine Books
(Division of Willam Morrow & Co., Inc.)
1350 Avenue of the Americas
New York, NY 10019
212-261-6661 • 800-843-9398
Fax: 212-261-6668

Ticknor & Fields Books for Young Readers
(Division of Houghton Mifflin Co.)
215 Park Ave. South, New York, NY 10003
212-420-5800 • Fax: 212-420-5850

Timun Mas (Editorial Timun Mas SA)
Ediciones Ceac SA, Calle Perú 164
Apdo 926, 08020 Barcelona, Spain
(93) 3075004 • Fax: (93) 3084392

Tundra Books, Inc.
345 Victoria Avenue, Suite 604
Montreal, FQ H3Z 2N2, Canada
514-932-5434 • Fax:514-484-2154

Unicorn Books
16 Laxton Gardens, Paddock Wood
Kent, TN 12 6BB, England
(01892) 833648 • Fax: (01892) 833577

Usborne Publishing
(dist by EDC Publishing, Division of Educational Development Corp.)
10302 East 55 Place, Suite B
Tulsa, OK 74146-6515
918-622-4522 • 800-475-4522
Fax: 918-665-7919 • Fax: 800-747-4509

Viking Children's Books
(See Penguin USA)

Viking Kestrel
(See Penguin USA)

Viking Press
(See Penguin USA)

Walker & Co.
(Division of Walker Publishing Co, Inc.)
435 Hudson St., New York, NY 10014
212-727-8300 • 800-AT-WALKER
Fax: 212-727-0984

Fredrick Warne & Co. Ltd.
(Penguin Books Ltd.)
27 Wright's Lane
London W8 5TZ, England
(0171) 4163000 • Fax: (0171) 4163099

Albert Whitman & Co.
6340 Oakton Street
Morton Grove, IL 60053-2723
708-581-0033 • 800-255-7675
Fax: 708-581-0039

Charlotte Zolotow Books
(See HarperCollins Children's Books)

MULTIMEDIA RESOURCE SUPPLIERS

AIMS Multimedia
9710 DeSoto Avenue
Chatworth, CA 91311-4409
800-367-2467

Bröderbund Software
P.O. Box 6125, Novato, CA 94948-6121
Fax: 415-382-4671

Carousel Film and Video
250 Fifth Avenue, Room 705
New York, NY 10001
212-683-1660

Coronet/MTI
108 Wilmot Rd., Deerfield, IL 60015
800-777-8100

Direct Cinema Limited
P.O. Box 10003
Santa Monica, CA 90410-1003
800-525-0000

Educational Software
4213 S. 94th St., Omaha, NE 68127
800-955-5570

Encyclopaedia Britannica Educational Corporation
310 South Michigan Avenue
Chicago, IL 60604
800-554-9862

GPN
P.O. Box 80669
Lincoln, NE 68501-0669
800-228-4630

GPN University
University of Nebraska-Lincoln
P.O. Box 80669
Lincoln, NE 68501-0669
800-228-4630

Listening Library
One Park Avenue
Greenwich, CT 06870-1727
800-243-4504

Macmillan/McGraw-Hill
220 East Danieldale Road
De Soto, TX 75115
800-442-9685

MECC
6160 Summit Drive North
Minneapolis, MN 5430-4003

National Geographic Educational Services
Washington, DC 20036
800-368-2728

PBS Video
1320 Braddock Pl., Alexandria, VA 22314
800-344-3337

Phoenix/BFA
468 Park Avenue South
New York, NY 10016
800-221-1274

Pied Piper/AIMS Multimedia
9710 DeSoto Avenue
Chatsworth, CA 91311-4409
800-367-2467

Reading Rainbow/GPN
P.O. Box 80669
Lincoln, NE 68501-0669
800-228-4630

Tom Snyder Productions
80 Coolidge Hill Road
Watertown, MA 02172-2817
800-342-0236

SRA/McGraw-Hill
P.O. Box 543, Blacklick, OH 43004
800-843-8855

SVE
6677 North Northeast Highway
Chicago, IL 60631
800-829-1900

Troll Associates
100 Corporate Dr., Mahwah, NJ 07430
800-929-TROL (8765)

United Learning
5633 West Howard Street
Niles, IL 60714-3389
800-424-0362

Weston Woods
339 Newton Turnpike
Weston, CT 06883-1199
800-243-5020

Index

Scope and Sequence

Overview

The skills and strategies of Macmillan/McGraw-Hill Reading/Language Arts are organized into five categories, or domains.

The domains represent the major areas of literature-based, integrated language arts instruction and assessment. Within each domain, there are sub-categories of specific strategies and skills.

The instructional design of the program is a recursive one; that is, the same major strategies and skills are taught across units in a grade level and across grade levels in the program.

The emphasis is the progress students make in applying strategies in increasingly sophisticated contexts. The emphasis is also on students personalizing strategies and transferring them to different contexts, not only other reading contexts, but also other curriculum-area contexts.

CATEGORIES

READING
- Comprehension Strategies
- Vocabulary Strategies
- Phonics and Decoding
- Print Literacy

WRITING
- Written Expression
- Conventions of Language

LISTENING, SPEAKING, AND VIEWING
- Listening
- Speaking
- Viewing

APPRECIATING LITERATURE AND LANGUAGE
- Multicultural Perspectives
- Writer's Craft/Artist's Craft
- Personal Interests and Attitudes

STUDY SKILLS AND INFORMATION RESOURCES
- Study Skills
- Information Resources

Reading

Ⓖ **These skills are tested in the Unit Progress Assessment.**   ▨ **Skills, strategies, and other teaching opportunities.**

COMPREHENSION STRATEGIES

	GRADE			1			2		3		4	5	6
LEVEL	1	2	3	4	5	6	7	8	9	10	11	12

USE PREREADING STRATEGIES

	1	2	3	4	5	6	7	8	9	10	11	12
Preview												
Activate prior knowledge												
Set purposes												

USE COMPREHENSION MONITORING STRATEGIES

	1	2	3	4	5	6	7	8	9	10	11	12
Ask questions												
Paraphrase												
Visualize												
Adjust reading rate												
Reread												
Use decoding and vocabulary strategies												

USE COMPREHENSION STRATEGIES

RELATE IDEAS

	1	2	3	4	5	6	7	8	9	10	11	12
Make inferences				☑	☑	☑	☑	☑	☑	☑	☑	☑
Make, confirm, or revise predictions	☑	☑	☑	☑	☑	☑	☑	☑	☑	☑	☑	☑
Analyze story elements (character, plot, setting, narrative or character's point of view, tone, mood, theme, style)	☑	☑		☑	☑	☑	☑	☑	☑	☑	☑	☑
Recognize literary genres (narrative, expository; fiction, nonfiction)												

ORGANIZE INFORMATION

	1	2	3	4	5	6	7	8	9	10	11	12
Main idea and supporting details	☑		☑			☑	☑	☑	☑	☑	☑	☑
Cause and effect	☑	☑	☑	☑	☑	☑	☑	☑	☑	☑	☑	☑
Problem and solution				☑	☑			☑	☑	☑	☑	☑
Categories	☑	☑	☑			☑	☑	☑				
Sequence of events	☑	☑			☑	☑	☑	☑	☑	☑	☑	☑
Steps in a process						☑	☑	☑	☑	☑	☑	☑
Comparison and contrast			☑	☑	☑	☑	☑	☑	☑	☑	☑	☑
Spatial relationships	☑	☑			☑	☑	☑	☑				
Use illustrations, photos, headings, subheadings, typefaces, maps, captions, diagrams				☑	☑	☑	☑	☑	☑	☑	☑	☑

SYNTHESIZE IDEAS

	1	2	3	4	5	6	7	8	9	10	11	12
Summarize					☑	☑	☑	☑	☑	☑	☑	☑
Make, confirm or revise predictions	☑	☑	☑	☑	☑	☑	☑	☑	☑	☑	☑	☑
Draw conclusions					☑	☑	☑	☑	☑	☑	☑	☑
Form generalizations							☑	☑	☑	☑	☑	☑

EVALUATE IDEAS

	1	2	3	4	5	6	7	8	9	10	11	12
Distinguish between important and unimportant information						☑	☑	☑	☑	☑	☑	☑
Make judgments and decisions								☑	☑	☑	☑	☑
Distinguish between fantasy and reality			☑		☑	☑	☑	☑	☑			
Evaluate fact and opinion										☑	☑	☑
Evaluate fact and nonfact								☑		☑	☑	☑
Recognize techniques of persuasion and propaganda											☑	☑
Evaluate author's purpose and point of view								☑	☑	☑	☑	☑

GENERATE AND APPLY IDEAS

	1	2	3	4	5	6	7	8	9	10	11	12
Reflect and respond to literature												
Extend meaning												

VOCABULARY STRATEGIES

	GRADE				1		2		3		4	5	6
	LEVEL	1	2	3	4	5	6	7	8	9	10	11	12
USE VOCABULARY STRATEGIES													
CONTEXT CLUES FOR:													
Unfamiliar words						✓	✓	✓	✓	✓	✓	✓	✓
Multiple-meaning words, including homographs							✓	✓	✓		✓	✓	✓
Homophones													
Figurative language							✓			✓	✓	✓	✓
Content-area and specialized vocabulary							✓			✓	✓	✓	✓
STRUCTURAL CLUES FOR:													
Inflectional endings (-er, -est, -s, -es, -ed, -ing)		✓	✓	✓	✓	✓	✓	✓					
Plurals (regular, irregular)		✓	✓										
Compound words									✓	✓			
Contractions													
Possessives			✓		✓	✓							
Prefixes and suffixes							✓	✓		✓			
Root words and combining Forms/Etymology										✓			
RELATE WORDS AND CONCEPTS													
Synonyms and antonyms													
Denotation and connotation													
Word categories													
Analogies													

PHONICS AND DECODING

		1	2	3	4	5	6	7	8	9	10	11	12
RECOGNIZE LETTERS, RECOGNIZE SOUNDS													
Recognize letters: Aa-Zz													
Recognize discrete sounds in words (phonemic awareness)													
RECOGNIZE SOUND/LETTER RELATIONSHIPS													
Consonants, blends, digraphs		✓	✓	✓	✓	✓	✓	✓					
Vowels (short, long, diphthongs, variants)		✓	✓	✓	✓	✓	✓	✓					
Vowels and phonograms		✓	✓	✓	✓	✓	✓	✓					
USE DECODING STRATEGIES													
Use phonetic cues													
Use semantic cues													
Use structural cues													
Blending													
Substitution													
Rhyming													
Known words/word parts													
Consonant and vowel patterns													
Syllable generalizations													
PRINT LITERACY/CONCEPTS OF PRINT													
Directionality													
Letter, word, sentence													
Punctuation													

Integrated Language Arts

☑ These skills are tested in the Unit Progress Assessment.   ▨ Skills, strategies, and other teaching opportunities.

WRITING

	Grade	1			2		3		4	5	6	
USE COMPOSITION STRATEGIES	Level	1	2	3	4	5	6	7	8	9	10	11	12
PREWRITING													
Generate Ideas (brainstorm, visualize, make a list, etc.)					■	■	■	■	■	■	■	■	■
Choose and narrow topics					■	■	■	■	■	■	■	■	■
Identify purpose and audience					■	■	■	■	■	■	■	■	■
Select writing mode: narrative, descriptive, expository, persuasive					■	■	■	■	■	■	■	■	■
SELECT WRITING FORM													
Journal		■	■	■	■	■	■	■	■	■	■	■	■
Message/list		■	■	■	■	■	■	■	■	■	■	■	■
Paragraph		■	■	■	■	■	■	■	■	■	■	■	■
Multi-paragraph composition					■	■	■	■	■	■	■	■	■
Essay						■	■	■	■	■	■	■	■
Story		■	■	■	■	■	■	■	■	■	■	■	■
Description			■	■	■	■	■	■	■	■	■	■	■
Personal narrative				■	■	■	■	■	■	■	■	■	■
Autobiography						■	■	■	■	■	■	■	■
Biography							■	■	■	■	■	■	■
How-to						■	■	■	■	■	■	■	■
Play (scene)							■	■	■	■	■	■	■
Advertisement							■	■	■	■	■	■	■
Editorial									■	■	■	■	■
Summary						■	■	■	■	■	■	■	■
Critique/review							■	■	■	■	■	■	■
Comparison/contrast						■	■	■	■	■	■	■	■
Book report					■	■	■	■	■	■	■	■	■
Report					■	■	■	■	■	■	■	■	■
Invitation				■	■	■	■	■	■	■	■	■	■
Thank-you note				■	■	■	■	■	■	■	■	■	■
Friendly letter				■	■	■	■	■	■	■	■	■	■
Business letter							■	■	■	■	■	■	■
Gather ideas and information		■	■	■	■	■	■	■	■	■	■	■	■
WRITING FIRST DRAFT													
Draft compositions for specific purposes and audiences, and to capture ideas					■	■	■	■	■	■	■	■	■
Use different organizational techniques to support and develop a central idea						■	■	■	■	■	■	■	■
REVISING													
Evaluate content, topic development, transition, clarity, appropriateness of language, word and sentence variety, and appropriateness to the purpose and audience					■	■	■	■	■	■	■	■	■
Add information and ideas					■	■	■	■	■	■	■	■	■
Eliminate unrelated details and sentences					■	■	■	■	■	■	■	■	■
Rewrite to include a variety of word choices and sentence types/structures						■	■	■	■	■	■	■	■
Clarify and refine ideas					■	■	■	■	■	■	■	■	■
Combine sentences						■	■	■	■	■	■	■	■
Evaluate revisions made by self and others						■	■	■	■	■	■	■	■

	GRADE LEVEL	1					2		3		4	5	6
		1	2	3	4	5	6	7	8	9	10	11	12
PROOFREADING													
Proofread and edit a composition						■	■	■	■	■	■	■	■
Check spelling, punctuation, and capitalization						■	■	■	■	■	■	■	■
PUBLISHING													
Share compositions with others		■	■	■	■	■	■	■	■	■	■	■	■
Use appropriate manuscript style						■	■	■	■	■	■	■	■

CONVENTIONS OF LANGUAGE

GRAMMAR AND USAGE

	1	2	3	4	5	6	7	8	9	10	11	12
Recognize types of sentences: declarative, interrogative, imperative, exclamatory												
Recognize complete and incomplete sentences												
Recognize sentence structures: simple, compound, complex												
Recognize sentence parts: complete, simple, compound subject/predicate; clauses												
Recognize nouns: common, proper, singular, plural, possessive; appositives												
Recognize verbs: action, helping, linking, irregular												
Recognize complements: direct/indirect object; predicate nominative/adjective												
Form verb tenses: present, past, future												
Form contractions												
Recognize pronouns: subject, object, possessive, indefinite												
Recognize subject-verb agreement												
Recognize adjectives: common, proper, articles, demonstratives												
Form comparative & superlative adjectives												
Recognize adverbs of place, time, manner, degree												
Form comparative adverbs												
Recognize negative words and avoid double negatives												
Recognize prepositions and prepositional phrases												

MECHANICS

	1	2	3	4	5	6	7	8	9	10	11	12
Use standard capitalization, punctuation, spelling					■	■	■	■	■			

SPELLING

	1	2	3	4	5	6	7	8	9	10	11	12
Sound-letter relationships												
Spelling generalizations												
Word analysis												
Word structure												
Study methods and strategies												

HANDWRITING

	1	2	3	4	5	6	7	8	9	10	11	12
Use legible handwriting (manuscript, cursive)												

Listening, Speaking, and Viewing

☑ These skills are tested in the Unit Progress Assessment.   Skills, strategies, and other teaching opportunities.

LISTENING

	GRADE LEVEL	1	2	3	4	5	6	7	8	9	10	11	12
LISTENING SKILLS													
Demonstrate listening skills (focus attention, organize information)													
Respond to speakers in a variety of ways (ask questions, think aloud, contribute ideas, retell what is heard)													
Listen for a specific purpose: information, appreciation, entertainment, directions, persuasion													
Apply comprehension strategies in listening activities													
Participate in listening activities related to reading and writing													

SPEAKING

	1	2	3	4	5	6	7	8	9	10	11	12
SPEAKING SKILLS												
Demonstrate speaking skills (volume, intonation, enunciation, appropriate rate, fluency)												
Organize and present ideas in a variety of oral presentation formats												
Speak for a specific purpose: inform, entertain, give directions, persuade, express personal feelings and opinions												
Apply composition strategies in speaking activities												
Participate in speaking activities related to reading and writing												

VIEWING

	1	2	3	4	5	6	7	8	9	10	11	12
VIEWING SKILLS												
Demonstrate viewing skills												
Respond to audiovisual media in a variety of ways												
Explore a variety of audiovisual media (television, film, photography, expressive arts)												
Use viewing for a specific purpose: information, appreciation, entertainment, directions, persuasion												
Compare and contrast the characteristics of print material and audiovisual media												
Apply comprehension strategies in viewing activities												
Participate in speaking activities related to reading and writing												

Appreciating Literature and Language

✓ These skills are tested in the Unit Progress Assessment.

▓ Skills, strategies, and other teaching opportunities.

MULTICULTURAL PERSPECTIVES

GRADE LEVEL	1					2		3		4	5	6
	1	2	3	4	5	6	7	8	9	10	11	12

ENHANCE MULTICULTURAL AWARENESS

	1	2	3	4	5	6	7	8	9	10	11	12
Appreciate and value diverse points of view												
Become aware of cultural backgrounds, experiences, emotions, and ideas of self and others through literature												
Appreciate the literary expression of our contemporary multicultural society and multicultural heritage												
Appreciate the universality of literary themes in many cultures and in many different times												
Appreciate the significance of traditional literature within a culture												
Recognize cultural attitudes and customs in literary selections												

WRITER'S AND ARTIST'S CRAFT

	1	2	3	4	5	6	7	8	9	10	11	12
WRITER'S CRAFT												
Appreciate the sound of language												
Appreciate literary devices and techniques												
Appreciate literary forms												
Appreciate words (unusual words and word combinations, word relationships and word histories)												
ARTIST'S CRAFT												
Appreciate artistic styles, media, and techniques												

PERSONAL INTERESTS AND ATTITUDES

INTERACTING WITH LITERATURE

	1	2	3	4	5	6	7	8	9	10	11	12
Select stories and books for personal interests												
Develop personal reading and writing interests												
Make connections between one's personal life and literature												
Choose to read and write for a variety of purposes												

SHARING THROUGH LITERATURE

	1	2	3	4	5	6	7	8	9	10	11	12
Develop an awareness of the classroom as a community of learners which values cooperation, fair play, and respect for others and for oneself												
Share, review, and recommend books to others												
Participate in reading, writing, listening, speaking, and viewing activities												
Appreciate the artistic interpretation of literature through film, illustration, photography, dance, oral presentations, and other forms of expression												

Study Skills and Information Resources

Ø These skills are tested in the Unit Progress Assessment.   ▢ Skills, strategies, and other teaching opportunities.

STUDY SKILLS

USE STUDY SKILLS

	GRADE		1					2		3		4	5	6
LEVEL	1	2	3	4	5	6	7	8	9	10	11	12		
Follow directions				Ø	Ø	Ø	Ø	Ø		Ø	Ø	Ø
Use alphabetical order				Ø	Ø			Ø	Ø	Ø	Ø	
Skim and scan for information												Ø
Organize information: classification, note taking, outlining									Ø			
Complete forms and applications							Ø		Ø	Ø	Ø	Ø
Use test-taking strategies												
Develop personal habits of self-assessment												

INFORMATION RESOURCES

USE INFORMATION RESOURCES

	1	2	3	4	5	6	7	8	9	10	11	12
Book concepts: cover and title, author and illustrator												
Parts of a book: title page, index, copyright page, bibliography, table of contents, glossary, footnotes				Ø		Ø		Ø			Ø	Ø
Reference sources: dictionary, thesaurus, encyclopedia, almanac, atlas, readers' guide and other periodical indexes, card catalog/library classification systems, library resources, nonprint media, telephone directory, calendar, textbook (organization), newspapers and magazines, guide books, technology, recipes					Ø	Ø	Ø	Ø		Ø	Ø	Ø
Graphic aids: charts and tables, diagrams, maps, cartoons, graphs, schedules, time lines, advertisements, menus, labels, brochures, signs						Ø	Ø	Ø	Ø	Ø	Ø	Ø